HANG GLIDING

THE BASIC
HANDBOOK
OF SKYSURFING

By
Dan Poynter

HANG GLIDING

THE BASIC HANDBOOK OF SKYSURFING

Published by Daniel F. Poynter
P.O. Box 4232
Santa Barbara, California 93103, U.S.A.

Copyright ©1973 and 1974 by Daniel F. Poynter

First Printing 1973

Second Printing 1974, Revised

Third Printing 1974, Revised

Fourth Printing 1974, Completely Revised

Fifth Printing 1974, Revised

Sixth Printing 1975, Revised

Printed in the United States of America

Library of Congress Catalogue Card No. 74-77827

ISBN 0-915516-02-0 Paperback
ISBN 0-915516-03-9 Hard Cover

FOREWORD

Dan Poynter is a man who happened onto hang gliding and became very excited just as you probably did. He searched for more information and discovered the need for a basic handbook on the subject; he soon became deeply involved.

As an author, pilot, (rated for both power and gliders), parachutist and now skysurfer, he is not only well qualified to write this handbook but he brings much new talent and experience to the hang gliding movement.

He can trace his interest back to 1967 when he began running down hills with experimental gliding parachutes and he not only flew, he wrote about it.

He has designed, built and flown numerous gliders in the course of his work, has traveled extensively gathering information and is well known for his work.

Carrying on his life's mission to help others through information, he has thoroughly researched the whole area of hang gliding and for the first time, lays it out for all to read, enjoy and dream.

This handbook should foster the safe growth and orderly development of this exciting and recently reborn aviation sport.

ACKNOWLEDGEMENT

For photographs, many thanks to Richard Jenks of the Register, Floyd Clark of Cal Tech, Doug Morgan, Bill Allen, J. Sheridan, James Gerstner, Dick Mascuch, Margaret Fronius, Norton Bell, Bob Etchells, Katherine Kiceniuk, Steven Keull, Dave Quiggen, Don James, Rick Poynter, Alasdair Russell, Carl Moe, Peter Menzel, and Mike Ramirez. Mike Riggs, Eddie Paul and Eipper-Formance provided outstanding drawings while technical data and/or moral support were given by the Industrial Fasteners Institute, Joe Faust, Doug Garr, Bill Ottley, Waldo Waterman, Kaz De Lisse, Jack Hall, Herman Rice, Chuck Stahl, Mouse Cossey, Chandelle-San Francisco, The Experimental Aircraft Association, Peter Brock, Michèle Gratton, Dave Barish, Parachutes Incorporated, F.M. Rogallo, John McMasters, Pioneer Parachute Co., Jim Spurgeon, Barry Palmer, Grant Smith, Mike Markowski, Ted Strong, Andy Simon, Bob Newman, Joanne Faust, Pat MacDonald, Hugo Sandroni, Ed Vickery, Richard Miller, Rich Piccirilli, Ted Webster, Bob Lovejoy, Jerry Theriault, The United States Hang Gliding Association, Low and Slow Magazine, Skysurfer Magazine, the Soaring Society of America, the Self Soar Association, Ground Skimmer Magazine and various branches of the U.S. Government. Particular thanks to the many manufacturers who contributed material, took part and are mentioned in the text.

Very special thanks to George Uveges and Jack Buckley for their great photography, Bill Allen and Tom Peghiny for technical proofing and Lloyd Licher for opening so many doors.

I sincerely thank all these fine people and I know they are proud of the part they have played in the development of hang gliding, the sport, the science and the industry as well as their contribution to this work.

Covers by George Uveges and David Seagoe.

TABLE OF CONTENTS

Locking pins, quick release
Rapid links
Ripstop tape
Shackles
Speed-Rail fittings
Turnbuckles
Velcro tape
Washers

Over 40 models listed generally in alphabetical order.

Body english vs. control surfaces
Airfoils and coefficients of lift
Rogallo sails
Wing area
Wing loading
Planform
Wing slots
Sweepback
Cantilever
Cylindrical and conical
Dihedral
The tail
The rudder
Sink rate
Aspect ratio
Glide angle
Streamlining
Limp vs. rigid
Strength
The cockpit
Center of gravity
Trapeze bars
Wheels
Pilot suspension systems
    Seats and harnesses
Buoyancy
Tomorrow
Instrumentation
Models
Testing

Man power
    Kremer competition
Ornithopters
Machine power

FAA Advisory Circular 60-10
Hang gliding organizations: clubs and associations

Magazines and newsletters
Local contacts - for more information

**THIS BOOK IS DEDICATED
TO
SAFETY THROUGH EDUCATION**

HANG GLIDING **IS ALWAYS
UP TO DATE; IT IS REVISED
WITH EVERY PRINTING.**

**FOR MORE INFORMATION ON
TOW LAUNCHED HANG GLIDING,
READ** *KITING* **BY DAN POYNTER**

Kent Trimble flies toward the Golden Gate Bridge.

CHAPTER I

LAUNCHING AND FLYING

HANG GLIDING, WHAT IS IT?

Everywhere you go from Torrey Pines in southern California to the sand dunes of Cape Cod, a rapidly growing hoard of enthusiasts are leaping from the tops of slopes, sand dunes and cliffs with fierce ape-like cries in an attempt to clear the lumps from their throats, desperately clutching aluminum and Dacron bat-like contraptions with serious intent to commit aviation. They can also be found in Colorado, the Pacific Northwest, the Lookout in the Ortegas over Lake Elsinore, in the Rockies of Alberta, in Australia and New Zealand, on the shores of Lake Michigan and jumping from piers into the water in Selsey, England. And the skysurfer has even returned to the site of early hang gliding and man's first powered flight, Kitty Hawk in North Carolina. The sport is spreading faster than a brush fire.

These are the "Hang Glider" pilots, the new pioneers on the last frontier of aviation. This new breed with high hope and low incomes, these men and women, mostly young (some say childish) are picking up the art of building and flying light weight, foot launched, man carrying wings; an art such historic aviation giants as Lilienthal, Chanute and Montgomery had laid to rest at the advent of the gas-powered airplane.

If you haven't already figured out just what this sport entails, Skysurfing consists of flying one-man (usually), ultra light (normally), gliders (hopefully) at altitudes near the earth's surface (It is usually recommended that, to begin, one keep this flying activity low and slow).

Actually, "hang gliding" may be accomplished in a no wind condition and consists of a slow descent to a lower altitude while "hang soaring" requires wind and allows man and machine to remain aloft for quite some time. "Hang" does not refer to the standing position supported only by the arm pits on the parallel bars but rather that the pilot is suspended below the wing so that he may avail himself to foot launching and landing. Hang gliders have been defined as "aircraft in which the undercarriage and take off power are provided solely by the legs of the pilot; landings with the legs retracted are permitted" — but watch out for "runway rash" in these cases. In any case, hanging prone in a harness and "flying like Superman" is still hanging. *"Hang glider"* comes from the German word *"hangegleiter"*.

Often, hang gliders are called "kites" because many of the first ones were kited or towed and the trapeze bar control system was borrowed from the water ski kite people. Now, of course, "kite" is simply easier to say than "glider" or any other alternative.

Hang gliding brings the age of flight to the public, it makes personal flight available without high material costs, costly student instruction, federal licensing or contributions to

1

air pollution. It is the closest thing yet to imitating the birds; it is flying in the true sense of the word: competing and working with mother nature for sustenance in the ocean of air is a compelling and unique experience.

Hang gliders weigh in between 15 and 100 lbs. with most in the 35 lb. range. They can be easily transported by car top methods. They are easy, fun and instructional to construct, quickly assembled on site, a bare minimum of aeronautical knowledge is required to operate one and they're just plain fun!

The amount you wish to spend will depend largely on how much of the work in building you wish to do yourself. Study the models in Chapter VI and send off for information sheets and plans of the most interesting ones. The cost is usually $5 or $6. Decide how much work you want to do yourself and what tools can be eliminated if you purchase certain parts already fabricated. For example, if you purchase the tubing cut to length, there is no need to buy a tubing cutter.

Those selling plans usually offer a kit which includes all the hard to find hardware items, pre-bent tubing etc., so that all you'll need is a drill, wrench and a hacksaw to build your glider. You can purchase your sail ready made or just buy the cloth and sit at the sewing machine yourself. Most designers also offer a completely built unit broken down for shipment and ready for instant erection.

This is a mighty inexpensive introduction to aviation when one considers that only the aircraft must be purchased; there is no requirement to spend some $800.-$900. to qualify for a license.

Hang gliding is a reality, not just a dream. Pilots have climbed on currents of air to over 1000', have stayed up over eight hours, have made spiral turns and have glided for miles. To start from a higher altitude, some have been towed with rope to several thousand feet, leaped from mountain peaks and released from hot air balloons. Hang gliding may start with low, slow ground bounding but the skysurfer soon develops a desire to find the bigger hill, the stronger air currents, and join the birds.

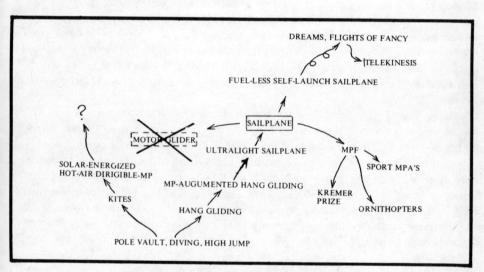

John McMasters lays out the entire eco-flight spectrum

"The charm of such flight is indescribable, and there could not be a healthier motion or more exciting sport in the open air" – Otto Lilienthal

Now that the craft is ready and you have convinced yourself that you are too, mount the glider on top of the car. Use a roof rack or sufficient padding so as not to scratch the paint. Wrap it securely so that it won't be torn up in the breeze while driving; one small piece of flapping fabric will completely destroy itself in the wind in a short time. A cover will not only protect the craft during transport to the site, but it will shed water from that unexpected thundershower. Lash it securely to the car top; use buffers where the rope passes around the bumper or the constant joggling will create a sawing action and your glider's first flight may be with wings folded on the freeway. Attach a red flag to each end. Some states, such as California, require a flag on any item which overhangs more than 18''. Such an eye catcher also aids in steering foreheads away in the parking lot.

Assemble a flight kit of spare parts, tools, instruments, clothing, etc. Be prepared! Fifty miles from home is no place to discover you need a jacket, fifty feet in the air is no place to be looking for a wrench.

Paint removable parts such as bolts a bright color to help locate them when dropped into the sand and carry some extras in case you can't. Turnbuckles may be tied on with a piece of string so they won't be lost if vibration unthreads them during transport. If a turnbuckle barrel is lost during transport to the flying site, look for it inside the carrying bag.

Inexpensive racks may be fashioned to fit any car.

The less the disassembly, the easier the assembly. Note the use of hooked bungee cord to keep the tubes together and the sail wrapped.

Roof racks are a great help. Watch the side overhang especially in parking lots and on narrow roads.

The glider should be mounted on the car nose forward so the sail won't fill.

"In developing aviation, in making it a form of commerce, in replacing the wild freedom of danger with the civilized bonds of safety, must we give up this miracle of the air? Will men fly through the sky in the future without seeing what I have seen, without feeling what I have felt? Is that true of all things we call human progress —Do the gods retire as commerce and science advance?" – Charles A. Lindbergh

Most Rogallo type gliders weigh about 35 lbs.

A full cover provides wind protection during transport. Most wear occurs during car top carrying and ground handling.

SITE SELECTION

Torrance Beach, California. A good intermediate slope; a little steep for beginners.

Dillon Beach, North of San Francisco. Excellent for student and intermediate flyers. This high conical sand dune permits flying in any direction.

The ski jump in Lake Placid, NY is for advanced flyers only; it's steep and landing areas are limited.

The dunes of Cape Cod are fine for learning and the soaring is good when the wind is up.

"The air! Man has visions of flight — not the roaring progress of heavy sinking machines, but that silent loveliness of gliding on outstretched arms that comes to everyone in dreams" — Frank S. Stuart, <u>City of the Bees</u>

Escape country in Southern California caters to hang gliders. The area has been cleared off and transportation is provided to the top.

Sylmar, site of the first National Championships is only for the most experienced. Take off is from the mountains in the background.

Hang gliding does not require an airport with its special facilities and personnel but certain conditions are necessary. The most ideal situation for learning would be a high, 60 degree conical shaped sand dune with a constant, smooth 10 mph breeze. Sand is forgiving and many of the bumps and scrapes which ordinarily come with learning to fly can be avoided. Unfortunately, few areas fit this description or they turn out to be jealously guarded by land owners or park rangers. In the Eastern US, the problem is trees, everywhere; they cover every hill. This often means that numerous sites must be located and logged with map and compass; sites can then be determined once the wind direction for that particular flying day is known. In the Western US, there are fewer trees and the wind is nearly always from the west and this permits the establishment of permanent flying sites.

The flying site should have a good launch area and a good landing area. If the slope is a long one, there should be a road from bottom to top. The area must be clear of power lines, fences, trees and rough terrain.

The wind direction should be within 15 degrees of running straight up the hill and less if the site is narrow such as an eastern ski slope. Flights are made into the wind and one should fly down the slope, not across it. Turbulence is caused by uneven terrain; hills, trees and so on. If the site is a narrow ski slope, the wind will come over the trees and spill down into the cleared area and tumble all around. Even the birds won't fly there. Stakes with ribbons placed at intervals from bottom to top of the hill will give a good idea as to the direction of the wind in each area. These wind indicators are especially useful just below the launch point and in the landing area.

Too much wind may lift the nose flipping man and machine up and back. Check the wind, keep the nose down and wear a helmet.

Keep the glider faced into the wind.

"I wanted to do that since I was a little kid, just to climb up the top of a mountain and then go off it . . . I just looked around me as I was flying and I could see all directions and I said, 'This is the finest thing I've ever done.'' — Rich Kilbourne.

The wind speed should be between 5 and 15 mph to start and gusts should not exceed 5 mph. If the wind is a problem during assembly of the glider, it is probably too windy to fly. Check it. Use a hand held wind meter to check the wind speed and a streamer or hand full of dirt to check direction. Experienced pilots can sometimes handle steady winds to 30 mph but this sort of flying is tricky and potentially quite dangerous. Over 15 mph, the wind approaches the flying speed of the glider and the ground speed may be reduced to zero or become negative.i.e.,the wind may lift it and flip it backward carrying the pilot up and maybe over the hill rather dramatically. The result is often serious damage to both.

The slope should be about 30 degrees (from the horizontal, think of a 30-60-90 triangle) and about 50 feet high. If it is higher, one may start at a lower spot, there is no need to go to the top.

This is steeper than the glide of the kite but it must be remembered that because one can only run so fast, the launch is usually in a semi stalled condition and it will be necessary to get the nose down to pick up flying speed before pulling away from the hill.

Ski hills are becoming more and more attractive. They offer a good slope, outstanding support facilities and that all important chair lift back up the hill. Many ski areas are looking into hang gliding as a summertime activity.

Just as in skiing, the easiest and fastest way to learn is to take lessons.

SETTING UP

These instructions and photographs for setting up the Chandelle glider are generally applicable to all Rogallos.

1. Remove the carrying bag and lay the glider on the ground with the nose into the wind.

2. Separate side, front, and rear wires. The front wires are shorter than the rear wires.

3. Attach the control bar, being certain that the pip pin is completely through the hole.

4. Attach the nose wires, being certain that the wires are not twisted.

5. Attach the rear wires, being certain that the wires are not twisted.

6. Place the glider in an upright position with the nose down and into the wind.

7. Rotate the cross bar being careful not to pinch the sail.

8. Raise the king post and attach the front upper wire.

9. Remove the tie from around the tubes and unfold each wing out to the end of the crossbar being careful not to scrape the fabric.

10. Secure the wing to the cross bar with wing bolts. Attach the tangs and lower wires to the bolt.

then tighten the palm grips securely. (Note: a partner may be needed in a wind.)

11. Adjust the upper, side turnbuckle until the lower wires are taut. Tune the fore-aft turnbuckle so that approximately 1-1½" of upward reflex occurs when sighting down the keel tube.

For dissassembly, detune the turnbuckles and reverse the procedure. Be sure to carefully roll each side of the sail to the center, avoiding any sharp fittings.

PRE-FLIGHTING

After assembling the new glider on site, "pre-flight" it; inspect it in every detail, you could be hanging your life on it. Develop a system, walk around it the same way every time. See that all structural members are in order, that the sail is not torn or distorted, that all fasteners are secure and that the craft is properly rigged. A simple check list makes the task easy and assures that nothing is left out. For example, with the common Rogallo:

CONTROL BAR:	On forward (front wires to the front)
TUBES:	Sight down them checking for bends. The Keel must not bend down. Check for depressions and cracks.
SAIL:	Make sure it is secure at all ends. Check for pinching between the keel and cross tube and between cross tube and leading edges. Check for wear.
NOSE PLATE:	Not distorted.
KINGPOST/CONTROL BAR:	Aligned.
BOLTS:	In place, not bent, secure, threads not stripped.
TURNBUCKLES:	Tight and safetied.
CABLES:	Snap each wire checking tightness and making sure they aren't caught around a bolt or tang. Check for wear especially around the thimbles. Nico sleeves secure.
HARNESS/SEAT:	Straight, adjusted to proper height (seated-just above belt buckle, prone - 2''-3'' above bar), secure.

Harness adjustment for prone flying.

Stand back and sight for overall balance and rigging. Pick up the glider and fill it slightly with wind. Check the harness length. Rotate the nose up and down several times; the craft should be tight and responsive.

First the aircraft must be tested to prove that it will fly and then the new pilot must learn to fly it. If the glider is not properly constructed and trimmed, no amount of running or elevation will prompt flight. New craft should be flown first by an experienced pilot who may pronounce it flyable.

Make a thorough damage check after each hard landing.

GROUND HANDLING

Just as the parachutist finds that packing his parachute takes longer than unpacking it, the skysurfer is confronted with a trip back up the hill which is more difficult, longer and less enjoyable than coming down.

Keep the glider faced into the wind at all times; during setting up, launch, landing, carrying and disassembly.

Carry it up if the winds are low.

"If a new wing doesn't fly, check the rigging then check yourself" – Russ Velderrain

To carry the Rogallo type glider back up, turn around and rest the top of the control frame on the shoulders with the glider pointing down hill (into the wind). If the up-slope wind is sufficient, the breeze may be trapped and will actually assist you in lifting the wing's weight while you walk along with it. Do not carry it while still connected to it as a sudden gust will pick both of you up and off the ground; the landing may be rough. Some designers have added wheels to the corners of the control frame to save the fingers from "road rash" and these same wheels are very helpful in trailering the glider back up the slope.

Fly it up if the winds are high. Walk the wires and find the best position.

A friend or two can be a great help particularly when the wind is up. Now is when you find if you really have any friends.

If the glider's wing tip catches on the ground and the wind wants to tip it over, it is best to let it go. If you don't, the wing tip will probably be bent. On the other hand, if it flips too fast, the king post may be smashed. It is wise to carry spares.

To turn the kite back over, swing it around until it is less than perpendicular to the wind line. Lift the down hill leading edge and the wind will turn it over into an upright position. If winds are high, solicit help.

While the trek up the hill may be good for you, it is often quite demanding. The new flyer will push himself lost in the excitement discovered in this new sport. Carrying a kite is like muscling a large umbrella in a windstorm; for most, climbing up a hill naked would be enough. Carrying a kite up a hill along with the wind pushing down on it is hard on the leg muscles, particularly the upper legs. A weekend of excited, intense flying will provide not only some souvenir scrapes and bruises but a couple of painful charley-horses.

"Being prepared to fly" means, among other things, having the body and mind in top shape to coordinate the controls without error. Take a rest at the top of the hill. It's been a lot of work, a long tough hike, now make the best of it; make this the best flight of all.

FOOT LAUNCHED hang gliding is the most popular and most closely reflects the activities of the birds. Many skysurfers frown on other launching methods; they feel that running down hill on your own is the only way. Remember that even small birds must learn to fly and you too will stumble before you soar. The foot launch is the best way to acquire this knowledge and one should not go on to other altitude gaining methods until man is master of the machine. So foot launching and flying will be discussed here and other methods of launching will follow later in the chapter.

To learn the fundamentals, many begin with the original hang glider system: parallel bars. They hang by the armpits and grasp the bars to maintain control. All the control is

"The idea is to teach people how to feel the kite, how to feel the wind" – Dave Kilbourne.

effected through weight shifting. The swing seat or harness arrangement with the trapeze bar gives more control since the craft may be tilted as the weight is shifted. Both systems will be discussed here and a thorough understanding of both will help in flying either system.

There are two basic camps when it comes to describing the guidance of the glider: one prefers to think in terms of pointing the ship in relation to themselves and the other visualize themselves as shifting weight beneath the glider. It has also been suggested that one think with the first group when standing on the ground and with the second once airborne.

FLYING WITH THE TRAPEZE BAR

Fasten yourself into the seat or don the harness and snap it to the frame, as applicable. Place a foot on, or in back of, the trapeze bar and pull on the uprights rotating the glider to where the keel is parallel to the ground.

With the hands spread wide, lift the trapeze bar to waist level and balance the kite by resting the two upper angled bars on the shoulders.

Now lift the kite into the full up position until you feel tension on the swing seat or harness. Pulling up further will raise the nose while pushing forward on the upright bars with the shoulders will lower it. Lean into the wind; bend the body forward slightly in order to assume a comfortable running position.

Face into the wind and hook up.

Place one foot on the bar and pull on the uprights to rotate the nose up.

Grasp the bar and prepare to lift.

Preparing for launch with the prone harness. Note the position of the elbows and the streamer dangling from the fore wires.

"In order to practice flying with these sailing surfaces one first takes short jumps on a somewhat inclined surface till he has somewhat accustomed himself to be borne by the air" – Otto Lilienthal

Holding the glider in the neutral position and preparing to launch. Note that the straps of the swing seat are routed in front of the shoulders.

When the trapeze bar is very wide, hold the cross bar with one hand and the upright with the other. It is a bit awkward at first but pitch control is better.

The one-shoulder method commonly used for launching today's large trapezes, which are too wide for balancing against both shoulders.

Hold the glider in this neutral position with the sail quiet or flapping slightly; there should be no tendency for the kite to rise or be forced down.

Recheck the wind direction. You must run straight into it and it may not be coming directly up the hill. You may have to run at an angle and you should avoid the tendency to dip a wing into the wind or to tilt the glider to stay level with the hill. Fly the wind, not the ground. If the take off run is not directly into the wind, there may be a tendency to drop one wing and it may catch on the ground and result in a ground loop.

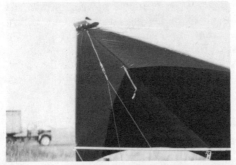

Tie a ribbon or piece of string to the wires near the nose; it will be very useful to assure a straight, into the wind launch as well as to help in judging wind velocity. If attached to the sail fabric under the keel, it won't catch on the cables as often.

11

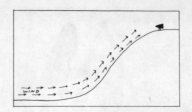

Run forward, fill the sail, nose down slightly to gain speed. Raise the nose for lift off and then drop it slightly to gain flying speed and plane through (over) the air (wind).

An Eipper-Formance drawing of the flight sequence. When starting on the slope rather than at the crest, level the keel with the horizon.

With the sail just slightly filled, get the straps tight, elbows out, lean into it and GO! Once committed, don't hesitate, run as though you planned to run all the way to the bottom.

Once off the ground, pull the control bar back to bring the nose down and pick up flying speed.

Ready? Now the pre-launch check list: Helmet on, harness tensioned, wind line, cleared flight path. Glance side to side: wing level. Raise the nose just very slightly above the neutral position to barely fill the sail and start running. Build up speed while controlling the pitch of the glider. Run smoothly, don't bounce up and down. Lean forward into the kite and pull upward to maintain tension on the suspension system. If the nose tends to rise, push forward with the elbows, if the nose tends to drop, pull up harder on the bar. If you have trouble running, the nose is too high and you are pulling the air with you. If the nose is too low, it will want to nose into the ground. Your glider is a flying bird, not a chicken and this taxiing is awkward but you must do your best. Get the feel of it; you must be able to control the kite while running full tilt down the hill.

The higher the wind, the shorter the run before lift off. Gently push the bar forward to lift the nose and fill the sail. It will become taut and quiet and you will lift off. If you push away too early or too much, the nose will go up too far and the glider will stall, falling back to earth. Once off, relax the upward pull and pull the bar back to get the nose down and pick up some flying speed. If using a prone harness, pick up the legs and lie down. Make sure you are flying as nose-ins are common at this point.

Now feel the air and adjust the glider angle for flying speed. Keep the nose low to avoid

12

the stall but keep it up to avoid luff. Don't porpoise by making radical pitching movements, take it easy.

Don't be anxious for altitude,at this level it is more important to go for speed. Try to fly just a few feet off the ground and keep the speed up. Speed may later be traded for altitude if needed. Speed gives control.

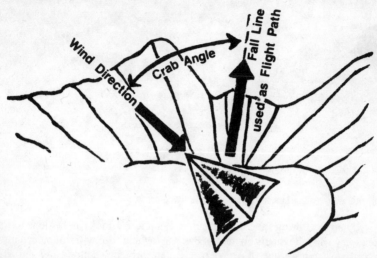

Intermediate fliers will want to try Dave Kilbourne's method for cross-wind takeoffs; handy when the wind is not coming directly up the slope. Face the glider directly into the wind and then run straight down the slope.

In learning, it is best to build confidence by mastering the landing before acquiring the ability to take off. The first flight should be very short; run and push forward on the bar so that the glider pitches up and stalls perhaps lifting the pilot a foot or two off the ground. Follow this with the take off instruction above and make a very short flight. Then lengthen the flights. It is comforting to know when running full tilt down a slope that you have the ability to stop at any time.

It is very important to note the relative positions of the bar, hands and shoulders. If you are leaning back with feet out front, you won't be able to push the bar forward as far as when leaning into it. In fact, probably not forward far enough to get the nose up. Also one must push out, not down. Think about this.

> *"You may see others flying off high hills and others soaring. You, the new flier, cannot do this and if you are foolish enough to try, you violate Murphy's law and the laws of Mother Nature will take their course"* – Larry Mauro.

Tom Peghiny initiating a right turn at Cape Cod while flying prone.

Crashes will happen during the learning stages but a few things can be done to minimize or eliminate injury. Install wheels on the trapeze bar so the glider will roll on ground contact instead of coming to an abrupt stop. Wear adequate protective clothing such as gloves, helmet and knee pads. When the crash is inevitable, aim your body between the bars, don't hit them. Some padding on the bars will be paid for the first day out.

Once up and flying, listen for the flapping of the sail's trailing edge. If it is flapping loud and violently, the speed is too high, push the bar forward. If it is quiet and there is little or no wind in your face, you are near the stall. Pull back and get the nose down to pick up flying speed. The sail should flutter lightly and there should be a light breeze in the face. As you become more experienced, you'll gauge speed more by feel than sound. Do not push the bar up or down, push it forward or pull it back to adjust flying speed.

Turning is easy but takes some practice to make the movements come naturally. Remember that the body is plumb and it is the wing that is tilted into a turn; the kite goes in the direction your weight goes. Body left and the kite turns left, body right and the kite turns right. The same also applies to the pitch of the nose: Body forward and the speed increases as the kite dives, body pushed back and the speed decreases as the kite flares. So to make a turn, move the bar to the opposite side. When approaching a hazard such as a tree, simply move the bar in its direction as if to push yourself away from it.

Gauge and monitor the turns with care; centrifugal force may pull you to the side and aggravate the turn. Tight turns are desired by the more experienced: Wills uses an extra wide control bar and Kilbourne has been known to step on a cable to bend the keel. But tight turns while sometimes helpful, reduce the lift and these maneuvers are reserved for those who have mastered the art.

360 degree turns should only be executed by the experienced and then only with sufficient altitude and room. Do not look back over the opposite shoulder in a turn, it is easy to become disoriented and crash.

The flying speed must be maintained during turns and this means the flying speed of *both* wing tips. When flying slow and close to the stall point, it is common to stall out one tip in a turn because one tip speeds up while the other slows down. Once a tip stalls, its loses lift,

"A wise man is cautious and avoids danger; a fool plunges ahead with great confidence" – Jim Diffenderfer

Tom Peghiny making a small turn over Torrance Beach seated.

Kent Trimble in a tight turn. Centrifugal force swings the body off plumb and further increases the bank. Pushing the bar forward will further increase the bank and tighten the turn. This type of overcontrol is reserved for the experts.

quits flying and drops. The remedy is simply to keep the speed up for turns and this means pulling the bar back slightly before moving it to one side. In a turn, the glider banks and the lift force generated is less so more speed is required to keep above the stall. Higher flying speeds also provide faster turns; if the turns are sluggish it's probably because the flying speed is low.

If the glider starts into an unintentional turn, it may be stalling and falling off to one side. Pull in a little on the bar and push it in the direction of the turn. This should effect a turn in the opposite direction which will level the wings and return you to normal flight.

Make all turns into the wind. A great deal of altitude is required to turn and fly down wind and then turn back into it for landing.

To land, keep headed into the wind and get the nose down for a little extra speed. At 10' to 15' from the ground, push the bar forward slowly and then, depending on the speed of the wind as judged by your ground speed, push the bar way forward at 4' to 6' to produce a full stall landing. Get the feet down and forward preparing for ground contact. With practice, you will glide in and flare like the birds. Don't stall too high and fall and don't land with

15

more forward speed than you can run out. Practice pays off. If the flare is too high, the glider will stall and one nice thing about Rogallos is that you can ''parachute'' them in. Just keep the nose up, keep the kite level. The best approaches are hot and high.

The feet forward, butt skimming landings often produce injuries and they're very painful. They usually occur when flyers try to extend their flight rather than land when they should. Keep the landing gear down.

Immediately upon landing, put the nose down on the ground and into the wind and then disconnect from the glider. Disconnecting is more important than wind line orientation. Remember that birds fold their wings on landing so that they won't blow away.

To land,push forward and get the gear down and out front.

A sudden gust may flip the craft and it is best not to be attached to it during these unplanned maneuvers.

Always land into the wind. If a cross wind landing is necessary, keep the upwind wing lower than the down wind tip by shifting the weight in the direction of the wind.

Do not attempt a landing in a turn as you will be off balance after ground contact and the ground speed will be faster making a smooth landing difficult if not impossible.

Plan the landing by picking a spot, noting the wind line and setting up an approach. Diving will build too much air speed, use ''S'' turns to compensate for an overshoot.

The need for radical movement is rare and should not be attempted by the novice. Initially, only gentle corrections will be required to keep the craft flying into the wind. Avoid overcontrolling, make the movements smooth and gentle.

For both birds and aircraft, the takeoff and landing are the most dangerous parts of flying. It is at this point that the airspeed is low, the lift is weak and a mistake can be disastrous because the flying speed has been reduced making recovery and a new landing attempt difficult if not impossible. If the branch moves as the bird comes in for a landing, he's in trouble.

Getting up takes a lot more energy than staying up and both planes and birds use everything they can: flaps, angle of attack, slotted wings, facing into the wind, etc. The Condor has a wing span of some nine feet and he can't get airborne from level ground without some wind, he can't run fast enough to achieve flying speed and his wings hit the ground if he just starts flapping. Condors usually take off and land from cliffs. Herons use their legs to jump into the air while ducks push on the water with their wings. Some water birds run on top of the water with their webbed feet to pick up flying speed.

A ground crew assist can be very helpful when learning and when the winds aren't right.The keel assist is often used in schools and sometimes to help a friend get flying speed when the winds are low. If there is a good wind and the student is running as he is supposed to, pushing isn't necessary. The glider is guided, kept pointed into the wind and at the right pitch.

The tail man must let go gently with the craft in a level position. If he shoves down, the glider will go nose up and stall, and if he pushes the tail up, the craft will nose in to the ground. The problem is that the pilot tends to compensate for the mistakes of the pusher. Learning to control a keel is probably harder than learning to fly. Get a good tail man.

The keel assist.

The wire assist is helpful when the student is first getting the feel for the glider and is necessary to the expert when flying in high winds, particularly in the cliff launch. The assistant holds onto the front cables to steady the glider and when the pilot says he is ready and starts to run, he immediately releases the wires, moves to one side and ducks to miss the wing wires. Timing has to be good.

The wire assist.

"The gull sees farthest who flies highest" – Richard Bach

17

Monoplanes without elevator control need a crew of two during launch, one on the tail and one on a wing to steady it.

Ground crew tow assists with a short rope can be very dangerous; the transition from tow to gliding flight can be quite challenging and should not be taken lightly.

FLYING ON PARALLEL BARS

To begin with, a hill is not even necessary in order to get the feel of the glider. Start on level ground and run directly into the wind. If running is difficult, the nose is too high and you should move forward on the bars. If the front of the glider tends to nose into the ground, move back to pick it up. A good general rule is to keep the nose slightly high and you won't fly too fast or nose in. If the glider pulls to one side, make sure you are running directly into the wind; the wind doesn't always blow straight up the hill. You must position yourself perfectly in the balance point and this will take some time to locate. Note the position for the best speed, mark it and feel secure that you won't stall unless hit by a sudden gust. Many skysurfers like to mark this point with tape or they "red line" the limits with lumps.

It must be remembered that hang tubes offer less control (especially in roll) than the trapeze bar arrangement unless you have controls.

From time to time it is wise to check the sail symmetry and rigging alignment, particularly after hard landings. For the first few trials, it is best to "ostrich run" with a step-hop-glide-step-hop-glide to get the feel for the center of balance and the lifting power of the wing.

Richard Miller ground skimming in the Conduit Condor.

Chuck Slusarczyk shifts weight to effect a turn.

After feeling it out on the level, it is time to progress to the slope. That is a "slope" not a cliff; pick a gentle hill which matches the glide angle of the flying system. Gradually work your way up the slope making short check out flights as you very cautiously run once again but this time down hill. As you gain experience and feel for the lifting and balancing qualities of the wing, you will get to the point where you are pulled away from the slope. Lift off will come with the proper combination of speed, wind and slope. In general, the steeper the slope, the less wind is required for a good takeoff. Keep it low, keep it slow, make short practice hops until your guiding reflexes become natural. Again, even the birds must LEARN how to fly!

Ready for the big one? Back to the top of the slope. Position the armpits over the parallel bars and grasp the uprights. Face into the wind and run forward until the lift pulls you away from the earth. Now quickly adjust your position, and correspondingly the attitude of the wing, for flight: weight forward to counteract a climb or weight back to recover from a dive condition. Flight is controlled by body english. Shift the weight forward to drop and gain speed or back to level off from a dive, climb, go slower or stall. Very little movement to the front or rear is necessary, don't overdo it.

To turn, stick the feet out in the direction of the desired turn, both weight shift and air drag will help to effect it. If the turn tightens, it may be necessary to throw the legs in the opposite direction to counter it. This requires the experience of a gymnast and the turns are not coordinated, they're skidding, there is no bank.

By shifting your weight, you'll find it possible to maintain control of the glider in both altitude and direction.

Otherwise, the flying is very much like that described for the trapeze bar system earlier.

When you make up your mind to foot launch, do it, don't pussyfoot, don't become anxious. Run hard while holding the nose down and then slide back somewhat to get off in a non mushing attitude. Both running and flying are not so difficult but halfway in between is because as the wing provides lift, you lose traction.

To land, glide down and level off with your landing gear 3-5 feet from the ground. Gradually raise the nose and slow your descent by sliding rearward on the bars, reach back with the feet and with a few running steps you should settle gently to earth standing up. Such a flight may take you 20 seconds and 100 yards.

Caution must be exercised in controlling the flight path. Extremes in control can cause loss of flying speed and a drop to the ground. Especially to be avoided is the STALL which accompanies a sharp nose up condition with its inevitable loss of flying speed.

The nose up attitude is desirable only when making a flared landing as it results in zero forward speed at touch down.

Accidental or unplanned landings may be uncomfortable because one usually braces himself so as not to damage the glider; this weight shifting may affect the last few moments of flight and hasten touchdown.

If coming in too high and you have individually operated ailerons or spoilers, use them in unison to destroy some lift and drop down. Experiment with different body positions to increase and reduce drag.

The Icarus II uses parallel bars for the pitch (nose up and down) control but it also has rudders mounted at the wing tips.

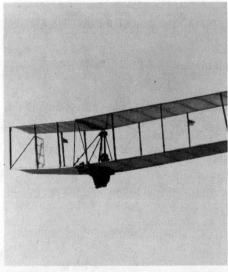

Launching the Icarus II is the same except that the rudders are used to keep the wings level and to keep the ship pointed into the wind. Once airborne, one can prop up his feet, sit back and fly.

"Be sensitive at all times to small changes in direction and altitude and apply small corrections early, rather than gross corrective effort later – Taras Jr.

19

Taras, Jr. landing the Icarus II.

On final.

Gear down.

Flaring.

Touch down.

THE CLIFF LAUNCH

The cliff launch is one of the easiest and it is one of the most desirable if there is a road from bottom to top. The launch is a little tricky and one must be sure to be flying once he leaves the ground; there is little margin for error. Ease the nose of the glider to the edge and feel for updrafts. Have an assistant hold the nose wires as you edge out.

If the wind is light, hold the glider in the neutral position, run and on stepping off, pop the nose up quickly to fill the sail and lift off. Then quickly get the bar back to drop the nose and pick up flying speed. If the wind is over 10 mph, be especially wary and get that bar back quickly. The wind will try to lift the nose and you must keep it down. Above 20 mph, the pilot requires a nose wire walker to hold the front wires and get the glider flying prior to release. Without this assistance, the glider will probably pitch up violently and toss the pilot back into the parking lot.

Remember: angle of attack is relative to the wind, not the ground.

From the Lookout in the Ortegas above Lake Elsinore, California, it is 1200 feet to the valley below.

And he's off. Notice the control bar pulled way back.

Initially, there is a drop as flying speed is gained.

Flights of 2-4 minutes are typical and if the wind is right, soaring is possible.

Like the water surfer searching for the larger wave, skysurfers are already combing the maps and mountains for the higher, steeper, better hill.

This, then is real bird-like gliding. With a good road for car top carrying, several flights can be easily made each day. But some search out the more remote flying sites and relish the challenge between man and mountain. For them, true sport is a long climb to the top of a mountain carrying the collapsed glider on the shoulder. Erecting it at the selected launch site and then with a strong and steady run, the pilot is off alternately skimming the mountain side and soaring out into the sky. The minutes and miles add up like the dials on a gas pump as he flies on and on with the cool breeze in his face. Ultimate freedom! Hopefully, flight will terminate near a road or in some sparsely populated area. With any luck at all, it will be a crowded beach and he will appear from nowhere, circle out over the water, come in seeming to skim the waves and performing a perfect standup on the beach in much the same manner that a seagull lands on a piling. Such a flight is exhilarating and what could be better than to climax it with an admiring audience.

The Author cliff launches at Torrance Beach.

Bill Bennett launches from Dantes View in Death Valley, California. The 6.2 mile flight took 11 minutes and 47 seconds to the valley floor 5,757 feet below.

And so the big problem is not so much in the flying but in the launch and in hang gliding there are many ways too.

THE KITE LAUNCH

The kite launch is simple and effective; it can be accomplished with a boat or a car. Hang Gliders have been kite launched by assistants on the ground with a short rope and even with an aircraft tow to several thousand feet. The kite launch owes its heritage to water ski kiting and it was the only way before Kilbourne tried the foot launch. But kiting is very dangerous particularly if the rope breaks or the release operates prematurely; very few experienced flyers will even consider it.

Kiting may have to return if hang gliding is to be enjoyed by those living in the Plains and some water skiers just aren't content with being on the water. Almost everyone in the hang gliding business agrees, if you must tow, go see Bennett or Moyes and learn to do it right. Kiting is regulated by the F.A.A. under Part 101.

Flexible wing tow gliders go back to the early 1960s. NASA built and flew the Paresev test vehicle while the US Army and Ryan Aircraft Co. developed and flight tested a variety of towed gliders for aerial delivery of cargo and equipment.

Both theory and statistics indicate that auto towing of hang gliders is perhaps the most dangerous mode of flight, and often the mode attempted by beginners. I will continue to advise against it, certainly for anyone short of an expert, and even experts have been killed doing it. – F. M. Rogallo

Bill Bennett kiting at Lake Tahoe.

Bill Bennett over the San Francisco-Oakland Bay Bridge.

The Bennett release.

Example of a towing accident about to happen. It was blowing 15 and a decision was made to kite this Rogallo. It shot quickly into the air and the pilot let go of the rope. He pulled the nose down and the wind pushed the glider into the ground. Result: one broken arm.

The Seasprite by Flight Dynamics under tow.

SKI LAUNCHING

Ski launching is easy, in fact it can be easier than the foot launch since one can ski faster than he can run but there are a few important rules. One should use a swing seat and regular or shorty skis. Flying prone is done on shortys only and should be left to the more experienced. Simply make a run down the slope holding the glider in the neutral position until the speed is sufficient for flight. Push out and rotate the nose up to fill the sail and lift off. With a few runs, both launching and landing will be smooth. Skis allow so much speed that even downwind takeoffs may be accomplished.

Remember the rules of the foot launch such as taking off into the wind and practicing on lower slopes to get the feel of skis vs. kite. Mountain winds are usually gusty and ski slopes have a lot of obstacles such as lift towers, trees, power lines and skiers. Ski slopes are normally perfect sites for hand gliding as there is a good elevation difference, outstanding support facilities and, of course, the all important lift back to the top. Many ski areas are looking into hang gliding as a summertime use for their real estate and demonstration flights are in great demand. Flyers must continue to approach the ski business professionally and to stay out of the way of the paying customers, the skiers.

When foot launching on snow or ice without skis, it is a good idea to have some sort of traction devices such as strap on spikes; traction is so poor that is is difficult to get up enough speed for take off.

Doug Weeks, Jr. at Brodie Mountain, Massachusetts.

Paul Laliberte over Maine's Sugarloaf ski area.

Setting up at Sugarloaf, Maine.

Dave Kilbourne balloon launches, one of many ways
to get up there.

STAYING UP-GLIDING

Many beginners believe that once launched, the glider will fly by itself; this is NOT so. This is not a parachute which depends only on drag and will lower you gently to earth. This is an aircraft which must be carefully guided, "flown" until it comes to a complete rest. Many perils lie ahead, most of which can only be appreciated by pilots, aeronautical engineers, and experienced skysurfers.

The most important thing to remember in flying is to *keep flying*. Keep your speed up, maintain your flying speed. If you slow to a point below your flying speed (probably between 15 and 20 mph), you will stall and drop to earth. To be safe, let's say that 20 mph worth of air must pass over the wings; this means *both* wings! We say "both" because in a turn, one wing slows down and if it does so to a point below the minimum flying speed, you're stalled! From what we can read, a stall in turning flight is what killed pioneer Otto Lilienthal and it has probably killed more pilots than any other maneuver since. The answer, of course is to keep the speed up for turns. The problem is particularly critical where hang gliders are concerned for a number of reasons which bear constant review.

It is very difficult to estimate airspeed. A Dwyer wind meter strapped to the front of the craft is helpful once well clear of the ground and flying but is difficult to read when attention is constantly directed to the terrain and changing air currents. Some sort of an audio noisemaker would help. When a pilot has accumulated a great deal of experience with the same ship, he may be able to rely on the natural noises of the wind through the ship's surfaces.

Since most hang gliders fly in the 20 mph range, most power plane pilots experience difficulty adjusting to this type of flight; they are not accustomed to remaining airborne in such low and slow conditions.

Flying near the stall point should be avoided unless the glider has full controls and there is ample altitude for recovery. When near the ground in turbulent conditions, a reserve of airspeed should be maintained in case of changes in wind direction and/or velocity.

STALLS involve loss of altitude and this loss occurs while out of control. The ailerons, if the craft has them, will be practically useless and they may even work the wrong way. The elevators won't make the ship respond. The rudder will have some control over rolling and

25

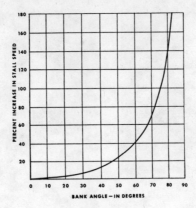

Stall speed chart.

not much over yaw (turns) but at least this will be of some help in bringing up a dropped wing. The first thing to do is to get the nose down in order to gain speed and get flying. Many pilots have a tendency to put the ship right back into the stall; as soon as they get some speed and feeling returns to the controls, they nose the craft back up again. Most hang gliders do not have controls and a stall means just one thing: a quick return to earth. As the wing drops, it loses lift and drops more turning the craft back into the hill.

The best recovery procedure for a standard Rogallo is to pull the bar back in an attempt to get the nose down and build up airspeed and then ease it forward.

Lower the nose slightly before turning. There is a tendency to push forward when making turns to gain more altitude or to avoid dragging a wing tip; both cost in airspeed.

Stalls also occur when the angle of attack is raised (nose up) above the stalling angle, the point at which the air ceases to flow smoothly over the wings and lift is reduced below the flying speed. Often pilots raise the nose in a turn or when they near the ground in an attempt to remain airborne. They only succeed in lowering the airspeed, stalling and dropping to the ground.

The angle of attack must be proper in relation to the wind, not with the horizon and it must be lower as the airspeed decreases for the craft to remain flying.

Stalls usually occur at a critical altitude above the ground: not high enough to recover flying speed and attitude but still high enough to gain speed and crash. Further, in the first tentative turn along the slope and off the wind line, the effect of a stalled inner wing tip will be to turn the glider further, heading it back into the hill. Now you're in real trouble because the flying speed of the glider is added to the speed of the wind and your ground speed could be 40 mph with the ground coming up fast.

Stalls may occur from changes in vertical winds. Flying near the stalling speed over a ridge can be a problem if one enters air rising more steeply because, in effect, the angle of attack has increased beyond the stalling angle without a change in attitude. Washout permits a gradual stall to occur and if recognized by the pilot, a recovery can be made prior to the full stall condition.

The Rogallo wing is very forgiving in that it will often "parachute" back to earth in a stall. It mushes into a stall; there isn't a sharp division between flying and stalling. First the sail goes quiet, then there is a loss of lateral control and the glide angle degrades. The glider wants to drop its nose and get up to flying speed again and this is fine if altitude permits. If near the ground, one must make large, exaggerated control movements to keep the wing level and stalled. Parachuting in is usually safe but the wing becomes very vulnerable to gusts. It is far preferable to make a normal landing with plenty of flying speed. If the descent rate is too great, try to make the glider hit first to absorb some of the landing shock. In gliders with parallel bars, one may be able to pull himself up within the cage structure.

SPINS are a continuous rolling and yawing (turning) motion with the nose down and recovery without controls and altitude are impossible . Briefly, they occur when a wing drops at low speed and stalls. This inboard wing meets the air with a large angle of attack but lift decreases since the wing is already stalled. It aggravates this condition, the up going wing gains lift and the glider begins to roll. The down going wing is creating more drag, however, and the upper wing will turn toward the down going one. This yawing will continue as long as the craft is rolling and a vertical corkscrewing motion is the result. The standard recovery is hard opposite rudder, pause, and get the nose down. Unfortunately, most hang gliders don't have controls or the altitude for such maneuvers. On the other hand, spins have not been a common hang glider problem. Remember: an aircraft must be stalled before it will spin.

Another problem encountered in turns is catching a wing tip on a bush or bluff. This most often happens during cliff launches and ridge soaring. Leave a good margin between the leeward wing tip and the slope. Anticipate bushes and cliffs and make turns to avoid them in plenty of time. If the winds die and there is a chance of wing tip/ground contact, straighten out and fly to the beach.

HIGH SPEED DIVES are sometimes deliberately entered into when the pilot wants to drop down a steep slope to gain enough air speed to leave the slope and begin a normal glide. In these dives, the hanging or swinging pilot tends to permit his weight to shift forward which maintains or increases his dive. The steeper the dive, the more muscle power required to move the weight back. If he should move back too fast, however, high stresses may be placed on the structure of the craft. It is preferable to gain flying speed by running down the slope so that steep diving launches are not necessary.

Stall recovery and steep turns also place additional loads on the structure; it is best to make all maneuvers gently.

Another high speed dive problem has come to be known as "Dive Syndrome" and it may occur in a couple of different ways. In the early stages of flying, a pilot may be reluctant to gain too much altitude and he ground skims, following the shape of the slope rather than trimming the glider out for maximum glide. On a steep slope, he can build up a terrific amount of speed. Sometimes, those making their first high flights become anxious because the ground under them doesn't seem to be moving as it was on the previous lower flights and they dive to get moving. The ground *seems* to move slower and slower the further away one moves from it. And the wind may actually equal or exceed one's ground speed at the higher altitude so one could actually be standing still or moving slightly backwards with relation to the ground. This is not a stall — we are talking of *airspeed* not *groundspeed* — listen to the wind and the sail and fly by ear.

These high speed dives create a shift in the center of pressure and the shape of the sail changes. It may take a tremendous amount of forward pressure on the trapeze bar to push the nose up. In fact, some pilots have reported the necessity of "standing" on the bar with their feet.

The solution, of course, is to fly the air, not the more visible and more familiar ground. Feel the wind on the face and listen for the flap of the sail; don't look to the ground as an indication of speed. After all, if the wind is blowing twenty, you may hover in one spot.

This is a good place to mention that those with prior aviation experience have a bit of an advantage; they learn faster. A pilot will have to learn new movements for control but he already knows that he must keep his airspeed up. A parachutist must learn to work with pitch (nose up-down) control but he is used to hanging in a harness with nothing between himself and the ground. Consequently when he takes off, he doesn't become anxious about being in the air and he can better concentrate on flying.

Until now, we've preoccupied ourselves with gliding; a launch and then a slow glide back to earth. The next step is soaring; to get aloft and remain aloft in one manner or another. As Lord Rayleigh stated way back in 1883, soaring flight requires a wind that is not horizontal or one that is not of uniform velocity. Soaring can be broken into two groups, static and dynamic; static exhibits itself in three basic forms: ridge soaring, wave soaring and thermal soaring.

Chris Wills at Sylmar.

RIDGE SOARING may be accomplished where the prevailing winds strike a sharp slope, ridge or cliff and deflect upwards such as is found on the coast with an on-shore breeze. As long as this upcurrent is greater than your sink rate, you can ride it back and forth all day and that is what real "skysurfing" is all about.

All turns must be made into the wind, away from the ridge and the pilot must be careful to remain in the upcurrent of air. Even with some altitude this rule must be followed as a down wind turn will quickly send the glider into the lee. Feel it out, find where the currents are. Carefully drift in and out with the contours of the slope maintaining the same distance from it. The upcurrent is strongest close to the ridge but one runs the risk of catching a wing tip. The stronger the wind, the farther away from the ridge one may venture. The wind becomes rougher the closer one flys to the ridge and is aggravated under thermaling conditions. Keep the speed up; a gust may suddenly reduce the air speed leaving you in a stalled condition.

Avoid rounded hill tops and ridges as the air often comes up one side and then "waterfalls" down the other. Flat top ridges are far better.

The lift band may reach well over the top of the ridge but one cannot count on it; it is best to stay away from the lee side of the ridge.

In ridge soaring, one dreams of returning after a long flight to land back on top of the cliff but there is often a lot of sink and turbulence as you go inland. To execute it properly and land into the wind, one must fly down wind over the cliff and then turn back into the wind for the landing on the cliff and this requires wind speed and altitude. Launching and landing at the same elevation is not just a dream but doing it at the exact same point is because of the different wind requirements.

If the wind is high enough to soar, the launch will be tricky. Follow the instructions for cliff launch and question other flyers at the site. An assistant on the nose wire is a necessity and this is a dangerous proposition as he must hold the glider steady as he backs to the cliff's edge. Good launch timing is essential and the pilot should hold the nose neutral or a bit

28

low, charge forward and "hang" on the bar; lean way forward and hold the bar all the way back. The sudden up rush of air will strike the nose first and attempt to lift it so the pilot must get high penetration speed once off the ground and he will move quickly away from the cliff. Trim out and turn to quarter the wind moving parallel to the cliff. To gain altitude, pump the nose up for just a second and bring it back down to flying speed. Experiment and get the feel of it. Listen for the flap of the sail, feel the wind on the face. Pump the nose up and down. Adjust the angle to the wind and ridge and alter the forward speed to fly back and forth.

Altitude may be lost in turns. Depending on the speed of the wind, one may face into it and remain almost motionless or quarter it and ride the ridge back and forth. From time to time, direction will vary from directly into the wind to almost parallel with the ridge. If the wind should die, soaring flight is over. Face into the wind and glide to a landing below.

Taras Kiceniuk, Jr. and his Icarus II without visible means of support.

Bob Wills flies the up-rushing air for hours.

Typical flight path for beach soaring.

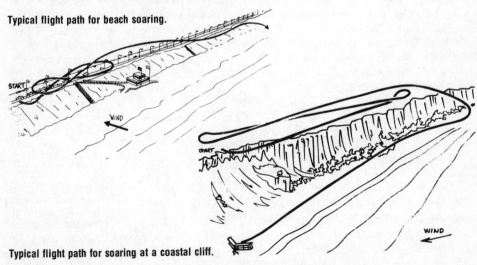

Typical flight path for soaring at a coastal cliff.

"In order to imitate the birds, observe them" - Chuck Stahl

29

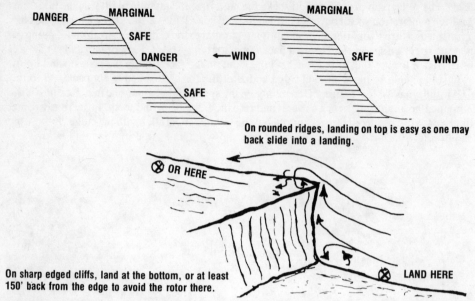

DANGER MARGINAL

SAFE

DANGER ←—WIND

SAFE

MARGINAL

SAFE ←— WIND

On rounded ridges, landing on top is easy as one may back slide into a landing.

⊗ OR HERE

On sharp edged cliffs, land at the bottom, or at least 150' back from the edge to avoid the rotor there.

⊗ LAND HERE

WAVE SOARING conditions can be found on the leeward side of a range of mountains. Initially the wind strikes the mountains and rises producing a ridge soaring condition. Then the wind moves down the other side and rises again. It is in this second rise that one wave soars. Waves are used by sail planes to gain altitude and they can be very dangerous as the rising air mass may be great and violent; some sailplanes have reached more than 45,000 feet. The lee side of the mountain often has downdrafts as well which should be avoided.

THERMAL SOARING takes place in areas where air is rising because it is warmer than the surrounding air. The lift is generated by the sun's heating of ground areas which in turn heats the air which then rises. As can be expected, thermals are usually best during the middle of the day. The air may rise in bubbles or in a column and is normally topped by a condensation phenomenon known as a cumulus cloud. Sail plane pilots search for them under clouds but, unfortunately, the cloud often indicates only where the thermal HAS been and one should, therefore, search for it along the course of the formation and get up front. Thermals often occur over plots of plowed land, roof tops, highways and runways. Fields, trees and rivers, on the other hand, should be avoided. Thermals are often evidenced by a hole in a cloud formation.

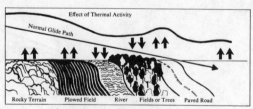

Effect of Thermal Activity

Normal Glide Path

Rocky Terrain   Plowed Field   River   Fields or Trees   Paved Road

The hang glider has the advantages of low speed and a small turn radius but must contend with the disadvantages of low L/D (glide angle) and high sink rate. The chart distinguishes the good areas from the bad. Hang glider flights will at least be prolonged by favoring the good even if the up coming air does not more than match the sink of the craft and keep man and machine aloft. It should be remembered that thermals occur down wind of their cause (highway, etc) and one should hunt for them there.

Hunting for thermals is like groping around in a dark room; they can't be visualized. They must be felt and only trial and error will keep you in it or help you to relocate it after passing through. The thermal usually announces itself with a mild bump and thereafter, you can feel the rise only slightly. Dust devils are really dusty thermals and are much easier to locate. A column of rising, spiraling birds is a sure sign of thermal activity, head for it.

When flying along the edge, the thermal may lift one wing slightly. Bring the nose down and turn into it. If the nose bumps up, you're in it. Turns should be made as soon as the thermal activity begins to slack off. But remember, altitude will be lost in a steep bank.

The air on the outside of a thermal goes down, particularly on the down wind side. The trick is to turn and remain inside.

Again, fly over the better areas to take advantage of any rising air which may be there and will extend the flight.

DYNAMIC SOARING is encountered most often by the academician and probably hasn't been mastered by anyone outside the bird family. It is, however, fun to speculate; it's food for thought. Dynamic soaring is remaining aloft by using winds of different horizontal velocities. Wind flows across the earth at different speeds in different areas. The surface of the earth offers resistance in the form of friction and it is common to find the wind standing still at the surface, moving slowly a few feet up and briskly at 50 feet. Rarely do "wind shears" occur, usually it is a gradual change. It is speculated that if the glider were to descend downwind in the high/upper wind to gain speed and then turn to fly into the slower wind near the surface, lift will be gained. If the craft ascends into the upper wind again, it could be turned to repeat the feat indefinitely. The secret is to use the energy of one wind to fly in another.

For more information, write for the Soaring Society's publication list. (P.O. Box 66071-P, Los Angeles, CA 90066).

MORE ON WIND

Wind under specific gliding and soaring conditions has been discussed but some more general information on this subject is in order.

Wind is simply air in motion. If man could see the air around him instead of just its effects, he might better use the moving air to this advantage. Winds of varying velocities occur around uneven terrain: ridges, gullys, trees, etc. and their prediction is subject to much study. Because man has been involved in high, powered flight for the last seventy years, far more is known about upper winds than those closer to the earth. There are four general rules about winds which affect the overall weather:

Rule 1. Wind blows from high to low pressure. Rule 2. The greater the difference between high and low pressure centers, the stronger the wind. Rule 3. In general, the prevailing winds that move storm systems across North America blow from west to east. Rule 4. Winds blow clockwise around a high pressure system and counterclockwise around a low.

Wind is very necessary to hang gliding and particularly to soaring but it can also be very dangerous. The energy contained in a wind is proportional to the *square* of its velocity. ie., the power of the wind increases much faster than the speed. A 10 mph wind is four times as strong as a 5 mph wind. At 20 mph it is 16 times stronger and at 30 mph it is 36 times more powerful. Remember, if the speed of the wind goes up a little, the force of it goes up a lot!

There has been considerable speculation regarding the practical applications of hang gliding.

However, it has also been theorized that the MOST practical application is the speculation itself . . .

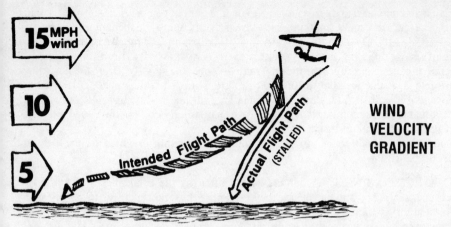

WIND VELOCITY GRADIENT

15 MPH wind
10
5

Intended Flight Path
Actual Flight Path (STALLED)

Always try to land INTO the wind to minimize ground speed and the necessary running to remain upright. (Headlong dives and three point landings - hands and nose - are not only frowned upon, they're uncomfortable). But beware of the wind gradient; the decrease in wind as you near ground level. The wind flows over the ground much as water moves in a stream: faster in the middle and slower at the sides. The wind drops off as you approach the ground. Be ready for it as it will affect your ground speed prior to touch down. It is very common to have a wind blowing 20 at the top of the hill and yet be virtually still at the bottom and it is easy to stall out and land short.

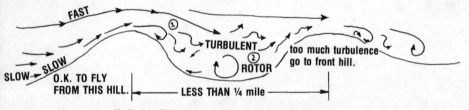

FAST

TURBULENT

too much turbulence
go to front hill.

SLOW

SLOW O.K. TO FLY FROM THIS HILL.

ROTOR

LESS THAN ¼ mile

1) Air is spilling down the hill. 2) Air is too turbulent.

When the flowing wind encounters an obstacle in its path, it tries to move around it, if it can't, it moves over it. This may cause lift or turbulence or both. When the wind encounters a tree, it flows through it and reduces in velocity. Keep the flying speed up when descending into no wind areas such as behind a tree line or the sudden drop in wind will get you. Wind is more turbulent near the ground.

On the lee side of a hill, the wind is usually going down, especially if it is strong. Stay away from the lee side or you may be caught in this downward moving air and forced into a severe crash.

On conical shaped hills, the wind often goes around each side and then rises when it meets again on the lee side.

Wind flowing up a ravine produces a small amount of lift over it and a little more on each side; most of the lift is concentrated at the top. But if the wind shifts just a few degrees so as to flow across the ravine and its ridges to either side, everything changes. This is not the time to fly down the center of tl   vine.

During the early morning and late afternoon, the sun heats one side of a hill while the other side is shaded. This causes the air to rise on the heated side and fall on the cool one. Don't fly down a "shadow line" during the morning or afternoon.

> *"Birds cannot soar to leeward of a descending slope unless high in the air"* – Wilbur Wright.

The wind is rarely straight up the hill and in ridge soaring this means that one flies faster (ground speed) going one direction (quartered down wind) than the other (quartered up wind). What might be a good wind for soaring if coming straight up the ridge may not be enough if coming at an angle. A wind direction shift of just 26 degrees reduces the lift component by one third.

Downdrafts are simply air moving down and it has to stop because the ground is in the way. When caught in a downdraft, it is best to maintain flying airspeed even if it is necessary to dive so as to have enough speed to maintain control once out of it. If not out by 30 feet above the ground, it is best to pitch the nose up and stall the glider if necessary; the landing should be reasonably good under the circumstances.

Down wind flying requires plenty of altitude and room and should not be attempted by the novice. The sudden increase in ground speed is terribly unnerving and it becomes difficult to remain cool. It is common to stall out and the turns are much different.

The keys to ridge lift are the steepness and height of the ridge and turns should be made in the more favorable lift areas. Know the wind's direction and the way it is affected by different types of terrain. Fly over the good areas and your flight will be greatly extended.

GROUP FLIGHTS

When there is more than one glider using the same piece of airspace, some general rules of the road are necessary.

Here are the FAA right of way rules extracted from Part 91 and slightly edited:

(a) General. *When weather conditions permit, regardless of whether an operation is conducted under Instrument Flight Rules or Visual Flight Rules, vigilance shall be maintained by each person operating an aircraft so as to see and avoid other aircraft in compliance with this section. When a rule of this section gives another aircraft the right of way, he shall give way to that aircraft and may not pass over, under, or ahead of it, unless well clear.*

(b) In distress. *An aircraft in distress has the right of way over all other air traffic.*

(c) Converging. *When aircraft of the same category are converging at approximately the same altitude (except head-on, or nearly so) the aircraft to the other's right has the right of way.*

(d) Approaching head-on. *When aircraft are approaching each other head-on, or nearly so, each pilot of each aircraft shall alter course to the right.*

(e) Overtaking. *Each aircraft that is being overtaken has the right of way and each pilot of an overtaking aircraft shall alter course to the right to pass well clear.*

(f) Landing. *Aircraft, while on final approach to land, or while landing, have the right of way over other aircraft in flight or operating on the surface. When two or more*

aircraft are approaching an airport for the purpose of landing, the aircraft at the lower altitude has the right of way, but it shall not take advantage of this rule to cut in front of another which is on final approach to land, or to overtake that aircraft.

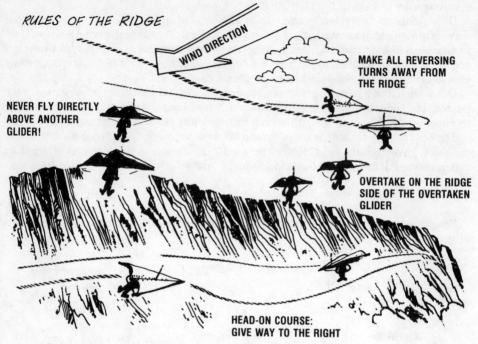

RULES OF THE RIDGE

WIND DIRECTION

MAKE ALL REVERSING
TURNS AWAY FROM
THE RIDGE

NEVER FLY DIRECTLY
ABOVE ANOTHER
GLIDER!

OVERTAKE ON THE RIDGE
SIDE OF THE OVERTAKEN
GLIDER

HEAD-ON COURSE:
GIVE WAY TO THE RIGHT

Four *Rules of the Ridge* govern nearly all slope soaring:

1. Make all reversing turns away from the ridge, i.e., into the wind. A downwind turn toward the slope is liable to force the glider into the hillside.
2. Never fly directly above or beneath another glider. The pilot below cannot see the upper glider and might rise up into it.
3. Gliders approaching each other head-on give way to the right (As in a car).
4. An overtaking glider passes between the slope and the overtaken craft. With the slope on the left, this means passing to the left, contrary to the rules of general aviation. This is a necessary deviation from general practice to avoid having the overtaken glider turn in front of the other.

When passing another glider on the downwind (upslope) side one often encounters a sudden jolt as he penetrates the other's wake.

When thermaling, gliders always turn the same direction, that way established by the first one in it.

Ground traffic control is also necessary when more than one hang glider is on the hill. On landing, the glider should be moved quickly out of the landing area so that others may fly. At the top of the hill, one should have everything ready before moving into the launch point. When it is your turn to fly - fly.

Right of way between aircraft also is determined by their ability to maneuver and avoid other categories of aircraft. Users of the airspace generally relate to each other in the

"Aviation is not in itself inherently dangerous. But to even a greater degree than even the sea, it is terribly unforgiving of any carelessness, incapacity or neglect"

following order: Balloon, parachute, sailplane, hang glider, airship, airplane, rotorcraft. The hang glider might even move one step farther from the sailplane due to its lack of a requirement for a prepared landing area (airport) and its ability to maneuver is better than an airship except that being unpowered, it can't go back up under normal conditions.

MOUNTAIN FLYING can be the ultimate in gliding and soaring but there are also great dangers. The winds in the mountains are tricky and very strong. Mountains provide turbulence, downdrafts, trees and rough terrain and one must know what to look for and how to avoid the problem areas. Learn to fly mountains from others. Go to a school such as Muller's in Calgary or Chandelle's in Golden. Ask and learn before you fly.

WATER LANDINGS can be extremely dangerous; they aren't so funny when they terminate a flying career. Flotation gear is a nice piece of equipment when flying near water and a quick release system on the harness is an absolute must. On approaching the water, take a big lungfull of air. This is hard to remember and is rarely done in the excitement of a water landing; it doesn't come to one's attention until he is under water where he can't get the air. As soon as you hit the water, reach up and activate the harness or seat release; you should have a single motion type such as made from a parachute quick ejector snap. A jerk on the lanyard is all that is required to disconnect from the glider. Get out from under the craft unless the waves are bouncing it around violently. If it is breaking up, hide under the center bolt, the strongest point. If in the surf, keep the glider level so that the waves won't roll up it and crush it. Water is very heavy. Never try to disconnect in the air. Judging altitude over water is very difficult and you might be releasing at 50' rather than 10'. Try some pool practice: get air, don't panic, disconnect and get away.

COMPETITION

The whole subject of competition in hang gliding is a new one but important if this aviation activity is to be called a "sport". Hang gliding competitions usually consist of spot landing, flying for distance or duration, number of 360 degree turns or style but other prizes are invariably given for best workmanship, most attractive, etc. Such meets give contestants a chance to get together, exchange information and show off their latest offspring.

"I wish to warn all fliers to beware of mountain flying. The winds are tricky and very strong" – Jim Galbreath

New competitions and fly-ins are being scheduled all the time and one should contact the organizations listed in the back of the book for schedules.

SHAPE AND WEIGHT (of the pilot)

Most discussion of strength increases and weight reductions concern the hang glider itself and often the pilot is overlooked. Higher performance is promised those who lower the gross weight; either the ship's or their's will affect the total package. A flabby pilot is not a healthy pilot and a few extra trips up and down the hill will be all to his benefit. Flab not only increases weight but it makes the pilot larger and contributes to drag; streamlined muscles fly better. Lightweight, smooth clothing will actually reduce drag.

Over exertion and heat exhaustion are not to be overlooked in a good day of skysurfing. Fatigue and the hot sun can take their toll. Water, shade and rest must be considered between flights and on long flights, some pilots recommend a canteen.

There is a story about an experienced Rogallo pilot who soared for over an hour and crashed while attempting to land. The most likely cause was fatigue. Flying takes its toll both physically and mentally, particularly during the learning stages and a tired pilot will experience some impairment to judgement. The blood flow is also reduced on long flights. Imagine what Bob Wills went through on his record breaking eight hour flight. There is a need to move about and change flying positions.

PUBLIC RELATIONS

Skysurfers, well aware of the power of politics and public opinion, are an unusually helpful and polite group. Natural exhibitionists, they explain the sport to anyone who will listen and are very considerate of the spectators and landowners.

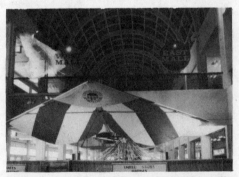

Booths at sport shows and displays in shopping malls publicize the sport and attract new hang glider pilots.

"Man need not accept all the shortcomings of present day aviation to enjoy the miracle of flight" – Taras Sr.

ACCIDENTS are bound to happen whenever man ventures out of his element particularly during the learning stages and, of course, when he tackles problems beyond his capabilities.

Most hang gliding fatalities are really kiting accidents which occur when the tow line breaks or when the release activates prematurely. But don't be mislead, people do get killed in foot launched hang gliding. Most hang gliding accidents are not fatal but are confined rather to scratches, bruises and the occasional broken leg. Common sense and few basics will contribute to many hours of safe and happy flying.

One should never fly alone, he may be injured and require assistance. Always consider the site, will help be able to reach the injured? Stay away from power lines. Aluminum is an excellent conductor and is often used in place of copper in high voltage transmission lines. Nylon, normally an insulator, becomes a conductor over 600 volts. If you go into power-lines, disconnect and get away. Do not tug on a trapped kite; electricity does not approach gradually, it strikes! Let the power company do it, it is their kind of work.

Adequate protective clothing is another important consideration; helmet, gloves, a jumpsuit with knee pads, etc. particularly at first. Later you may want to remove certain articles but the all important helmet should be maintained.

Wear a helmet at all times. Put it on BEFORE attaching the body to the glider; a gust might dump you at any time. Do not remove it until disconnected and away from the glider. If you should land in a tree, keep the helmet on until you reach the safety of the ground.

When the winds are coming from the wrong direction or are gusting, watch the more experienced skysurfers. If they are waiting the winds out, now is the time for a little fear and common sense to come into play.

HANG GLIDER TRANSITION FOR PILOTS

Pilots, both power and glider, will find the transition to Rogallo flight easy and rewarding. While the controls are backward (push forward to pitch the nose up, etc) and speeds are slow, these inconsistencies may be easily overcome with some ground exercises and careful thought. Flying low, slow and with the breeze in one's face is a fantastic new experience.

Flying a hang glider is far simpler than piloting one of their heavier, faster and more expensive brothers for a number of reasons and the pilot is already schooled to maintain his airspeed, especially in turns.

The most critical part of flying full size aircraft is in the ground contact, normally during planned landings. The novice must coordinate the controls to guide the plane to a smooth, safe landing and this takes much practice until these guiding movements become "natural". The hang glider does not require control coordination; it doesn't even have a rudder. Even most of the monoplane hang gliders have their rudder control connected to the pilot's seat so that it moves with him automatically as he moves the trapeze bar to the side for a turn.

The absence of spoilers and flaps further adds to the simplicity and makes learning easy.

The Rogallo is very forgiving, especially in a landing. Full stall landings leave zero roll out after touch down and are often on one foot. If the landing area is approached too high and the wind is smooth, slow up a Rogallo into a stall and then "parachute" it in vertically.

The sound of the sail's trailing edge flapping in the wind provides a perfect audio wind speed indicator and this makes the recognition of the stall point easy.

Hang gliding is introducing millions to aviation inexpensively and easily (no license is required), millions who would not have looked to the sky otherwise. The natural desire to go higher, farther and faster will eventually graduate today's hang glider enthusiast into other aviation sports: sail planes, parachuting, ballooning and powered aircraft.

> *If the good Lord had wanted man to stay on the ground, he would have given us roots.*

The Quicksilver.

Doug Fronius in his Waterman **Biplane**.

38

CHAPTER II

HANG GLIDING
FROM THE START

A brief history

To fly like the birds has been one of mans' great dreams, probably from the time the first man saw the first bird. Many aerial devices have been born of these desires to duplicate birds' airborne achievements. Initially, men fashioned wings of feathers and other material and strapped them to their arms but they soon found that arm power was insufficient to maintain flight; it worked only in legend for Icarus and his father Daedalus and it was Icarus who fell into the sea when he ventured too close to the sun and his wax melted.

The next step in development was the glider and this opening of a new era in aviation was pioneered by Otto Lilienthal of Germany in 1891. He ran with the craft on his shoulders and after lift off, he literally hung from the glider and hence the name "hang glider". Lilienthal started something and the following pages provide a closer look at these hang gliding pioneers.

A number of drawings are reproduced here from their original patents. Patents have a life of 17 years and copies, with both drawings and text, are available at .50 each by writing U.S. Patent Office, Washington, DC 20231; delivery takes about four weeks. Order by number.

Some of the earliest designs of flying machines were sketched and described by Leonardo da Vinci in the late 1400's but while this genius was clearly on to something, there is no evidence that any of his designs were ever built or flown.

Sir George Cayley contributed a great deal during his life time and his work with gliders was of major importance. Unfortunately, the records are sketchy since flying was considered more of a family embarrassment than a source of pride. However, Cayley did write about his work and his claims seem to be accepted as authentic.

"Wilbur and Orville Wright, Glenn Curtiss, Ferdinand Ferber, Percy Pilcher, Otto Lilienthal, Octave Chanute, John Montgomery, James Doolittle, Charles Pretzwer, Eddie Allen, the Schweizer Brothers and the Voisin Brothers, all started their aviation careers in SKYSURFING".— Tom Peghiny

Cayley's sketch of a glider

Cayley first proposed flight in 1799 and he went on to describe a glider in 1804. In 1809, he laid down the principles for heavier than air flight and numerous papers were published over the next forty years.

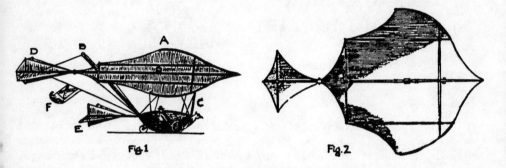

There are some gliding accounts in 1849 and some well documented evidence that he persuaded his coachman to pilot the craft in 1852.

F.H. Wenham originated the biplane in 1866; he noted that several pelicans can fly one above the other without interference. And while he never produced a practical application of his theory, Hargraves developed the box kite and others went on to produce aircraft with two stacked flying surfaces.

LeBris Glider

Captain LeBris reportedly flew a wing warped glider in 1867.

L. P. MOUILLARD.
MEANS FOR AERIAL FLIGHT.

No. 582,757   Patented May 18, 1897.

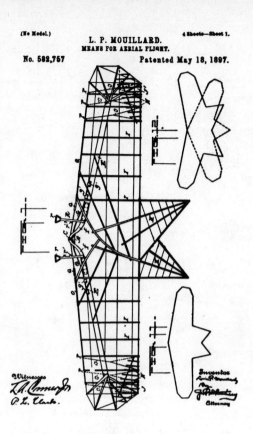

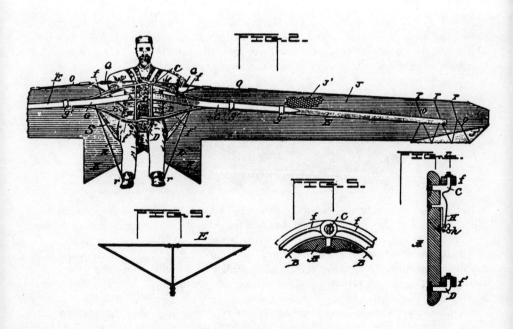

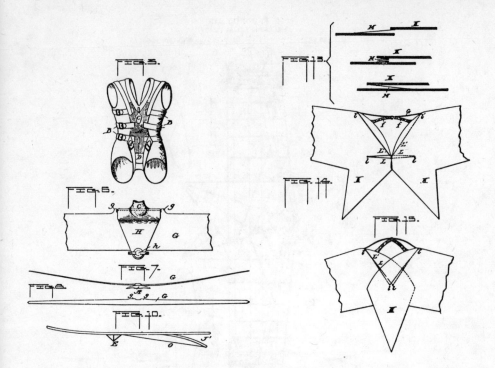

Louis Pierre Mouillard of Egypt published "L'Empire de l'Air" in 1881 and described his gliding flight; its been called "one of the great classics of aeronautical literature". His patent filed in the U.S. in 1892 notes his appreciation of one type of wing warping.

John J. Montgomery is credited with being the one who contributed the most significant early contributions by making the first flight under complete control.

But there is a great deal of controversy here. Some claim there is no evidence of his early flights other than his own undocumented claims many years later.

In 1950, a monument was erected on the rim of Otay Mesa where John Montgomery reportedly took off in 1883 and flew some 603 feet. It is located at the Northeast corner of National and Coronado avenues, south of San Diego.

The International Aerospace Hall of Fame has established a $1500. Montgomery Glider Flight Competition. To win, one must build a replica of the 1883 glider and fly it over the course for 600'. The results of this competition should help to prove or disprove Montgomery's claims.

Montgomery continued his experiments at Santa Clara College where he was a professor. There, he built the tandem wing bi-planes which he towed to 4000 ft. altitude under a hot air balloon and cast off to glide gracefully back to Earth.

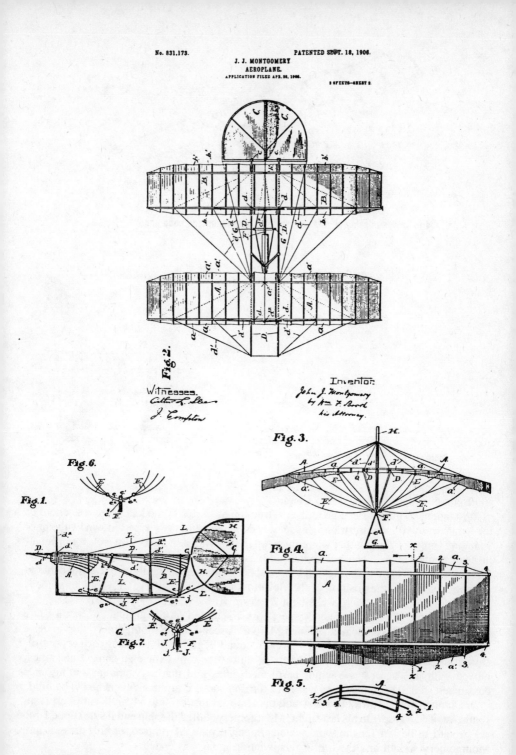

43

Jim Spurgeon's model of Montgomery's 1883 monoplane hang glider.

Maloney flying the 1905 Santa Clara.

Jim Spurgeon writes of the Santa Clara:

"A tandem bi-plane, same general construction as the 1883 model except, the chord of the wings were 40" and the trailing edge of each wing could be 'warped' down by the pilot 'standing' on wire rigging that was connected to the wing rear spars thru a clever arrangement of control wires. The horizontal tail was movable, up and down, and had a fixed vertical 'fin' built rigid to the elevator. A 'snubber' was used on the elevator control cable so the pilot could 'set' the position of the elevator and let it 'free wheel'. Overall length was 180" and total wing loading was about 2 lbs/sq. ft."

On 29 April, 1905, thousands of spectators assembled on the grounds of Santa Clara College to watch the parachutist Daniel Maloney ascend in the Montgomery ship under a hot air balloon. He cut loose at some 4000 feet and began to glide under perfect control. During the twenty minute descent, he made numerous turns, traveled some eight miles, moved with and against the wind, performed dives and made a standup landing on a designated spot. The Santa Clara was not a terribly stable craft; maneuvers had to be mild.

In October of 1911, Montgomery and his assistant made some 54 flights at Evergreen, southeast of San Jose. On his last flight, Montgomery stalled the ship and it side slipped into the ground to be left for the wind which flipped it over. A protruding bolt pressed into Montgomery's skull and the life of this aviation great was ended.

"This flight of Montgomery's was 'the most daring feat ever attempted." —Octave Chanute

"The 'Evergreen" and the wooden launching track set up for it on Ramonda Ranch Hill (renamed Montgomery Hill in 1961).

For more information on Montgomery and his work, write: Waldo Waterman, PO Box 6532p. San Diego, CA 92106 and Jim Spurgeon, 5590p Morro Way, La Mesa, CA 92041.

The two major collections on Montgomery are at the University of Santa Clara and at the San Diego Junior Chamber of Commerce.

Horatio Phillips investigated wing sections to a greater extent than anyone else between 1884 and 1891 and produced slat-like multiplane models of extraordinary lifting capacities.

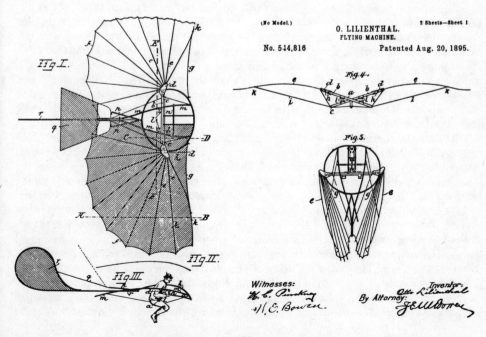

Otto Lilienthal began his work on gliders in 1871. Twenty years later he began piloting his craft and during the next 15 years he made over 2000 flights, some to 1000' and as fast as 22 mph.

Even when they were school boys in Pomerania, Otto (1848-1895) and his brother Gustave (1849-1933) began experimenting with model gliders. It wasn't until much later though, that they became serious enough to design and construct a full size machine.

Prior to going to full size crafts, the brothers conducted an intensive study of bird flight, but unlike most of their contemporaries who merely pointed out the general fundamentals, they discovered the definite factors and relationships. They learned precisely what a bird does with its wings . . . how it alters dihedral for changes in stability, and how it varies its wing camber to change the lift and drag relationships in a given flight situation. During these observations they evolved the theory of flight which is the foundation for the modern science of aerodynamics. Then in 1889, Otto published his book, "Der Vogelflug als Grundlage der Fliegekunst (Bird Flight as the Basis of Aviation). The book appears to have been read by nearly everyone who had a serious interest in building and flying heavier-than-air craft.

It was during his studies, that Otto came to realize the tremendous importance of curved wing surfaces. He also made many other interesting aerodynamic observations; for example, he discovered that natural wind, with its unsteadiness of flow is more favorable for soaring flight than a strictly uniform flow. The advantage of the non-uniform flow conditions arising because of the upward components of wind in the airstream. Furthermore, he found that even in the absence of the so-called upward components of wind, the lift in a natural wind was still superior to that in a strictly uniform stream. This effect has only been recognized during recent times due to a cross-velocity gradient, which generally prevails in a natural wind, at least in the air near to the earth's surface. The type of soaring done under these conditions is referred to as "dynamic soaring".

All that the brothers thought however, was not sound, in fact they had one rather nebulous "theory". They had devoted much thought to the possibility of creating negative drag, (propulsion) by designing a suitable airfoil shape. Needless to say, this idea violates the basic laws of physic. But even so, several years after Otto's tragic death, Gustave actually published a "theory" for negative drag which obviously didn't accomplish very much.

Lilienthal's first glider was a monoplane built in 1891. It had a slightly dihedraled wing of some 23 feet in span, made of willow wands covered with waxed cotton cloth. Flight path control being accomplished solely by center of gravity shift through proper body movements. His weight was supported by an arrangement of parallel bars contained within the wing center section. The craft weighed but 40 pounds, thus enabling him to launch himself into the air from a hill top by running down the slope. Before he began leaping from hills though, he relied upon a springboard in his back yard! Then in a short while he began jumping from mounds in the nearby fields between Gross Kreutze and Werder. It was here that he discovered that wind gusts could become too much for the wing so he added a tail to aid stability.

In 1893 he set up a base of operations at a hill top near Steiglitz, including a shed to house his creations. He even went so far as to make the wings foldable for more compact storage.

After a year at Steiglitz, Otto began to search for a location where the prevailing winds would be more favorably suited to his needs. He found his site in the Rhinow Mountains, near Rathenow. Up until this time he had experienced no serious accidents, but at Rathenow during one of his glides the wind caught him off-guard, over turned the craft and sent him headlong to the ground, from a height of about 60 feet. The glider had been travelling at 35 miles an hour! Fortunately, he escaped with but a sprained left arm and a flesh wound on the side of his head.

Lilienthal described some of his flights.

Lilienthal moved once again in 1894, to a hill he had constructed specifically for gliding at Gross Lichterfelde. At the base of the hill was a storage space for his gliders. During experiments here, he came to the conclusion that he could attain greater stability with a biplane configuration and so began to build and test some model biplanes. Following these tests, he constructed a full size version with 194 square feet of wing area. During some practice sessions, he was able to glide distances approaching a quarter of a mile at heights of 75 feet!

Otto still wanted more control and he eventually came to realize that this might be accomplished with a movable elevator. So, he fitted one to one of his gliders. It was connected to his head and controlled by movements thereof. At about this same time, 1896, he planned to fit a 2¼ horsepower carbonic motor weighing 88 lbs. to a newly completed biplane which had movable wing tips controlled by hand operated valves.

True to his methodical way of doing things, Otto tested everything on the ground before venturing aloft. But he never had a chance to test his new rig! During a practice session in one of his monoplane gliders, near Stollen, on Aug. 9, 1896, he lost control of his craft and fell to the ground to his death from a height of 50 feet. He had broken his spine and died the following day. Before he passed away he uttered these immortal words: "Sacrifices must be made".

Even though Otto was actively involved in actual gliding operations for only five years, his continuous flight tests, insights, visions, modifications as dictated by flight experience, and a willingness to share his findings with others, most definitely gives Otto Lilienthal a special important place in the history of skysurfing. Of special importance, Lilienthal was the first man to soar; to use the upward moving wind to gain altitude.

Percy Pilcher, England's pioneer skysurfer designed, built and flew several hang gliders prior to his fatal crash in 1899, his 33rd year. He was close to powered flight at the time of his death. His activities were reported by his sister Ella Tidswell in the *Aeronautic Journal*, July 1909 as follows:

From Pilcher's earliest boyhood he was entirely wrapped up in the idea of flying, and from the time he was thirteen, when he joined the Britannia, he made small experiments. I remember when he was fifteen, a cadet in the Royal Navy, his explaining to me what he believed would be the shape and working of the flying machine of the near future.

At nineteen he left the Navy, worked through Elder's Shipbuilding Yard at Govan, Glasgow, and afterward went to the University of London. In 1893, when he was assistant lecturer in Naval Architecture and Marine Engineering at the University of Glasgow, he began his experiments in aeronautics.

During that winter of 1892-93 he built the machine we called the Bat. The body piece was, as far as I remember, 11 feet 8 inches long and 2 feet 4 inches wide.

The wings were laced to two rather heavy spars crossing a triangle in front of the machine, and guyed by wires to the triangle which reached 2 feet 6 inches below the body piece and about the same distance above it. When the lacing to the front spars was undone, the wings folded back like a fan.

It was necessary to have it so, in order that it would pack easily as Pilcher was obliged to live in town on account of his work. In Glasgow he had the loan of a large room under the roof as a workshop, while we had to go down to the country for the experiments.

In his first experiments the wings of the Bat were very much raised-almost V-shaped-and the rudder in this instance was shaped like the outspread tail of a crow, with a small vertical rudder to keep the machine head to wind, the horizontal rudder working up and down on the vertical one.

The very first day of the experiments, which were made in the beginning of '93 near Cardross, from a slight elevation and against a slight wind, Pilcher was raised twelve feet from the ground, where he hovered without any forward movement for between two and three minutes and then descended by tilting the machine forward quite successfully. But the next time he rose the wind caught the machine sideways, and his weight being insufficient to restore the equilibrium it tipped forward and sideways in landing, breaking one of the front spars.

After this he lowered the wing tips and had some very good results such as from 30 to 40 yards about 10 to 15 feet from the ground, starting from the top of a hill and gliding against the wind, the angle, we reckon, being approximately 1 in 10.

He also altered the rudder, which was now made of two round disk sails, one vertical and the other horizontal, really formed of two large hoops, covered with sail silk, each of about 15 feet in area, the vertical one being fixed, and the horizontal one working on it.

We took a farmhouse with a very large, empty barn at Cardross, on the Clyde, where we got nice, clear wind on the hills, and he was able to practice almost daily, his longest soar with no motive power being about sixty yards, and greatest height about twenty feet.

It is very difficult to gauge the height accurately, as there must of necessity be no trees or anything nearby which one might hit.

At Cardross he built two more machines. One was never quite finished as the framework, which was built to carry an engine, proved too heavy for soaring.

It was a monoplane, the wings being very square cut and the body piece much the shape of the Bleriot short span flyer.

He then went rather to the other extreme, influenced, no doubt, by a month of very light winds, and the Gull was built with a wing area of 1½ feet to the pound weight, (wing loading

= 2/3 pounds per sq.ft.) and was so light as to be cumbersome and impossible to use for practice except with the very light breeze.

The Bat

The Gull

The Hawk

Pilcher's gliders

The Hawk-the most successful of all-was the last machine that Pilcher built. The Hawk was built at Eynsford, in Kent with a wing area of ¾ foot to the pound weight, (wing loading = 1.333 lbs/sq. ft.) and was estimated to carry one man and an engine-about 250 pounds.

The ribs of the wings are of pine, each rib slipping into a long pocket, and the sail lacing on to the body piece.

The curve of the wings is 1 in 20, and apex of the curve about 1/3 from the front of the wing.

The wings are guyed to two uprights, and the machine runs on very small bicycle wheels.

With this machine Pilcher had many very successful flights, notably one at Eynsford, from the top of one hill to the top of the next across a valley, when, as a substitute for power, he had a light rope attached to the machine, which was hauled in on a pulley on the far hill.

This flight was over 250 yards-nearly 300 yards-and of course, in this case, across the valley, the flight was a high one. The balance was perfect, and so was the steering gear. The machine rose high, making a great upward curve from hilltop to hilltop, and landing beautifully.

Pilcher had hoped to add a motor engine to this machine the following winter. Drawings for it had been made and the work of construction begun at his works-Wilson and Pilcher, Ltd., Westminster- when his career was cut short in his thirty-third year by the fatal accident at Stamford Hall, Yelvertoft, caused by the snapping of one of the rudder guys during a flight, after a heavy rain, on September 30, 1899.''

Octave Chanute who was hang gliding at Dune Park,Indiana on the shores of Lake Michigan prior to the turn of the twentieth century has been called the "scientific skysurfer"; the following accounts show why:

From the FAA Aviation News/November 1973

The success of the Wright brothers in achieving controlled, powered, man-carrying flight in 1903 came after years, indeed centuries, of human struggle to master the realm of the sky. Orville and Wilbur freely acknowledged their indebtedness to many earlier designers and inventors, but if there is one man amongst all the pioneers of aviation who might have claimed with justification to have been their aeronautical godfather, it would have been Octave Chanute.

Born in Paris on February 18, 1832, the son of a university professor, Octave Chanute came to this country with his family at the age of seven. He went to work as a chainman on the Hudson River Railroad in New York City at age 17, and was promoted to division engineer by the time he was 21. Moving west with the railroads at midcentury, Chanute became an eminently successful and ingenious construction engineer who laid out many miles of track toward the Pacific. He is credited with inventing the technique of preserving wooden railroad ties by impregnating them with creosote. Other works of his fertile mind included the famed Union Stockyards in Chicago, and the elevated train system of New York City.

O. CHANUTE.
SOARING MACHINE.

No. 582,718.   Patented May 18, 1897.

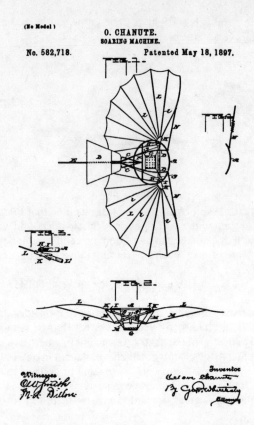

He left the railroad industry in 1883 to begin a new career as a bridge builder, and soon was spanning the Missouri and Mississippi River with his designs.

In 1889 Chanute retired from construction work and settled down in Chicago. His attention turned to what had been a subject of increasing interest to him over the past 15 years: the theories of European aeronautical pioneers. He was particularly interested in the theories of the Englishman Francis Wenham, who stressed the need for developing a systematic approach to flight.

Chanute proceeded to do just that. After poring over all the historical accounts he could get his hands on, both in the United States and abroad, he began to publish a series of articles on "Progress in Flying Machines" in the *Railroad and Engineering Journal* of New York. The first article appeared in 1891; the entire series was later published as a book. This was the first comprehensive and systematic review ever to appear on human flight, and it was a masterful achievement, complete with many detailed drawings as well as photographs, aerodynamic formulas, graphs, and propulsion designs, stress tables, wing-loading calculations, etc. as well as accounts of various lengthy studies on the flight of birds species. Chanute began by collecting data on the earliest mythological and legendary figures, and he concluded with a lengthy description of the work of Otto Lilienthal, currently at the height of his fame.

Although an admirer of Lilienthal, Chanute believed that a practical airplane could not be properly controlled by the pilot flinging his body about as required in the German's hang gliders, and that some form of "automatic and voluntary" stability should be designed into the aircraft — i.e., controllable airfoils were needed. His first original design, a multi-winged (5) glider, apparently permitted the pilot to move the wings horizontally around a vertical axis. The multiplane glider did not fly well, and Chanute went on to produce a biplane, probably the most successful and influential airplane ever built before the Wright glider.

The two wings were fastened together and braced by what was known as a "Pratt truss" (a bridgebuilding concept) which increased stability of the airfoil without loss of lift. This method of rigging the wings proved to be the prototype of all the biplanes later developed. Beneath the wings Chanute positioned the pilot in an open cage, with horizontal bars supporting him under his armpits and two vertical bars to grasp with his hands; there was also a small seat slung below, which few pilots apparently ever had time to use (most flights lasted only about 10 to 12 seconds). The tail was fastened to a boom extending aft behind the pilot; the boom was flexible enough to allow for some vertical movement of the tail, but there were no hinged planes.

In 1896 Chanute, then aged 64, flew this glider from the sandhills of Lake Michigan, about 30 miles west of Chicago. His choice of a flying site with the "forgiving" sand and water available for crash landings, showed excellent judgment, as well as some deference for his aging bones. According to reports, this biplane glider was so inherently stable that not only did Chanute and his co-workers fly it without accident, but they also allowed "amateurs" to take it up on occasion, when the wind was slight. They estimated it to achieve a ground speed of 17 to 20 mph., and an airspeed of about double that. They logged nearly 1,000 flights, many of them well over 100 feet in length. On very windy days they "sat around and watched the birds", and Chanute apparently learned how to make full stall landings from observing a sparrow alight on pavement.

The success of his biplane glider, as reported in the press, together with the widespread interest in his "Progress in Flying Machines", made Chanute into a public figure, much in demand as a speaker for, and correspondent to, aeronautical and scientific societies throughout the world. He also received hundreds of letters from youngsters asking, in effect: How does one go about building an airplane?

One such letter, describing the author as "afflicted with the belief that flight is possible to man" was datemarked Dayton, Ohio, May 13, 1900. It was signed by Wilbur Wright, and it was the beginning of an extraordinary correspondence that lasted until Chanute's death in 1910. The older man quickly recognized the quality of genius in the Wright brothers, encouraged them, visited them, supported them and advised them on financial as well as theoretical and practical matters. Over the ensuing decade some 400 letters passed between the Wrights and their mentor in Chicago.

During this period Chanute gave up his own experimentation and threw himself into the task of supporting the efforts of others elsewhere in America, in England, on the European continent, and in Australia (Hargrave). Without question his efforts to bring about the free

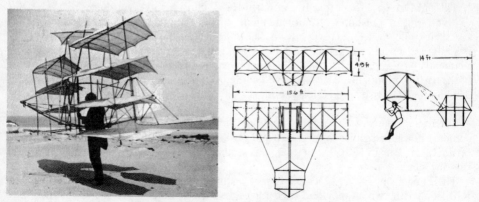

Chanute began with a multi-plane glider, later shifted to a biplane with a specially designed "truss" that braced the wings.

exchange of experimental results among independent workers in aviation hastened the advent of successful human flight.

Wilbur noted admiringly, "What one man can do himself directly is but little. If however he can stir up ten others to take up the task (of mastering flight) he has accomplished much. I know of no man in America so well fitted . . . to do this missionary work."

Chanute's inability to take the final step in the perfection of the glider, as perceived by the Wrights (controllable, movable planes), cost him any claim to immortality as an inventor; but it may very well be that his willingness to formulate the problem for the benefit of others made it possible for Wilbur and Orville to grasp the solution.

The Wright Brothers, Orville and Wilber, made history as the inventors of powered flight but they started with hang gliders. Modern skysurfers owe the Wrights a debt of gratitude; their methods set the pace for those who followed. They considered safety in flight above all else and never suffered a serious gliding accident. And with the mounting of an engine on their ultra-light glider, they catapulted into the realm of powered flight and pushed aside further development in the area of skysurfing. This new/old sport lay dormant for nearly seventy years with only occasional arousals. As a result, today's skysurfer is a pioneer experiencing the same thrill as the Wright Brothers as they discovered flight. The following account of the Wright's activities is reprinted from Wright Brothers: National Park Service, Historical Handbook Series No. 34.

Glider Experiments, 1901

In July, 1901, the Wrights returned to Kitty Hawk during a downpour of rain immediately after a storm had broken anemometer cups at 93 miles per hour. There followed a miserable week spent fighting mosquitoes, "which came in a mighty cloud, almost darkening the sun." They attempted to escape by going to bed early, wrapped up in blankets with only noses protruding cautiously from the folds. But the July heat became unbearable beneath the blankets. When they partly uncovered, the mosquitoes again swooped down upon them, forcing a perspiring retreat once more behind blankets. But Wilbur and Orville pushed forward good-humoredly and energetically to solve the problem of flight.

During the 1900-1902 experiments, the Wright family, and the Brothers themselves, considered the brother's stay in camp at Kitty Hawk simply as pleasure trips or vacations. Everyone in the family was glad to have them go to their North Carolina camp. The advantages of the sunshine, sea breezes, and outdoor exercise outweighted the occasional discomforts and seemed to be good for their health. Indeed, their sister Katherine wrote, "Will and Orv . . . think that life at Kitty Hawk cures all ills, you know."

Being sons of a bishop who enjoined them "to honor the Sabbath," the brothers did not test their gliders on Sundays while in camp. On those days they often visited with the friendly and hospitable people in Kitty Hawk, and at nearby lifesaving stations. They frequently wrote home. One of Orville's hobbies-photography-also resulted in a fine record of the early experiments. They observed while in camp, "This is great country for fishing and hunting. The fish are so thick you see dozens of them whenever you look down into the water.

For living quarters the Wrights continued using a tent. To provide more space they erected a combined glider storage shed and workshop, the building of which they undertook on arrival at camp in 1901. Fresh water was secured nearby by driving a pipe 10 feet or more into the sand.

Their new campsite was located 4 miles south of Kitty Hawk, about 1000 feet north of Kill Devil Hill, which they had used for gliding the season before and which they now realized offered the best test opportunities. Near the camp were four dunes formed of sand heaped by the winds. These dunes were collectively named Kill Devil Hills. They were constantly changing in height and slope according to the direction and force of the prevailing winds. Using three of the four Kill Devil Hills for gliding experiments during the period 1901-1903, the Wrights called these the Big Hill, the West Hill, and the Little Hill.

On the 1901 trip to camp, the brothers brought with them parts to be assembled into a larger glider than the one tested in 1900. Knowing it would be impractical to house the larger glider with them in the tent, as they had done with the smaller one, they built a rough frame shed for the new glider and for use as a workshop.

When assembled, the new glider had a wing span of 22 feet. It weighed 98 pounds, nearly double the weight of the earlier glider. To give it greater lifting power, the glider had a total lifting area of 290 feet, considerably larger than the 165-foot wing area of the previous glider. The 1901 glider was a much larger machine than anyone had ever dared try to fly. It had the same system of control and general design as the first one. The Wrights increased the camber in this glider from 1 in 22 to 1 in 12 to conform to the shape prescribed by Lilienthal's tables of air pressure. Chanute and others had used these tables, and the brothers were rudely surprised upon finding that the wings with a camber of 1 in 12 were even less efficient than the 1-in-22 camber wings they had used in 1900.

The Wrights were also dismayed to discover that the fore-and-aft control was not as effective in a machine with wings of 1-in-12 camber. At times when gliding, they were required to use all their skill and the full power of the rudder to prevent the glider from rearing up so sharply as to lose all headway and then to plunge toward the ground (a dangerous condition which they later referred to as "stalling"— an aeronautical term still in use). The brothers reduced the camber of the wings by adding little "trussing posts" to wires to depress the ribs and flatten the curvature from that used by others to 1 to 18 to make the wings more like those of their 1900 glider. This change resulted in control as good as it had been the year before.

Several hundred glides were made by Wilbur and Orville during the 1901 season of experiments. Using the slopes of Kill Devil Hill and West Hill, they sailed along in winds up to 27 miles an hour, breaking all records for distance in gliding. But the brothers were far from satisfied. They had learned a great deal about control, though their glider was still too feeble in lifting itself off the ground and staying aloft.

Occasionally in free flight, the warping of the wings to increase the angle of attack to recover lateral balance did not produce the desired result. The wing having the greater angle sometimes lost speed as it lifted, compared with the opposite wing having a lesser angle of attack. The brothers then realized that the greater angle of the wing on one side gave more resistance to forward motion and reduced the relative speed of that wing. This decrease in speed more than counterbalanced the effect of the larger angle of the wing in producing lift. The Wrights determined that they must add something to their method of controlling equilibrium to insure that equal speeds at the wingtips would be maintained. However, a vertical tail as a solution to the problem was left for the next glider.

Contrary to the scientific texts they had read, it was becoming evident to the Wrights that the travel of the center of pressure on curved or cambered surfaces was not always in the forward direction as on a plane surface. They observed that when the angle of attack on a plane surface was decreased, the center of pressure did move toward the front edge; but on cambered surfaces this was true only when large angles were being decreased.

Wilbur and Orville were discouraged that the ideas about pressures on curved surfaces and travel of center of pressure, concepts advanced by most reputable writers on the subject, including Langley, were unreliable. So perplexing did the problem seem that the Wrights considered dropping their experiments altogether. It was apparent, then, that better scientific data were needed before the problems of flight could be solved.

On their way to Dayton from camp, Wilbur declared his belief to Orville that not within a thousand years would man ever fly. He later reduced his prophesy to 50 years. When they made known their discouragement to Chanute, he urged the brothers to continue their researches, arguing that if they stopped experimenting it might be a long time before anyone else would come as near to understanding the problem or know how to work toward its solution. The admonitions of Chanute and their own intense interest in scientific inquiry led them to continue their research.

Always practical, the brothers did not take up the problem of flight with the expectation of financial profit, and they had no intention of ruining their bicycle business in pursuit of a dream. When Chanute, who was kept fully informed of their researches offered financial assistance, Wilbur wrote:

"For the present we would prefer not to accept it for the reason that if we did not feel that the time spent in this work was dead loss in a financial sense, we would be unable to resist the temptation to devote more time than our business will stand".

Glider Experiments, 1902

The Wrights had faith in the tables of air pressure compiled from their wind-tunnel experiments of 1901. Their new knowledge was incorporated into a larger glider which they built based on the aerodynamic data they had gained. Now they wanted to verify those findings.

It was the 1902 glider that the Wrights pictured and described in the drawings and specifications of their patent, which they applied for in March of 1903. Their patent was established, through the action of the courts in the United States and abroad, as the basic or pioneer airplane patent.

Richard Miller's model of a Sellers quadraplane hang glider. It flies well.

Matthew B. Sellers began his gliding experiments in 1903 with a Lilienthal glider and then went on to design, build and fly a number of gliders and powered aircraft including some stepped multiplanes with as many as five wings. According to an article authored by Sellers in *Aviation Magazine* dated 28 February 1927, he found the Lilienthal glider difficult to control as did Chanute. He then turned his attention to Phillips and the multiplane. In his design, he offset each wing under the other in a stepped fashion and the result resembled a flying staircase.

In the article, Sellers claimed that sometime prior to 1908, he "built, among other, a full-size quadraplane glider, and easily made long flights with it". The four wings which appear to be identical, in all respects are of constant chord and have no dihedral nor sweep. Each wing has two spars of small dimensions, strip ribs, and appears to be covered on the top surface only. The tips are rounded. The planes are interconnected by a number of struts angled at 45 degrees so as to give the wings the desired relationship to one another. The photographs are not clear enough to show the rest of the bracing detail. Dimensions given were Span 16', chord 2.5' and total area 140 sq. ft. The hang bar structure was positioned about 6'' below the lower surface. A large vertical fin with a 3' chord spans the upper wing bays. Another photograph showed Sellers in flight in a five wing model without a vertical fin.

> *"Few people realize that the first heavier-than-air flights in the states of Vermont, North Carolina, California and Michigan were made by skysurfers"* Tom Peghiny

Louis Bleriot's contribution to hang gliding read like this:
Bleriot I, 1901, a flapping wing machine-failed
Bleriot II, 1905, a towed biwing glider mounted on hydroplanes.
Bleriot III: A double biplane; like a box kite but with semicircular instead of vertical ends. Sported a motor but didn't fly.
Bleriot IV, 1907, A modified III. It flew but it was motorized.

Francis M. Rogallo has carved his nitch in the annals of hang gliding not as a pilot but because his kite has been adapted and is the most popular form of hang glider seen on the slopes today. Rogallo went to work at the Langley Center in Hampton, Virginia, as a scientist in 1936 and recently retired as head of the 7 by 10 foot tunnels branch, Full Scale Research Division. During the mid forties, Rogallo and his wife experimented with kites and they filed for a patent in 1948. It was granted in 1951 and another was granted in 1965; about twenty patents were taken out in all, some solely in Rogallo's name and some jointly with others. The idea of a limp para wing was presented to NASA as a reentry vehicle and millions of dollars were spent in research and tests. The highest L/D obtained on a completely limp model was about 3.5 and this was of a twin keel design (see NASA Report T.N. D-5965).
Stiffened Para Wings have performed much better than the limp models.
In 1966, the U.S. Army looked into the para wing and several were quickly produced by Pioneer Parachute Co. and Irvin Industries for tests. Irvin went on to manufacture them; they were marketed to the sport through Steve Snyder Enterprises as the "Delta II Parawing" in 1969.
Snyder had taken the basic para wing and added slots to reduce opening shock, steering slots, a blunt nose and an anti stall nose flap.

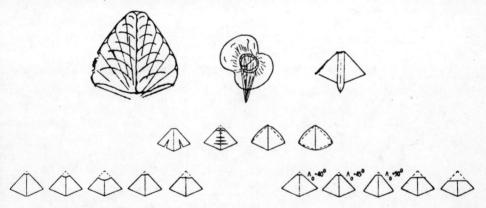

So the Wrights added power to their glider and aviation technology galloped off madly in all directions. Except for Pelzner in Switzerland and Hasselbach at Cape Cod, hang gliding activity was pretty quiet. Then there arose some special circumstances. In 1941,the Government banned all flying within 150 miles of the California coast and a frustrated Volmer Jensen built a traditional hang glider but with full controls rather than rely on the usual weight shifting and wing warping. It flew! During the next 30 odd years, Jensen built more than a score more gliders, powered aircraft and amphibians. His modern hang gliders are some of the best designed and most professionally produced.
Dr. Horten flew a flying wing in Argentina in 1953 while Barry Palmer launched himself off a California hill in 1961. The modern sport of hang gliding, particularly with Rogallos, was reborn in 1964 and credit goes to Richard Miller, an extremely literate sky dreamer who built the "Bamboo Butterfly", a bamboo and polyethylene Rogallo wing for a total investment of about $9.00. Initial flights cost him many bruises as well as verbal abuse from

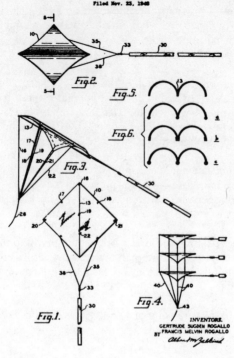

Fig.2.

Fig.5.

Fig.6.

Fig.3.

Fig.1.

Fig.4.

INVENTORS.
GERTRUDE SUGDEN ROGALLO
FRANCIS MELVIN ROGALLO
BY

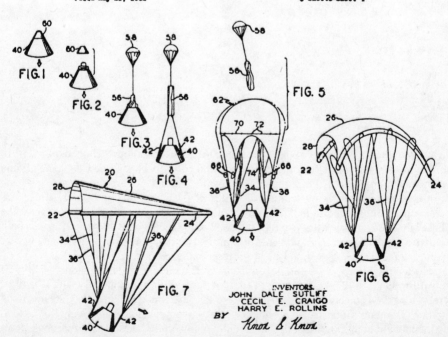

FIG.1

FIG.2

FIG.3

FIG.4

FIG. 5

FIG. 6

FIG. 7

INVENTORS.
JOHN DALE SUTLIFF
CECIL E. CRAIGO
HARRY E. ROLLINS
BY
Knox & Knox

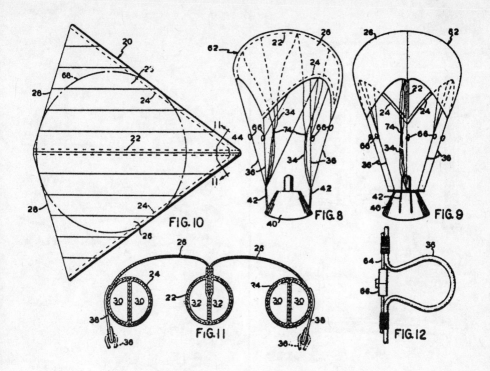

FIG. 10

FIG. 8

FIG. 9

FIG. 11

FIG. 12

Ryan version of the Rogallo wing with a 500 lb. payload. An electronic guidance unit in the cargo compartment homes in on a radio beacon at the target area.

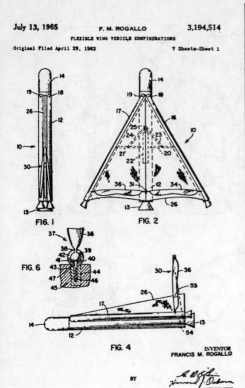

July 13, 1965   F. M. ROGALLO   3,194,514

FLEXIBLE WING VEHICLE CONFIGURATIONS

Original Filed April 29, 1963   7 Sheets—Sheet 1

FIG. 1

FIG. 2

FIG. 6

FIG. 4

INVENTOR
FRANCIS M. ROGALLO

BY

ATTORNEYS

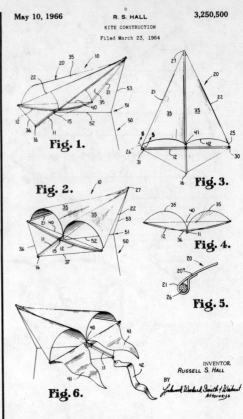

May 10, 1966   R. S. HALL   3,250,500

KITE CONSTRUCTION

Filed March 23, 1964

Fig. 1.

Fig. 3.

Fig. 2.

Fig. 4.

Fig. 5.

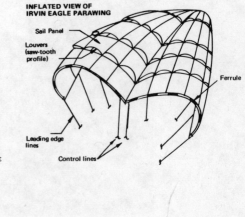

Fig. 6.

INVENTOR
RUSSELL S. HALL

BY

Attorneys

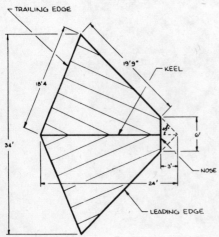

TRAILING EDGE

19'9"

KEEL

18'4

34'

6'

3'

NOSE

24'

LEADING EDGE

INFLATED VIEW OF
IRVIN EAGLE PARAWING

Sail Panel

Louvers
(saw-tooth
profile)

Ferrule

Leading edge
lines

Control lines

Hawk Parawing:
Solid fabric and a 24' referenced keel length. Very hard opening.
Never went into production.

GID76-120 Eagle Parawing. 400 square feet, 14 gores of five panels
each. 12 leading edge and 7 keel lines of 750 lb., 1,000 lb. and
1,500 lb. line. 24' referenced keel length. 2.25 ripstop nylon
fabric with a silicon treatment. Steering control lines go through
ferrules on the trailing edge.

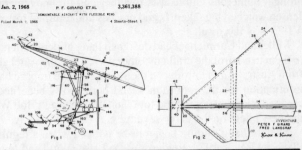

Jan. 2, 1968 P. F. GIRARD ETAL 3,361,388
DEMOUNTABLE AIRCRAFT WITH FLEXIBLE WING
Filed March 7, 1966 4 Sheets-Sheet 1

Fig I

Fig 2

INVENTORS
PETER F GIRARD
FRED LANDGRAF
Knox & Knox

GID76-130 Delta II Parawing. Circa 1969. Similar to the Eagle but the back section was removed, Snyder's wrap or "OSI" (opening shock inhibitor) and stall control panel were added. Referenced keel length is 19.5'. 10 leading edge and 6 keel lines of 1,000 lb. line. Control lines are Type IV suspension line, 750 lb. 254 square feet, 14 gores of four panels each.

bystanders but he learned to fly and, more important, wrote about it. The movement has been going down hill ever since.

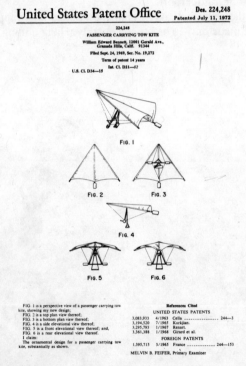

United States Patent Office Des. 224,248
Patented July 11, 1972

224,248
PASSENGER CARRYING TOW KITE
William Edward Bennett, 12001 Gerald Ave.,
Granada Hills, Calif. 91344
Filed Sept. 24, 1969, Ser. No. 19,272
Term of patent 14 years
Int. Cl. D21—02
U.S. Cl. D34—15

FIG. 1

FIG. 2 FIG. 3

FIG. 4

FIG. 5 FIG. 6

FIG. 1 is a perspective view of a passenger carrying tow kite, showing my new design;
FIG. 2 is a top plan view thereof;
FIG. 3 is a bottom plan view thereof;
FIG. 4 is a side elevational view thereof;
FIG. 5 is a front elevational view thereof; and,
FIG. 6 is a rear elevational view thereof.
I claim:
The ornamental design for a passenger carrying tow kite, substantially as shown.

References Cited
UNITED STATES PATENTS
3,083,933 4/1963 Cella .... 244—3
3,194,520 7/1965 Kurkjian.
3,295,793 1/1967 Renart.
3,361,388 1/1968 Girard et al.
FOREIGN PATENTS
1,395,715 3/1965 France .... 244—153

MELVIN B. FEIFER, Primary Examiner

In 1962, John Dickenson, a water skier/engineer known as "the father of kiting" was the first to put down his flat kite and try a Rogallo. The Rogallo kite's altitude could be varied by changing its pitch while flat kites depend on the speed of the boat (air). Bill Moyes began promoting and selling Rogallos the following year and in '67, he towed to 1000'. Bill Bennett, who worked with Moyes, brought the first water ski Rogallo kite to the US in 1969. Dave Kilbourne, a water skier/kiter, met Bennett and provided the boat on several demonstration flights in San Francisco Bay.

Jack Lambie sponsored a hang glider meet on Otto Lilienthal's birthday in 1971 which brought numerous enthusiasts together and the movement gathered momentum. Volmer Jensen watched the takeoffs and crashes and returned for consultations with Irv Culver; the VJ-23 was the result.

Miller and Carmichael had designed hang gliders with parallel bars and it never occurred to them to control the craft any other way. Then the water skiers, Bennett and Moyes, came from Australia and introduced the swing seat and trapeze bar. The US skysurfers traded this information for the foot launch and both sports benefited. Dave Kilbourne is generally credited with developing the foot launch and he and Bob Wills are most often referred to as the best pilots of the early seventies.

Modern hang gliding began to be noticed when a regular flying site was established at Playa del Rey in 1972. Velderrain, De Lisse, Weyl and Jensen were always in the air while Bill Allen caught it all on film. In fact, photographers Allen and George Uveges and Joe Faust through his magazine *Low & Slow* deserve much credit for spreading the word to the rest of the World.

Dave Kilbourne was the first to soar a Rogallo in the fall of 1971 and he was quickly followed by Taras Kiceniuk, Jr. in his Icarus I biplane. Bob Wills set the current soaring record of some 8.5 hours in 1973 in the strong, smooth winds in Hawaii. Rudy Kishazy set the altitude and distance record from Mt. Blanc in France: 13,152', 18 kilometers and 35 minutes. Mark Clarkson gained over 5700' in a Quicksilver near Phoenix in 1974 and flew some 16 miles to land at a gliderport.

Many names are in the news these days, many new hang gliders appear on the scene each weekend. Records are made only to be broken quickly. Hang gliding is on the move . . .

SKYSURFING- a sport is reborn

CHAPTER III

CONSTRUCTION AND MAINTENANCE

This chapter outlines some of the construction techniques common to hang gliders. Here one can find simple methods of joining load bearing members, working with cable and sewing sails.

Most of the discussion surrounds the basic Rogallo type glider but some of this information is applicable when considering alternative designs. eg, cable work is the same for all. Those considering building up a wing might consult a dope and fabric manual.

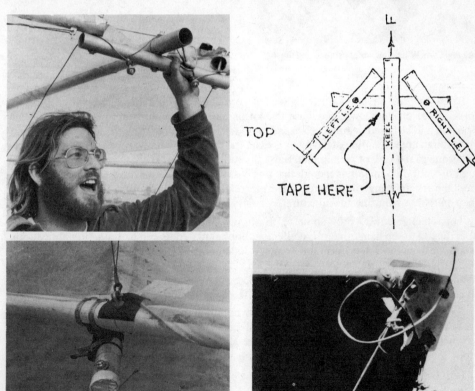

Fortunately, some of the more primitive materials and construction techniques are giving way as skysurfers fly higher and higher.

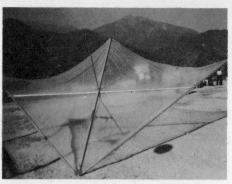

Even some of the newer designs still sport plastic sails to minimize cost.

Bob and Chris Wills aloft under bamboo and plastic.

After studying the plans for the glider of your choice, you may make up your mind to forge ahead on your own, purchase the kit or buy the complete unit ready to fly. This decision will be based on time, space and the existence or lack of that certain creative desire. A thorough understanding of the plans is essential because it may be necessary to modify the plans due to the lack of certain materials. If you have a lot of spare time, you may want to hunt up your own materials though this rarely saves any money over mail order purchases from the several hang glider firms. Some pieces are so applicable only to a certain craft that their purchase from the manufacturer is nearly mandatory.

This chapter covers only some of the basics and those building techniques relating specifically to the hang glider. Excellent additional materials can be found in publications available from the Experimental Aircraft Association, PO Box 229P Hales Corners, Wisc. 53130, and the Soaring Society of America, PO Box 66071P, Los Angeles, CA 90066. Write for their lists. Advisory Circular 43.13-1A, Aircraft Inspection and Repair is available from the Government Printing Office, see Chapter IV.

Very few tools are needed to construct the common hang glider. Aluminum is soft and easy to work. A hand drill, hacksaw, ball peen hammer, swaging tool, wire cutters, screwdrivers, awl and wrenches round out the basic kit. A large clean area such as a garage floor is nice but hang gliders have been built in bedrooms.

Building it yourself allows one to spread the payments. Build the frame first and then the sail.

Building it yourself is half the fun! and it gives you a greater understanding of both man and machine. There is something indescribably exhilarating about conquering gravity; flying on something you made with your own hands.

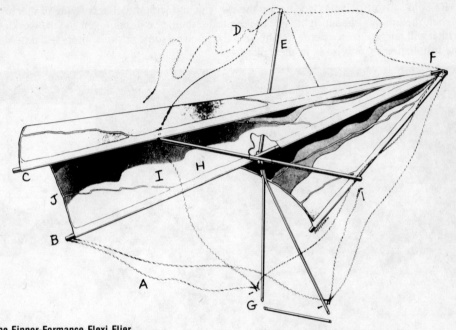

The Eipper-Formance Flexi Flier

THE BASIC COMPONENTS OF THE STANDARD ROGALLO

A. FLYING WIRES, or lower (or bottom) rigging (or wires or cables). These carry the normal flying loads.

B. KEEL, or keel tube or bar.

C. LEADING EDGE, or spar, or wing bar.

D. KINGPOST WIRES, or top (or upper or overhead) rigging (or wires or cables), or ground wires (opposed to flying wires).

E. KINGPOST.

F. NOSE PLATES, or hinge or apex plates.

G. TRAPEZE, or triangle bar, or A-frame, or control bar.

The bottom portion is the CROSSBAR while the sides are called UPRIGHTS or down tubes. Not all trapezes are triangular.

H. CROSS TUBE, or crossbar (which gets confused with the crossbar of the trapeze).

I. SAIL or wing. This has POCKETS through which pass the leading edge and keel tubes. Some sails also may have pockets for BATTENS, used to add a degree of stiffness to the sail.

J. TRAILING EDGE. The aft portion of the sail.

FLYING SURFACES, wings and sails

Basically, there are two ways to construct hang glider flying surfaces: the limp type from fabric as found on Rogallos and the fixed type built up with either single or double surfaces per most mono and biplanes.

> *"I have noticed that the press regards every man who builds a home built aircraft as an inventor, even if he has made no changes in someone else's design. It must make a better story that way, and probably very few people really care about the origin of technology, only about its final application. I can't say what motivated some other inventor to do what he did. Sometimes I don't know why I do what I do."* — F. M. Rogallo

Rogallo sails of polyethylene are on the way out and with the gliders flying higher and higher, the timing is about right. The use of plastic should be discouraged and the working with it will not be covered here. As a historical reference, some manufacturers still describe the installation of poly sails in their plans.

When it comes to performance and control, the sail is the most critical part of the glider; if it is off just the slightest bit, the craft will never fly right. While the amateur can often build an adequate sail, he can also waste a lot of expensive materials; most turn to the experienced sailmaker.

Sails are usually made of Dacron though some are of Nylon and some of the other interesting man made fabrics.

Remember that the sail will have a wider angle than the glider frame so that it will billow properly. To insure proper measurements and fit, build the frame first.

Sewing should be done with a Fed. Std. #304 zig zag stitch, 12-16 stitches per inch with size "E" thread (commercial #69) and the thread must be the same as the fabric. eg, using cotton thread on nylon fabric is asking for trouble because of the different rates of elongation. Fit the machine with a large #20 needle. If the needle is too small, it will "travel" in thick fabric, miss the hole in the throat plate and break. Some fabric specialists can achieve a good seam with two rows of straight stitching (Fed. Std. #301) and this with a folder and puller makes a good, more attractive joint. But without the proper equipment and techniques, straight stitches produce fabric take-up and the sail is warped since the seams are shorter than the fabric. The zig zag stitch does not take up the fabric and it stretches with the fabric,when loaded,like an accordian.Hence, the zig zag stitch is recommended. Always practice on test strips of material before committing needle to sail.

Use the same pattern for each half of the sail; it must be perfectly balanced. Exposed seams should be selvage edges or cut and seared with a hot knife. Turning it under will hide and protect the raw edge. Trailing edges are normally folded over twice in a ½" seam. All seams are double stitched with two rows side by side and all stress points should be reinforced.

The sail must be designed to achieve the desired flying shape which will be quite different than in its relaxed state. As the load is taken by the frame, it will flex and change the shape of the sail. The outboard tips will be flexed inward and upward and the leading edges between the cross tube and the nose will flex slightly down and out. If this condition is not corrected by outriggers or larger tubing, the sail must be shaped to compensate. Cutting for tip deflection is called putting in some "dog leg". A 6" elliptical cut in the trailing edge will reduce some of the flutter and most sails have this feature. The trailing edge must not be tighter than the adjoining sail or the cupping will make the glider dive.

Stitch up the long seams, then the leading edge seams and finally join the two halves together.

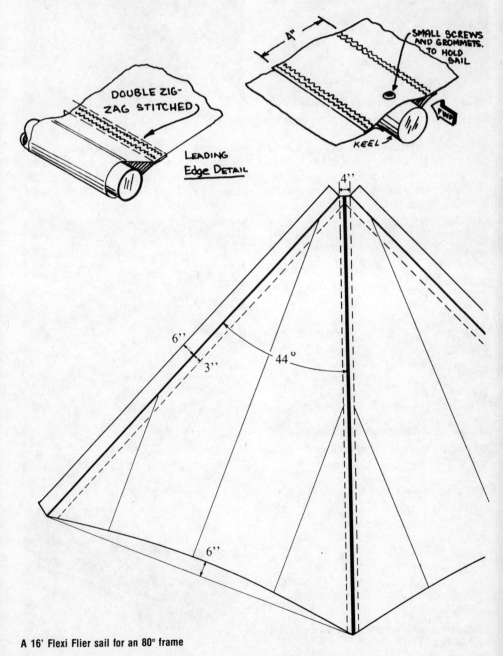

A 16' Flexi Flier sail for an 80° frame

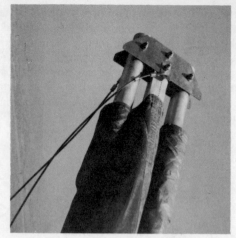

The sail must be securely fastened to the frame at each end.

Slide the sail on the frame making sure it is right-side-up and mark the areas where holes must be cut for joining members and grommets. The sail is normally attached to the frame with bolts or machine screws. A layer of duct tape on the top of the cross tube will reduce wear on the sail during set up and break down. Another way to compensate for the flexing of the frame under flying loads is to add deflexer assemblies or ''outriggers''.

The outrigger should be angled down about 45 degrees.

The Outrigger manufactured by Ultralite Products.

Attachment of the UP deflexer kit to the aft leading edge tube.

The fixed wing usually consists of two spars with formed ribs and a covering on top and sometimes on the bottom. Ribs may be constructed of bamboo, thin aluminum tubing, ⅛'' plywood or even ½'' foam plastic.

Both the Icarus and the VJ plans are well detailed and the extra work in wing construction is well worth the effort.

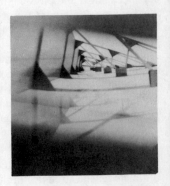

Construction details of the VJ-23 wing.

Construction details are easily seen in Ron Klemmedson's "A S Whooppee" biplane.

FORMING ALUMINUM

In the construction of most hang gliders there is considerable aluminum work. Most of the bends and curves are fairly simple but a basic understanding of the operation is advisable. Several basic factors should be considered such as the stresses set up by bending, the mechanical and physical properties of the alloy being bent, the bending technique and the bending equipment being used.

The proper alloy and temper must be selected and since strength is usually more important than forming qualities to the glider builder, a fairly hard 6061-T6 is normally used. Soft tempers will bend better than hard tempers but at a sacrifice in strength. The Materials chapter should be consulted for a fuller explanation of alloys and tempers. Know your alloys and tempers and stay within their limits.

"Springback" occurs in hard, high strength alloys. Compensation may be made for it by bending the material to a smaller radius than ultimately desired.

It is rarely necessary to bend aluminum hot but it will allow a smaller radii should this be necessary. If heat is used, it should not exceed 375 Fahrenheit degrees.

In bending, one side is stretched while the other is compressed. If the material's plastic (ultimate tensile strength) limit is exceeded, it will crack. If not exceeded, the piece may actually gain in strength through cold working.

Aluminum tubing is weakened when drilled or cut. Strength should be built up with wood plugs, aluminum bushings and/or sleeves.

Scratches should be watched closely as they provide a point for further tearing, bending, etc.

For further information, see *Forming Aluminum Shapes and Tube* available free from Reynolds Aluminum, 6601P West Broad St., Richmond, VA 23218.

NOSE PLATES

Nose plates join the leading edge and keel tubes and are normally made of stainless steel or 6061-T6 aluminum. They should be rounded or angled to form a skid plate to resist digging in when the nose touches down first. When drilling nose plates, drill both sides simultaneously to assure good bolt alignment.

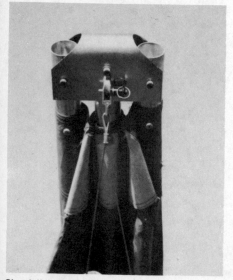

Chandelle's Nose Plate.

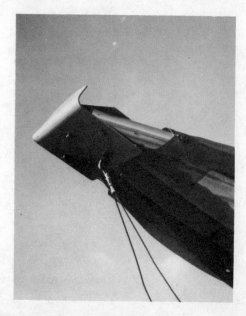

Top view of the one piece stainless steel nose plate from Ultralite Products.

A two piece braced, angled skid as found on the Skysurfer and the LARK.

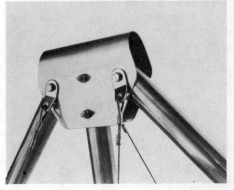

Top and bottom views of the UP plate.

THE KING POST

The use of a kingpost is mandatory with practically all models and they have been made in several different ways.

The cables should not be free to slide through the post as shown here.

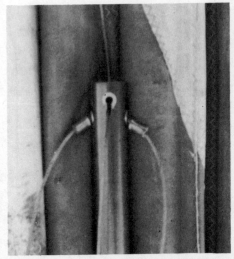

Or they may saw their way through as shown here. Worse yet, the king post can always slip and collapse.

The Skysurfer has a double king post.

The king post kit from Ultralite features a plug-in arrangement. When the wind flips the glider and smashes the king post, it takes just a couple of minutes to insert a new tube and get back into the air.

The Sky Sports LARK utilizes a set screw with a rubber pad to hold the cables in place.

Note the king post on the Icarus V. This external bracing is used to save weight; the alternative is a cantilever wing with heavier internal bracing.

CENTRAL STRUCTURE

The central structure is the heart of the glider and typically everything hangs on the one main bolt. Frequent inspection of this area is mandatory. Tubes at this juncture must be dowelled or sleeved to prevent deformation and rupture. Saddles facilitate set up and knock down since the cross tube must be rotated each time.

Typical set-up of the central juncture. King post mount, sleeved tubes set in plastic saddles, three position C.G. adjustable trapeze bar mount with locking pin for quick installation and removal. Note that locking pin has a safety cable to prevent loss.

Note the sleeved cross tube, trapeze bar spacers, adjustable CG mounting bracket and pilot support rope. From Ultralite.

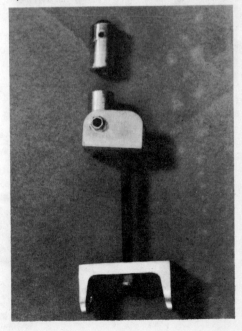

The central structure kit as found on the Sky Sports LARK.

TANGS

Tangs are used to make connections and may be flat, angled or saddled. They may be made from ⅛'' sheet aluminum but should be of stainless steel. They measure about 1'' x 2'' and the hole sizes vary according to the application.

Typical detail of a saddle tang which conforms to the round tubing. Note the turnbuckle with clevis pin and round safety clip. From Ultralite Products.

Typical detail of a standard angled tang with cable attached as produced by Ultralite Products.

Standoffs and saddles are available for various diameter tubing. They make a much cleaner joint and avoid deformation of the aluminum. From Ultralite. Made of plastic so as not to dent the aluminum tube.

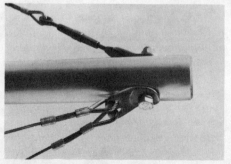

Double tang for the keel by Ultralite.

EYEBOLTS

Eyebolts may be substituted for the bolt/tang arrangement in some applications but care should be taken in angle loading. See the Materials chapter.

Typical eye bolt installation.

SPEED-RAIL HARDWARE

Speed-Rail fittings are easy to work with; simply drill out the rivet and set screws and substitute bolts.

Speed rail fittings are easy to work with; no fancy tools are required.

DOWELLING AND SLEEVING

Hardwood plugs or aluminum sleeves must be added to certain areas to add strength and prevent deformation. Dowelling in the ends of tubes also acts to keep out foreign matter. Bonn Industries uses aluminum plugs.

Note the plug in the cross tube and sleeve on the leading edge tube.

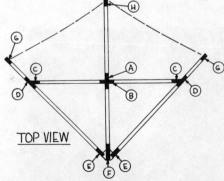

TOP VIEW

Reinforcing is recommended at all places noted in the above Whitney drawing but particularly at points A, B and D.

The tubing is weakened by drilling and a sleeve may be added to strengthen the area around the drilled hole. Now, however, the weak point is at the end of the sleeve as the tube, when forced, will bend around the end of the sleeving tube. Broken tubes may also be spliced. The splicing sleeve should have the same or greater wall thickness as the broken tube and it should cover the broken tube for a minimum of three diameters on each side of the break.

In-flight structural failures are what nightmares are made of. The most common failures are due to improperly attached nico press sleeves, shredding plastic or tape installed on the plastic sail incorrectly. Landing damage usually involves the aft end of the leading edge tube just beyond the cross tube. Occasionally when a kite flips over in the wind, the king post folds.

Bob Wills drills a trapeze bar. Note that a hose clamp is used to keep the two pieces together to assure hole alignment.

Extrusions may be cut, drilled and smoothed to form numerous parts.

PLUGS AND CAPS

Tubing plugs and caps dress up the ends of the tubes and keep out foreign matter. They may be dowelling, metal inserts or plastic caps and they all do the same basic job.

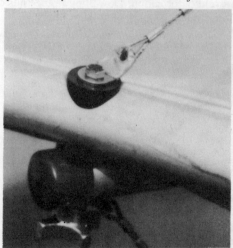

74

RIGGING

Typical cable structure as found on the Whitney Rogallo.

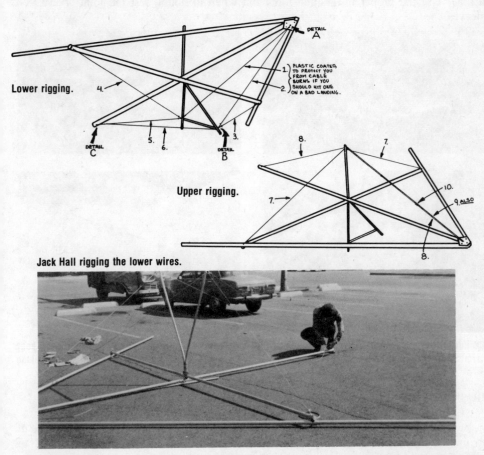

Lower rigging.

DETAIL
A

1.) PLASTIC COATED, TO PROTECT YOU FROM CABLE BURNS IF YOU SHOULD HIT ONE ON A BAD LANDING.
2.)

4.

DETAIL
C

5. 6.

DETAIL
B

3.

Upper rigging.

8.   7.

7.

10.

9 ALSO

8.

Jack Hall rigging the lower wires.

The lower "flying" wires take the load during flight. Turnbuckles and other separating hardware should not be used here. The upper "landing" wires keep the structure tight, making ground handling easier, keep the glider from folding up should it become inverted in flight and keeps it from folding up on landing or while on the ground in a strong wind. This upper bracing is very important. During rigging, the turnbuckles should be unscrewed to their ends so that maximum tightening will be allowed later. Manta has some interesting approaches to rigging, see Chapter VI.

CABLES AND SWAGING

Cables are attached to the structure by doubling them back on themselves and securing with a Nicopress sleeve. They must be protected with a thimble. A single sleeve provides a joint as strong as the cable itself but often two sleeves are used and the second overhangs the end of the cable's bitter end just slightly so as to cover the sharp wires. If not fabricated in this manner, wires should be covered with tape or shrink tubing.

A running splice may be used to connect two pieces of cable together by using two sleeves ½ " apart. This is good for 100% of the cable strength while a single sleeve will only hold 80%.

Cable is easily cut with cable cutters or with a cold chisel on a steel block. Don't use a cutting torch as the heat will damage the cable. Always use a thimble and make sure it is securely installed. Without it, the cable will be cut through one strand at a time. Use the proper installation tools and when in doubt, test the joint or use two sleeves.

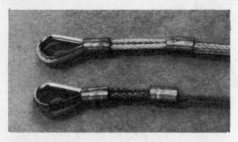

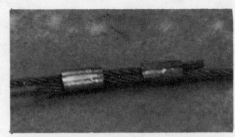

Chandelle uses swaged ball and shank fittings for a clean appearance.

These towers on Chandelle's Competition glider keep the cable off the sail while allowing a shorter king post.

BUSHINGS

Bushings add strength, resist compression and avoid tubing rupture. They are made of aluminum tubing of a size compatible with the bolt to be used.

As described by Eipper-Formance, bushings are made as follows:

Cut bushing and insert into tubing so that it protrudes about ⅛" on each side. Insert flathead screws on both ends of bushing and lay tube on a hard concrete surface. Pound with a hammer until bushing flares. Remove screws and finish flare by backing with a block of wood and flattening bushing ends.

The bushed tube may deform slightly and may have to be drilled out.

Bushings Installed.

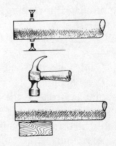

Bushing Installation.

"Hey Dad, look at that man trying to fly a broken kite".

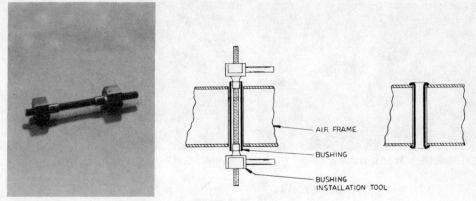

A bushing installation tool from Free-Flight Systems.

AIR FRAME

BUSHING

BUSHING
INSTALLATION TOOL

CARING FOR THE HANG GLIDER

The hang glider consists of many substances which may include Dacron,aluminum, copper, steel, wood, glues, etc. and they must be considered in storage and cleaning. Generally, a cover should be used in transport and a good storage place may be in the rafters of the garage. Most gliders will stand a lot of weather abuse but to keep it looking sharp and to retain the highest level of reliability, it should be stored out of the sun, dampness and dust. When transporting it on the car top, it should be covered to protect it from wind whipping.

Washing the sail will restore some of its color and will remove sand and foreign matter which cut the cloth fibers.Remove it from the frame and wash it in warm-to-hot water with a mild soap. A smooth bathtub makes a good washing area. Agitate and continue the soapy washings until the dirt is gone. Then rinse it several times in warm fresh water until the soap is out. Do not wring the sail with the hands but hang it in the shade to dry. Inspect the sail thoroughly , push firmly in questionable areas with the finger, and patch the small holes and tears.

While the sail is off the frame, inspect it carefully. Check the cables for wear around the thimbles and the tubing for cracks especially around bolt holes. Check the bolts for bends or cracks. Clean up the rusty areas and apply a light coat of oil. Take care of the glider and it will take care of you.

TOOLS

The tools required by the skysurfer vary according to whether he is building or simply maintaining and according to the materials if building, wood or metal. Some of the more common tools are listed here.

For an outstanding treatment of tools for the homebuilder, see *Basic Hand Tools* Vol. 1 and 2. They are available at $2.50 each from the Experimental Aircraft Association, PO Box 229P, Hales Corners, Wisc 53130. For information on fabric tools and sewing machine operation, see *The Parachute Manual* ($20.85pp), 48P Walker St, North Quincy, MA.02171.

PIPE BENDER for bending tubing and pipe.

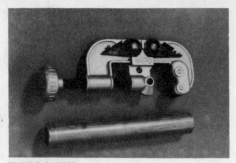

TUBING CUTTER

SWAGING TOOL, large bolt chopper type. From
National Telephone Supply, Cleveland, Ohio.

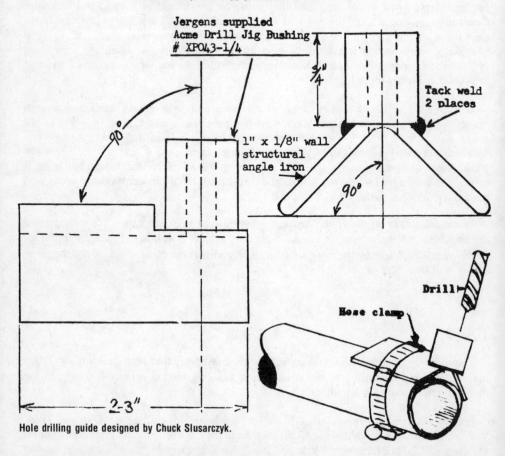

Jergens supplied
Acme Drill Jig Bushing
XP043-1/4

90°

3/4"

Tack weld
2 places

1" x 1/8" wall
structural
angle iron

90°

Drill

Hose clamp

2-3"

Hole drilling guide designed by Chuck Slusarczyk.

Plus assorted screwdrivers, wrenches, etc. Socket sets with a ratchet and brace or
"speeder wrench" speed work tremendously.

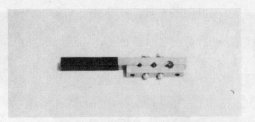

SWAGE-IT TOOL, No. 2 for 1/16" and 3/32" cable from S and F Tool Co., Costa Mesa, CA.

HOT KNIFE for cutting and searing synthetic fabrics.

Size No. 0 chuck and die set.

CHUCK. For the eyelet type washer. Tool for size No. 0:9191.

BENCH DIE. For the eyelet type grommet. Available for grommets in sizes No. 0 to No. 6. Tool for size No. 0:9192.

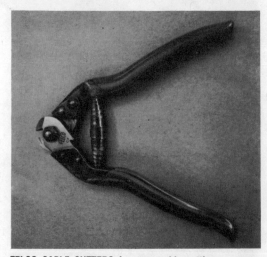

FELCO CABLE CUTTERS for easy cable cutting.

Grommet Punches. Grommet punches should cut a hole slightly smaller than the grommet to be used to provide a tight fit.

CHAPTER IV

HANG GLIDING AND THE LAW

One of the great attractions in hang gliding is freedom. One is free to soar with the birds; to get out into the open air, to do his own thing. When skysurfers gather to exchange experiences, they often find that there are other laws besides that of gravity affecting their activity. These range from park rangers to local ordinances and the attractive nuisance doctrine. Most have speculated as to the concern of the Federal Government and some have been bold enough to ask.

As far as certification of hang gliders as aircraft is concerned, there are three alternatives: No certification, the "amateur" built or "experimental" category and the standard production category as set forth in FAR Part 23. Each area is distinct and brings with it its own ramifications.

Currently, hang gliders do not require certification as aircraft. If they did, manufacturers would have to operate under FAR Part 23, a 99 page document entitled AIRWORTHINESS STANDARDS: NORMAL, UTILITY AND ACROBATIC CATEGORY AIRPLANES and covers flight characteristics, structure, design, construction, equipment, operating limitations, etc. Among a million other things, a compass would be required.

To better understand what all this regulation might mean to the manufacturers, read through FAR Part 23 at the nearest FAA General Aviation District Office and send $1. for the *Basic Glider Criteria Handbook* (FAA 5.8/2:G49/962) to U.S. Government Printing Office, Public Documents Department, Washington D.C. 20402. Hang gliding could wind up with something similar; manufacturers would be required to extensively document tests before any changes or improvements could be made and this would result in sharply higher prices and less progress.

If however, the major portion of the aircraft is built by the purchaser, it then becomes "amateur built" and may be registered as "experimental". This procedure isn't too difficult but the glider will still be required to have certain equipment such as an air speed indicator, altimeter, compass and an emergency locator beacon and then the only persons eligible to fly it would be pilots holding at least a student certificate. See Parts 61 and 91 at the local GADO for details.

"And to think that all you wanted to do was to run down a hill, skimming a few feet above the terrain, to the bottom"

In a letter to Mike Markowski, Editor of *Skysurfer,* A. McKay answered a letter for then FAA Administrator John Shaffer, as follows:

"We have been giving thought to the possible *need* for regulations on hang glider operations. At this moment, however, we feel that "skysurfing" is a sporting activity comparable to *intentional parachute jumping.*

It is not our desire to subject sporting activities which make *momentary or brief* use of the airspace to Federal regulations beyond what is necessary to *protect air traffic and the general public".* (emphasis ours).

So far, it would appear that most hang gliding activity is not subject to aircraft and pilot licensing requirements of any sort. The words "momentary" and "brief" were not defined in the letter but the comparison of hang gliding with parachuting would seem to indicate that flights of short duration would be acceptable. Parachutists normally make a freefall of up to a minute, open their parachutes around 2000 feet and then spend about two minutes in the final slower descent. They may, however, open higher and spend quite a bit of time in the airspace descending at about 1000 feet per minute. Some of the newer gliding canopies have quite a range and a somewhat slower rate of descent. In any case, assuming that the Administrator understood the capabilities of the parachute and the parachutist, there was no intention to place any altitude restriction on hang gliding and "brief" could be interpreted to be 15 minutes or even more.

The letter goes on to use the old familiar FAA bureaucratic legalese. "To protect air traffic and the general public". Keeping skysurfing activity low, slow and away from airports should solve the air traffic conflict concern. Those attempting to soar at higher altitudes might well consider a licensed craft and a pilot's certificate. By "general public", the FAA shows concern not just for "persons and property on the ground" (the gathering crowd)but also for those purchasing plans for hang gliders; especially when a pilot is injured.

If poor quality hang gliding kits are sold and a skysurfer gets injured as a result, FAA may suddenly require hang gliders to be licensed "to protect the public" and they mean the flying public here. If every piece of bamboo/polyethylene ground skimming contraption suddenly is required to be certificated and every user must be licensed as a pilot, the young and growing sport of skysurfing will die a very early death.

It has been suggested that the ultralight hang glider continue to be exempted from Federal control and be defined as "Gliders-Man Powered Aircraft" with wing loadings less than 3 lbs/sq ft and that they be limited to solo flight, self launched (minor assists O.K.) and flights under 500 feet AGL (above ground level.)

So far, the only collisions between hang gliders and other aircraft have been with radio controlled models, with usually fatal results to the model. Many flights are being made near airports without any reported conflict. Examples exist at Los Angeles International and Torrance County Airport in California.

In 1972, FAA Administrator John H. Shaffer, endorsing the petition for issuance of a stamp to commemorate ballooning, wrote:

"As you know, the Federal Aviation Administration promotes all facets of civil aviation-commercial and private flying, the air carriers, and general aviation--including sport ballooning.

We recommend publicizing this event with a stamp not only in the interest of international sportsmanship and world cooperation, but because it will also symbolize *how the air space over these United States is a national resource belonging to everyone."* (emphasis ours).

The FAA does not regulate other brief, low and slow users of the air such as ski jumpers, flying trapeze gymnasts, cliff divers, motorcycle slope jumpers, high jumpers, pole vaulters, wrecked car leapers or Tarzan. In fact, the only reason that skydiving is regulated is because the parachutists must use an aircraft to get up there and the aircraft are already regulated.

It is doubtful that the FAA or any state body could ever effectively control hang gliding anyway since it is too wide spread and can be done almost in secret. These officials do not have the required man power and, in fact, FAA's funds are being trimmed. The FAA has been ordered to "recover administrative costs"in the form of user charges so that general (private) aviation will pay for the airways system. Certainly it would be unfair to make the skysurfer pay for something he doesn't need or use.

The only real problems which have confronted the skysurfer so far are those with locating sites. It doesn't take long to draw a crowd and then the whole activity is stopped by a property owner, forest ranger or a representative of the park department. Some skysurfers have secret sites and jealously guard their location. It is particularly discouraging to climb to the top of a mountain only to be told by the ranger that you have to carry the 50 pounds of gear back down. While they are often sympathetic, they have to enforce the rules and if you get into trouble, they must perform the rescue. The best advice seems to be: Don't ask for permission, (the answer will probably be"no"), be inconspicuous(no camera crews)and get in and out as quickly as possible.

The beach is a good place to learn and fly but many people seem to think that they should only be used by bathers and they argue that skysurfers tear down the dunes. One solution is to use private property such as ski slopes where only one land owner need be consulted. Of course, ski hills also have tows which make hang gliding much more fun.

The following waiver submitted by Eddie Paul may be of some help when dealing with land owners:

Waiver of Legal Rights

I hereby acknowledge that I will take full responsibility for any injury that I may suffer while on your property. I further acknowledge any legal rights that may accrue as the result of any injury I may suffer while flying my "hang glider" on or across your property, and having acknowledged such rights I hereby waive them and any other legal rights related thereto.

This constitutes a waiver of my rights and is an agreement that I will not pursue any other legal remedies. I further agree that I will limit my use of the land to flying my "hang glider" and agree to use the land only at such time as may be designated.

Having considerable experience flying a "hang glider", I have the ability to determine where and how to fly the "hang glider" under any given conditions, thereby minimizing the possibility of any injury.

DATE _____

NAME _____

NAME _____

NAME _____

"The idea of building a hang-glider appealed to me greatly, first of all it was cheap, easy to build and there was no FAA that would say that I couldn't"

The Federal Aviation Administration

The Office of the Administrator of Civil Aeronautics of the Department of Transportation publishes laws as Federal Aviation Regulations (FARs);they are updated from time to time and one should be certain to obtain all the latest changes. Alterations to the FARs involve a very expensive and time consuming procedure consisting of thorough notification, comment and hearing process between the field and the FAA.

The Federal Aviation Regulations

The FAA issues the FARs on a volume system and they are sold on a subscription basis. The purchase of an FAR volume will establish your subscription service with the Superintendent of Documents for automatic receipt of changes to the volume as issued by the FAA. The volume structure is layed out below. Regulations which may pertain to hang gliders and hang gliding are marked with an asterisk; their purchase is highly recommended.

In 1974, the FAA decided once again, to sell the parts individually. Inquire at your local G.A.D.O.

Orders for the FARs should include remittance by cheque or money order made payable to the Superintendent of Documents and should be addressed to:

Superintendent of Documents
U.S. Government Printing Office
Washington, D. C. 20402

Be certain to include the GPO catalogue number: TD 4.6/3:v. Or FARs may be purchased from GPO Bookstores in Atlanta, Chicago, Boston, Dallas, Denver, Kansas City, Los Angeles, New York and San Francisco.

Orders from Foreign countries, except Canada and Mexico, should include an additional amount of one-fourth the purchase price to cover mailing. Remittance should be by International Money Order or by a draft on a U.S. bank.

STATUS OF THE FEDERAL AVIATION REGULATIONS
As of April 15, 1973
FEDERAL AVIATION REGULATIONS VOLUMES

Volume No.	Contents	Price	Transmittals
Volume I		$2.50 plus 75¢ foreign mailing	5
Part 1	Definitions and Abbreviations.		
Volume II		$10.50 plus $2.75 foreign mailing	31
Part 11	General Rule-Making Procedures.		
Part 13	Enforcement Procedures.		
* Part 21	Certification Procedures for Products and Parts.		
* Part 37	Technical Standard Order Authorizations.		
Part 39	Airworthiness Directives.		
* Part 45	Identification and Registration Marking.		
* Part 47	Aircraft Registration.		
Part 49	Recording of Aircraft Titles and Security Documents.		
Part 183	Representatives of the Administrator.		
Part 185	Testimony by Employees and Production of Records in Legal Proceedings and Service of Legal Process and Pleadings.		
Part 187	Fees.		
Part 189	Use of Federal Aviation Administration Communications System.		
Volume III		$13.50 plus $3.50 foreign mailing	12
* Part 23	Airworthiness Standards: Normal, Utility, and Acrobatic Category Airplanes.		
Part 25	Airworthiness Standards: Transport Category Airplanes.		
Part 36	Noise Standards: Aircraft Type Certification.		
Volume IV		$5.00 plus $1.25 foreign mailing	6
Part 27	Airworthiness Standards: Normal Category Rotorcraft.		
Part 29	Airworthiness Standards: Transport Category Rotorcraft.		
Part 31	Airworthiness Standards: Manned Free Balloons.		
Part 33	Airworthiness Standards: Aircraft Engines.		
Part 35	Airworthiness Standards: Propellers.		
Volume V		$3.50 plus $1 foreign mailing	12
* Part 43	Maintenance, Preventive Maintenance, Rebuilding, and Alteration.		
Part 145	Repair Stations.		
Part 149	Parachute Lofts.		

Advisory Circulars

Advisory Circulars (ACs) are published from time to time to explain the intent of the FARs, to clarify certain areas and to make notifications to the field. Advisory Circulars are not "law" but are offered as guidance and should be followed. Those Advisory Circulars which are free are available from:

D.O.T. Dist Unit
TAD 484.3
Washington, D.C. 20590

Advisory Circulars with a price are available from the Government Printing Office, address above. The following Advisory Circulars which might be of interest to those building or flying hang gliders are:

20-27B Certification and Operation of Amateur-Built Aircraft (4-20-72).

Provides information and guidance concerning certification and operation of amateur-built aircraft, including gliders, free balloons, helicopters, and gryoplanes, and sets forth an acceptable means, not the sole means, of compliance with FAR Part 21 and FAR Part 91.

20-28 Nationally Advertised Aircraft Construction Kits (8-7-64).

The AC says that nationally advertised kits that supply parts and materials may provide the builder with so many completed assemblies that his actual contribution may not be enough to qualify the finished aircraft as amateur-built.

20-45 Safetying of Turnbuckles on Civil Aircraft (9-17-65).

Provides information on turnbuckle safetying methods that have been found acceptable by the FAA during past aircraft type certification programs.

20-46 Suggested Equipment for Gliders Operating Under IFR (9-23-65).

Provides guidance to glider operators on how to equip their gliders for operation under instrument flight rules (IFR), including flight through clouds.

20-71 Dual Locking Devices on Fasteners (12-8-70).

Provides guidance and acceptable means, not the sole means, by which compliance may be shown with the requirements for dual locking devices on removable fasteners installed in rotocraft and transport category airplanes.

20-86 Aviation Education through Building an Airplane (5-11-73).   Provides information in high schools about the available assistance, resources, methods, and opportunities for attaining basic educational goals by building an airplane.

21-2B CH 2 (2-8-71).
21-3 Basic Glider Criteria Handbook (1962).

Provides individual glider designers, the glider industry, and glider operating organizations with guidance material that augments the glider airworthiness certification requirements of the Federal Aviation Regulations. Reprinted 1973. ($1.75 GPO.) FAA 5.8/2: G49/962.

21-12 Airworthiness Certificates.

Contains step by step procedures for obtaining the certificate. Especially helpful to homebuilders.

43.13-1A Acceptable Methods, Techniques and Practices — Aircraft Inspection and Repair (4-17-72).

Contains methods, techniques and practices acceptable to the Administrator for inspection and repair to civil aircraft. Published in 1973. ($3.70 — GPO.) TD 4.28/2:972.

43.13-2 Acceptable Methods, Techniques, and Practices — Aircraft Alterations (4-19-66).

Contains methods, techniques, and practices acceptable to the Administrator in altering civil aircraft. Published in 1965. ($3.50, $4.50 foreign Sub. — GPO.) TD 4.28:971. Subscription now includes: Changes 1 thru 14 Consoiidated Reprint in 1973.

61-43A Glider Pilot Written Test Guide — Private and Commercial (1-12-72).

Provides information, guidelines, and sample test items, to assist applicants for the Glider Pilot Certificate in attaining necessary aeronautical knowledge.

The FAA worked with the sport and the industry on an Advisory Circular entitled *Definition and recommended safety parameters for operation of hang gliders.* It was published in the summer of 1974 and is reproduced in the Appendix.

Currently Federal Aviation Regulations do not affect hang gliding and it should be emphasized that Advisory Circulars are not law. If rule making is enacted, hang gliders may be placed in the experimental category due to the obvious appeal to the homebuilder. Eventual regulation is virtually inevitable but inactment takes years and once hang gliding laws are made they will be nearly impossible to enforce. Hang gliding is not as visible as other aviation sports and it can be done on the other side of the hill, out of sight. And, of course, there is little need for regulation. The F.A.A. has traditionally recognized each individual's authority to subject himself to danger (but not to others).

The light weight, low speed hang glider rarely presents a hazard to ''persons and property on the ground''. A crash into a house may knock down the TV antenna but it won't injure the occupants.

Hang gliding is FREE!
Free of expensive aircraft, hampering regulations and pollution.

CHAPTER V

MATERIALS

The earliest aircraft used a lot of bicycle parts; no doubt, due to the influence of the Wright Brothers. Fortunately, knowledge was gained and materials improved; aircraft began to fly faster and metals were devel6ped to replace wood. Even today, the hang glider pilot is continually looking for lighter, stronger building materials. The most popular are aluminum and Dacron but some attention is being directed toward Nylon, magnesium, paper honeycomb and fiberglass. Here is a weight comparison of some common materials:

Material	Specific Gravity
Sitka spruce	0.43
Alloy steel	7.83
Aluminum (tubing)	2.80
Magnesium	1.75
Titanium	4.51
Fiberglass (general purpose epoxy)	1.80
Fiberglass (filament wound epoxy)	2.22

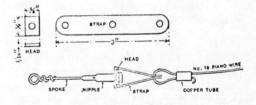

Bicycle spoke turnbuckle.

"In the early days we had to scrounge to find our materials. There were no such things as plans or kits, and there was no one to advise us on standards of construction. We had a lot of fun with bamboo and plastic and later with surplus tubing and plastic. We even trusted hardware store bolts and turnbuckles. But then, we also kept close to the ground-usually the beach. And it was a good thing because we rarely went home with an intact glider after a day's flying. In two years the sport has come a long way. Somebody's kite folding up in the air is no longer the joke it was when hardly anyone got more than 10 feet off the ground. Hang glider pilots need aircraft-quality materials which they can trust" - Dick Eipper.

Materials used in aircraft construction are not ordinary materials. One finds this out the first time looking for tubing. A very significant advantage to the modern hang glider is the utilization of modern high strength, light weight materials, and they are not found in the hardware store. It is likely that more time will actually be spent finding materials than spent in construction. And prices for small quantities can be somewhat higher than expected.

Here are some publications on materials which are helpful:
Airmart Hardware Digest ($4.95), Airmart, Hanger B4AP, Jefferson Co Arpt, Broomfield, Colo 80020, and
Aircraft Hardware Standards Manual and Engineering Reference ($5.50) Aviation Publications, PO Box 123P, Milwaukee, Wis, 53201

This chapter is your permanent reference source. The compiled data is the result of intensive research and the most up to date field trials. Special attention is called to the all-inclusive charts, tables, and photographs which provide a ready reference to useful statistical data.
Federal and Military Specifications and Standards
The materials used in hang glider construction are, and must be, standardized and of the very best grade obtainable. All of these fabrics, tapes, webbings, hardware, etc. are manufactured in strict accordance with Government regulations. These specifications are in the form of written descriptions,drawings,prints,commercial designations, industry standards and other descriptive references. These regulations set forth certain minimum standards and details of construction for each type of material or equipment. This is very necessary to insure that the item ordered meets the requirements and that the item will perform the functions for which it is rated.
Government specifications are divided into two principal groups: Federal Specifications and Military Specifications. Some items purchased by the Department of Defense, particularly those with no special military characteristics, can be described satisfactorily by Federal Specifications and the Department uses them rather than Military Specifications.
The armed forces now procure most of their materials and equipment under a coordinated program. All items procured in this manner are assigned Military Specification numbers. The "MIL SPEC" will be mentioned in the text where applicable. They have become a handy method of identification.

Military Specifications and Standards, Federal Specifications and Standards, AN and MS drawings, Qualified Product Lists, Air Force-Navy Aeronautical Specifications and Standards, Air Force-Navy Aeronautical Design Standards, U.S. Air Force Specifications and Specification Bulletins, Military Handbooks, Industry Documents, and Air Force-Navy Aeronautical Bulletins with all the latest revisions, are available from:

Commanding Officer
Naval Publications and Forms Center
5801 Tabor Avenue
Philadelphia, Pa 19120

They should be ordered by number and name and should be limited to five per request. There is no charge. DD Form 1425 in duplicate and double spaced should be used, if available, but a letter will do. Telephone requests may be made Monday-Friday, 8:00 am-4:30 pm: (215) 697-3321. There is an answering device for off duty requests, seven days a week.

Common AN and MS drawings referring to hang glider parts are listed here. Copies of the drawings may be obtained free as noted above.

A drawing guide. Courtesy of Airplane Supply Centre, 1104P Cambie Rd., Richmond, BC, Canada.

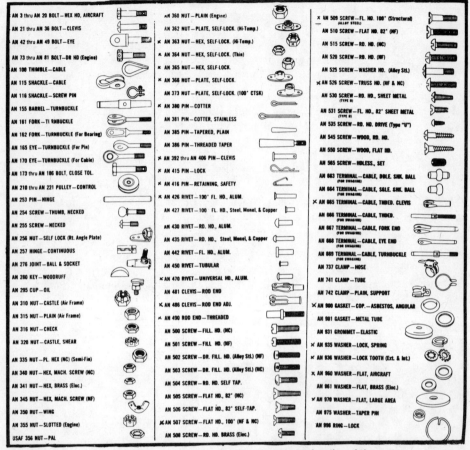

AN 3 thru AN 20 BOLT — HEX HD, AIRCRAFT	AN 360 NUT — PLAIN (Engine)	X AN 509 SCREW — FL. HD. 100° (Structural) (ALLOY STEEL)
AN 21 thru AN 36 BOLT — CLEVIS	AN 362 NUT — PLATE, SELF-LOCK. (Hi-Temp.)	AN 510 SCREW — FLAT HD. 82° (NF)
AN 42 thru AN 49 BOLT — EYE	X AN 363 NUT — HEX, SELF-LOCK. (Hi-Temp.)	AN 515 SCREW — RD. HD. (NC)
AN 73 thru AN 81 BOLT — DR HD (Engine)	A AN 364 NUT — HEX, SELF-LOCK. (Thin)	AN 520 SCREW — RD. HD. (NF)
AN 100 THIMBLE — CABLE	X AN 365 NUT — HEX, SELF-LOCK.	AN 525 SCREW — WASHER HD. (Alloy Stl.)
AN 115 SHACKLE — CABLE	X AN 366 NUT — PLATE, SELF-LOCK.	X AN 526 SCREW — TRUSS HD. (NF & NC)
AN 116 SHACKLE — SCREW PIN	AN 373 NUT — PLATE, SELF-LOCK. (100° CTSK)	AN 530 SCREW — RD. HD., SHEET METAL (TYPE B)
AN 155 BARREL — TURNBUCKLE	X AN 380 PIN — COTTER	AN 531 SCREW — FL. HD., 82° SHEET METAL (TYPE B)
AN 161 FORK — TURNBUCKLE	AN 381 PIN — COTTER, STAINLESS	AN 535 SCREW — RD. HD. DRIVE (Type "U")
AN 162 FORK — TURNBUCKLE (For Bearing)	AN 385 PIN — TAPERED, PLAIN	AN 545 SCREW — WOOD, RD. HD.
AN 165 EYE — TURNBUCKLE (For Pin)	AN 386 PIN — THREADED TAPER	AN 550 SCREW — WOOD, FLAT HD.
AN 170 EYE — TURNBUCKLE (For Cable)	X AN 392 thru AN 406 PIN — CLEVIS	AN 565 SCREW — HDLESS., SET
AN 173 thru AN 186 BOLT, CLOSE TOL.	X AN 415 PIN — LOCK	AN 663 TERMINAL — CABLE, DBLE. SHK. BALL (FOR SWAGING)
AN 210 thru AN 221 PULLEY — CONTROL	X AN 416 PIN — RETAINING, SAFETY	AN 664 TERMINAL — CABLE, SGLE. SHK. BALL (FOR SWAGING)
AN 253 PIN — HINGE	X AN 426 RIVET — 100° FL. HD., ALUM.	X AN 665 TERMINAL — CABLE, THDED. CLEVIS
AN 254 SCREW — THUMB, NECKED	AN 427 RIVET — 100 FL. HD., Steel, Monel, & Copper	AN 666 TERMINAL — CABLE, THDED. (FOR SWAGING)
AN 255 SCREW — NECKED	AN 430 RIVET — RD. HD., ALUM.	AN 667 TERMINAL — CABLE, FORK END (FOR SWAGING)
AN 256 NUT — SELF LOCK (Rt. Angle Plate)	AN 435 RIVET — RD. HD., Steel, Monel, & Copper	AN 668 TERMINAL — CABLE, EYE END (FOR SWAGING)
AN 257 HINGE — CONTINUOUS	AN 442 RIVET — FL. HD., ALUM.	AN 669 TERMINAL — CABLE, TURNBUCKLE (FOR SWAGING)
AN 276 JOINT — BALL & SOCKET	AN 450 RIVET — TUBULAR	AN 737 CLAMP — HOSE
AN 280 KEY — WOODRUFF	X AN 470 RIVET — UNIVERSAL HD., ALUM.	AN 741 CLAMP — TUBE
AN 295 CUP — OIL	AN 481 CLEVIS — ROD END	AN 742 CLAMP — PLAIN, SUPPORT
AN 310 NUT — CASTLE (Air Frame)	X AN 486 CLEVIS — ROD END ADJ.	X AN 900 GASKET — COP. — ASBESTOS, ANGULAR
AN 315 NUT — PLAIN (Air Frame)	A AN 490 ROD END — THREADED	AN 901 GASKET — METAL TUBE
AN 316 NUT — CHECK	AN 500 SCREW — FILL. HD. (NC)	AN 931 GROMMET — ELASTIC
AN 320 NUT — CASTLE, SHEAR	AN 501 SCREW — FILL. HD. (NF)	X AN 935 WASHER — LOCK, SPRING
AN 335 NUT — PL. HEX (NC) (Semi-Fin)	AN 502 SCREW — DR. FILL. HD. (Alloy Stl.) (NF)	X AN 936 WASHER — LOCK TOOTH (Ext. & Int.)
AN 340 NUT — HEX, MACH. SCREW (NC)	AN 503 SCREW — DR. FILL. HD. (Alloy Stl.) (NC)	X AN 960 WASHER — FLAT, AIRCRAFT
AN 341 NUT — HEX, BRASS (Elec.)	AN 504 SCREW — RD. HD. SELF TAP.	AN 961 WASHER — FLAT, BRASS (Elec.)
AN 345 NUT — HEX, MACH. SCREW (NF)	AN 505 SCREW — FLAT HD., 82° (NC)	X AN 970 WASHER — FLAT, LARGE AREA
AN 350 NUT — WING	AN 506 SCREW — FLAT HD., 82° SELF-TAP.	AN 975 WASHER — TAPER PIN
AN 355 NUT — SLOTTED (Engine)	X AN 507 SCREW — FLAT HD., 100° (NF & NC)	AN 996 RING — LOCK
USAF 356 NUT — PAL	AN 508 SCREW — RD. HD. BRASS (Elec.)	

A careful reading of the AN or MS drawing will reveal a complete explanation of the parts.

FASTENERS

BOLTS

One of the most common fasteners is the bolt/nut combination. Most of the bolts used to construct hang gliders will have a hexagon shaped head and are normally called "cap screws". These have a forged head and shaft and following forging, the shaft is threaded. In this condition, the bolt is a soft Grade 2 type, the kind found in hardware stores and often imported. Heat treating increases the strength and it may be heated and quenched once to make it a tougher Grade 5 or two or more times to make it a very tough Grade 8. Then they are electroplated, usually with zinc so they won't rust and immediately baked to relieve the hydrogen embrittlement introduced by the plating. The more work done to the bolt, the higher its price. Only the AN (military) or Grade 8 (commercial) bolt should be used.

There are so few bolts in a hang glider and their cost is so small that it is wise to purchase the best. One common bolt costs out in the three grades as follows:

Grade 2: .09¢
Grade 5: .10¢
Grade 8: .15¢

Grade markings are listed in the following tables.

Threads may be course or fine. Fine threads allow torquing the nut tighter but the course threads have more body and hold better. In hang glider work, tightness usually only results in bent tubing; the course threads are recommended, but are hard to find.

For further information on fasteners, contact the Industrial Fasteners Institute, 1505P East Ohio Bldg, 1717 E 9th St, Cleveland, Ohio 44114.

It is of the utmost importance to find and use the proper bolt. If identification is impossible, discard it and purchase a new one from a fastener dealer.

A bolt which is bent is very weak; often they crack along a thread in bending. It must be replaced. Bolts should be inspected periodically and replaced as required.

Fasteners securing critical parts should have dual locking devices such as a nylon lock and a safety wire per FAA Advisory Circular 20-71. It should be noted that nylon lock nuts are designed to be installed only once and that they will not hold well in a second installation.

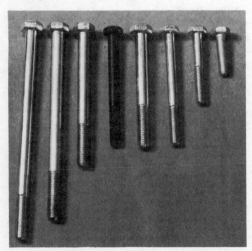

A-N Bolts

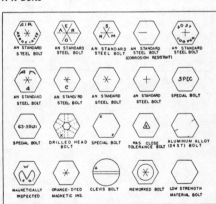

"See how the wings striking against the air hold up the heavy eagle in the thin upper air, near to the element of fire. And likewise see how the air moving over the sea strikes against the bellying sails, making the loaded heavy ship run; so that by these demonstrative and definite reasons you may know that man with his great contrived wings, battling the resistant air and conquering it, can subject it and rise above it."

Leonardo Da Vinci

ASTM AND SAE GRADE MARKINGS
FOR STEEL BOLTS AND SCREWS

COMMERCIAL BOLTS

Grade Marking	Specification	Material	Bolt and Screw Size, in.	Proof Load, psi.	Tensile Strength min., psi.
NO MARK	SAE—Grade 1		1/4 thru 1 1/2	33,000	60,000
	ASTM—A 307	Low Carbon Steel	1/4 thru 1 1/2	33,000	60,000
			Over 1 1/2 thru 4	. . . . .	55,000
	SAE—Grade 2	Low Carbon Steel	1/4 thru 3/4	55,000	74,000
			Over 3/4 thru 1 1/2	33,000	60,000
	SAE—Grade 3	Medium Carbon Steel, Cold Worked	1/4 thru 1/2	85,000	110,000
			Over 1/2 thru 5/8	80,000	100,000
	SAE—Grade 5	Medium Carbon Steel, Quenched and Tempered	1/4 thru 1	85,000	120,000
			Over 1 thru 1 1/2	74,000	105,000
	ASTM—A 449		1/4 thru 1	85,000	120,000
			Over 1 thru 1 1/2	74,000	105,000
			Over 1 1/2 thru 3	55,000	90,000
	ASTM—A 325	Medium Carbon Steel, Quenched and Tempered	1/2, 5/8, 3/4	85,000	120,000
			7/8, 1	78,000	115,000
			1 1/8 thru 1 1/2	74,000	105,000
	ASTM—A 354 Grade BB	Low Alloy Steel, Quenched and Tempered	1/4 thru 2 1/2	80,000	105,000
			Over 2 1/2 thru 4	75,000	100,000
	ASTM—A 354 Grade BC	Low Alloy Steel, Quenched and Tempered	1/4 thru 2 1/2	105,000	125,000
			Over 2 1/2 thru 4	95,000	115,000
	SAE—Grade 5.1	Low or Medium Carbon Steel, Quenched and Tempered with Assembled Lock Washer	Up to 3/8 incl.	85,000	120,000
	SAE—Grade 7	Medium Carbon Alloy Steel, Quenched and Tempered, Roll Threaded after heat treatment	1/4 thru 1 1/2	105,000	133,000
	SAE—Grade 8	Medium Carbon Alloy Steel, Quenched and Tempered	1/4 thru 1 1/2	120,000	150,000
	ASTM—A 354 Grade BD	Alloy Steel, Quenched and Tempered			
	ASTM—A 490	Alloy Steel, Quenched and Tempered	1/2 thru 2 1/2	120,000	150,000
			Over 2 1/2 thru 4	105,000	140,000

Chart Courtesy Industrial Fasteners Institute.

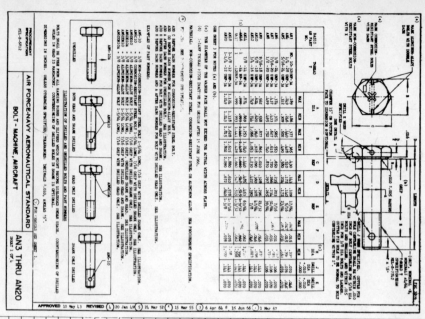

AIR FORCE-NAVY AERONAUTICAL STANDARD
BOLT - MACHINE, AIRCRAFT
AN3 THRU AN20
SHEET 1 OF 1

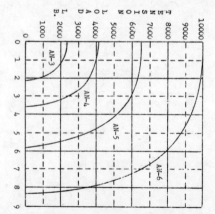

SHEAR LOAD X 1000 LB.

AN-3 AN-4 AN-5 AN-6

This graph shows the allowable loads for AN bolts in tension, shear or any combination of the two. The figures are valid only if regular nuts are used; thin shear nuts will fail at lower loads.

EYEBOLTS

Eyebolts come in very handy in assembling hang gliders and they can often serve double duty by replacing a bolt as well as being a cable juncture. Eyebolts should not be loaded at an angle greater than 45 degrees as the tensile strength is lowered; even at 45 degrees, the reduction is 25%. Both commercial and AN eye bolts are listed here. The commercial type is not graded and should not be used unless individually tensile tested. Commercial hardware store eyebolts with open eyes should not be used under any circumstances. They are made of softer materials, they aren't forged and the incomplete eye is certain to open up.

Aircraft Type.

Commercial Type.

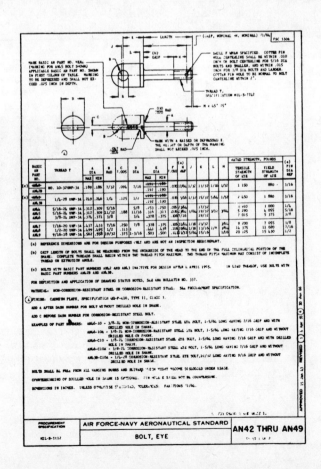

APPROVED 15 Jan 43 REVISED

NUTS

Nuts are made softer so that they will give before the harder, more expensive bolt. Most nuts are not graded and needn't be since their purpose is only to hold the bolt in place. On eyebolts and wherever a lengthwise pull is being made on the bolt, a graded nut should be used. Two nuts may be used as a safety factor. A "2H" marking on the nut indicates heat treating.

Where quick assembly and disassembly depends on nuts, wing nuts may be used. They should be tightened until they meet the end of the threaded shaft so they won't back off and then they should be safetied with wire or locking pins.

96

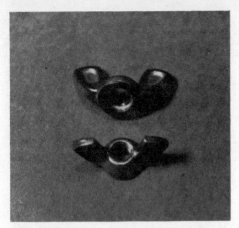

Wing nuts facilitate assembly and disassembly.

Use only AN wing nuts and then safety them with pins or locking wire.

Make certain the threads of the nut match the bolt, course or fine.

Hex nuts with nylon inserts may be more quickly installed with a brace or speeder wrench. Plastic insert bolts and nuts are designed for a single installation and do not hold as well screwed on the second time. Critical attachments should be secured with cotter pins or safety wire.

A "locknut" is one with a special means within itself for gripping the bolt so that relative rotation between them is impeded or prevented in use. It may have a plastic insert, the threads may be deformed, etc. Grace "C" locknuts should be matched to Grade 8 bolts.

Nuts come in numerous shapes and types and their grade is difficult to identify. When in doubt, ask a fastener dealer. Look up "Fasteners, Industrial" in the Yellow Pages.

For information on Elastic Stop nuts and other self locking fasteners, Write: Amerace Esna Corp, 2330P Vauxhall Rd, Union, NJ 07083

APPROVED 8 JUL. 43   REVISED ⑩ 29 DEC 72

AN PART NO.	THREAD T	ULTIMATE TENSILE STRENGTH MINIMUM POUNDS		A (a)	B APPROX	H
		STEEL	AL ALLOY			
AN315-640	NO. 6-40UNF-3B	-	-	.313±.002	23/64	7/64
AN315-3	NO.10-32UNF-3B	1 100	-	.375±.002	7/16	9/64
AN315-4	1/4 -28UNF-3B	2 210	1 100	.438±.002	1/2	3/16
AN315-5	5/16 -24UNF-3B	4 080	2 030	.500±.002	37/64	15/64
AN315-6	3/8 -24UNF-3B	6 500	3 220	.563±.002	21/32	9/32
AN315-7	7/16 -20UNF-3B	10 100	5 020	.625±.002	23/32	21/64
AN315-8	1/2 -20UNF-3B	13 600	6 750	.750±.002	7/8	3/8
AN315-9	9/16 -18UNF-3B	18 500	9 180	.875±.004	1-1/64	27/64
AN315-10	5/8 -18UNF-3B	23 600	11 700	1.000±.004	1-5/32	15/32
AN315-12	3/4 -16UNF-3B	30 100	14 900	1.125±.004	1-19/64	5/8
AN315-14	7/8 -14UNF-3B	44 000	21 800	1.313±.007	1-33/64	21/32
AN315-15	1 -12UNF-3B	60 000	29 800	1.500±.007	1-47/64	3/4
~~AN315-16~~	~~1-12UNF-3B~~	~~80 700~~	~~40 000~~	~~1.500±.007~~	~~1-47/64~~	~~3/4~~
AN315-18	1-1/8 -12UNF-3B	101 800	50 500	1.688±.007	1-61/64	13/16
AN315-20	1-1/4 -12UNF-3B	130 200	64 400	1.875±.007	2-11/64	7/8

(a) FOR ALUMINUM-ALLOY NUTS LARGER THAN -5 SIZE, TOLERANCES ON DIMENSION "A" MAY CONFORM TO APPLICABLE MATERIAL SPECIFICATIONS FOR BAR AND ROD.
(b) 1-1/4NF THREAD SIZE INACTIVE FOR DESIGN AFTER 27 MARCH 1967.

⑩ MATERIAL: STEEL, ALUMINUM ALLOY AND CORROSION-RESISTANT STEEL. SEE PROCUREMENT SPECIFICATION.
FINISH: STEEL-CADMIUM PLATE IN ACCORDANCE WITH QQ-P-416, TYPE II, CLASS 2. PARTS WITH CLASS 3 PLATING MAY BE FURNISHED FROM SUPPLIER'S STOCK UNTIL 1 JANUARY 1971.

ALUMINUM ALLOY-ANODIZE IN ACCORDANCE WITH MIL-A-8625, TYPE II.
CORROSION RESISTANT STEEL-PASSIVATE IN ACCORDANCE WITH QQ-P-35.

ADD C BEFORE DASH NUMBER FOR CORROSION-RESISTANT STEEL NUTS.
ADD D BEFORE DASH NUMBER FOR ALUMINUM-ALLOY NUTS.
ADD R AFTER DASH NUMBER FOR RIGHT-HAND THREAD.
ADD L AFTER DASH NUMBER FOR LEFT-HAND THREAD.

EXAMPLES OF PART NO.: AN315-7 = STEEL NUT, 7/16-20UNF-3B, RIGHT HAND THREAD
AN315C7R = CORROSION-RESISTANT STEEL NUT, 7/16-20UNF-3B, RIGHT HAND THREAD
AN315D7R = ALUMINUM-ALLOY NUT, 7/16-20UNF-3B, RIGHT HAND THREAD

DIMENSIONS IN INCHES.   UNLESS OTHERWISE SPECIFIED, TOLERANCES: FRACTIONS ±1/64, DECIMALS ±.005, ANGLES ±1.

FOR DESIGN FEATURE PURPOSES, THIS STANDARD TAKES PRECEDENCE OVER PROCUREMENT DOCUMENTS REFERENCED HEREIN.
REFERENCED DOCUMENTS SHALL BE OF THE ISSUE IN EFFECT ON DATE OF INVITATIONS FOR BID.

PROCUREMENT SPECIFICATION: FF-N-836
SUPERSEDES: FORMER USAF AND NAVY STANDARD ISSUES OF AN315

AIR FORCE-NAVY AERONAUTICAL STANDARD
NUT, PLAIN, HEXAGON, AIRFRAME

AN315
SHEET 1 OF 1

FED SUP CLASS 5310

THREAD T, SPECIFICATION MIL-S-7742 CSK 110° TO OD OF THREADS

CHAMFER ON BOTTOM FACE 15° TO DIMENSION A OPTIONAL

A plain nut.

AN310

THREAD T, SPECIFICATION MIL-S-7742.
CHK 110° ± .05 OF THREAD

FED. SUP. CLASS
5310

ROUND OR SQUARE BOTTOM
CASTELLATION OPTIONAL

15° ± CHAMFER ON BOTTOM FACE 15° TO
RAD DIMENSION A OPTIONAL

AN PART NO.	THREAD T	ULTIMATE TENSILE STRENGTH MINIMUM, POUNDS		A		B				
		STEEL	AL ALLOY	STEEL (a)	AL ALLOY	APPROX				
AN310-3	NO. 10-32NF3-3B	2 710	1 100	.375-.002	.375-.002	7/16	7/81	1/4	5/32	
AN310-4	1/4-28NF3-3B	3 080	2 020	.438-.002	.438-.002	7/16	7/81	9/32	5/64	
AN310-5	5/16-24NF3-3B	6 500	3 220	.500-.010	.500-.010	1/2	5/64	5/64	5/64	
AN310-6	3/8-24NF3-3B	10 100	3 965	.562-.002	.562-.002	7/32	7/32	5/64	1/32	
AN310-7	7/16-20NF3-3B	13 600	6 750	.625-.002	.625-.002	23/32	29/64	9/32	1/8	
AN310-8	1/2-20NF3-3B	18 500	9 180	.750-.012	.790-.012	7/8	17/64	7/32	1/8	
AN310-9	9/16-18NF3-3B	23 600	11 700	.875-.012	.895-.012	39/64	5/32	3/16	5/32	
AN310-10	5/8-18NF3-3B	30 100	14 900	1.000-.002	1.000-.002	1-5/32	5/32	1/68	5/32	
AN310-12	3/4-16NF3-3B	44 000	21 800	1.125-.016	1.125-.016	1-5/32	9/16	5/32	3/16	
AN310-14	7/8-14NF3-3B	60 000	29 800	1.312-.017	1.312-.003	1-33/64	21/32	5/32	3/16	
AN310-15	1-12NF3-3B	80 700	40 000	1.500-.017	1.500-.003	1-47/64	3/4	5/32	3/16	
AN310-16	1-1/8-12NF3-3B		48 900	1.688-.002		1-61/64	1	5/32	3/16	
AN310-18	1-1/4-12NF3-3B	101 800	50 900	1.875-.002		2-11/64	1-7/16	5/32	5/32	
AN310-20	1-1/4-12NF3-3B	130 200	64 000	1.875"-.002		2-11/64	7/8	5/32	1/4	

AIR FORCE-NAVY AERONAUTICAL STANDARD
NUT, PLAIN, CASTELLATED, AIRPLANE

PROCUREMENT SPECIFICATION
FF-N-836

SHEET 1 OF 2

APPROVED 5 Jul 43   REVISED (8) 29 DEC 72

AN320

THREAD T, SPECIFICATION MIL-S-7742.
CHK 110° ± .05 OF THREAD

FED. SUP. CLASS
5310

CHAMFER ON BOTTOM FACE 30°
CHK 110° ± .05 OF THREADS

AN PART NO.	THREAD T	ULTIMATE TENSILE STRENGTH MINIMUM, POUNDS		A		B			
		STEEL	AL ALLOY	STEEL (a)	AL ALLOY	APPROX			
AN320-1	NO. 6-40NF3-3B			.313-.002	.313-.002	5/64	5/64	5/32	
AN320-2	NO. 8-36NF3-3B			.344-.002	.344-.002	25/64	5/32	5/64	
AN320-3	NO. 10-32NF3-3B	1 105	550	.375-.002	.375-.002	7/16	3/32	3/16	
AN320-4	1/4-28NF3-3B	2 040	1 015	.438-.002	.438-.002	1/2	3/32	3/16	
AN320-5	5/16-24NF3-3B	3 230	1 610	.500-.002	.500-.010	37/64	3/16	5/64	
AN320-6	3/8-24NF3-3B	5 050	2 510	.562-.010	.562-.010	21/32	3/16	1/8	
AN320-7	7/16-20NF3-3B	6 800	3 375	.625-.002	.625-.002	23/32	7/64	1/32	
AN320-8	1/2-20NF3-3B	9 230	4 590	.750-.012	.790-.012	7/8	1/4	1/8	
AN320-9	9/16-18NF3-3B	11 800	5 850	.875-.012	.875-.012	9/64	3/16	5/32	
AN320-10	5/8-18NF3-3B	15 050	7 450	1.000-.002	1.000-.002	1-5/32	3/16	5/32	
AN320-12	3/4-16NF3-3B	22 000	10 900	1.125-.002	1.125-.016	1-19/64	1/4	3/8	
AN320-14	7/8-14NF3-3B	30 000	14 900	1.312-.017	1.312-.017	1-33/64	5/16	5/32	
AN320-15	1-12NF3-3B	40 350	20 000	1.500-.002	1.500-.002	1-47/64	3/8	1/2	
AN320-16	1-1/8-12NF3-3B	48 350		1.688-.002		1-61/64	13/32	1/2	
AN320-18	1-1/8-12NF3-3B	50 900	25 350	1.688-.002		1-61/64	13/32	9/16	
AN320-20	1-1/4-12NF3-3B	65 100	32 200	1.875"-.002		2-11/64	13/32	5/8	

AIR FORCE-NAVY AERONAUTICAL STANDARD
NUT, PLAIN, CASTELLATED, SHEAR

PROCUREMENT SPECIFICATION
FF-N-836

SHEET 1 OF 1

APPROVED 3 AUG 43   REVISED (10) 29 DEC 72

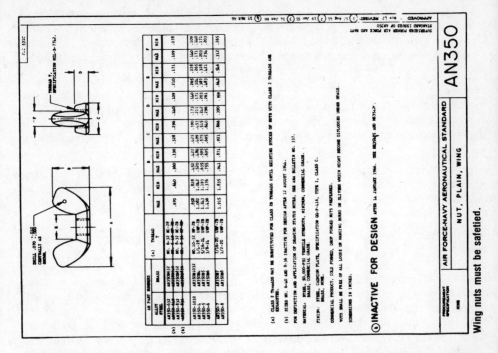

BAMBOO can usually be found by searching the ads in the hang gliding magazines. Other sources are carpet shops (carpets sometimes come wrapped on bamboo poles) and patio furniture suppliers. Most is 12' or 16' in length and splicing may be required. The lengthwise splits which appear in bamboo do not seem to affect the strength.

WING COVERINGS AND MATERIALS

Generally, there are two types of wing coverings: the single surface, flexible type as found on Rogallo type hang gliders and the single or double surface, non flexible type found on most mono and bi planes. For the single surface, flexible type, all that is needed is a sewing machine; for the more rigid wing skins, a book on aircraft recovering is recommended.

First, a general discussion of skin materials:

Tear Strength

Woven textiles possess certain unique mechanical properties unlike other sheet materials such as paper or film. The great improvement in the tear strength is due to the geometry of the matrix into which the fibers have been formed; the yarns have been twisted and then they have been interwoven at right angles into a material sheet. The crossing yarns are free to slide over one another. When a tear is started, the threads move and the stress is distributed around the end of the tear. The threads of a piece of plastic film or paper, on the other hand, cannot move or do not exist and continuing a tear is relatively easy. Any treatment or coating of the fabric which reduces this deformability will reduce the tear strength. Therefore, it is normally inadvisable to coat fabrics though sometimes very light coatings will reduce permeability with minimum reductions in tear strength.

Therefore, a woven fabric, while more expensive, is preferred over non-woven sheets.

Weight:

Cloth is usually weighed in ounces per *square* yard, i.e., "1.1 ripstop" is a ripstop weave fabric, one square yard of which weighs no more than 1.1 ounces. Note: the weight of the cloth has nothing to do with its permeability. Permeability of woven fabrics is determined by the calendaring (heat and pressure process)or coating given them. But be careful, some cloth is weighed by the running yard at a given width.

Finishing:

After weaving, cloth is sometimes scoured and dried. It is then calendered. This is a rolling process using pressure and heat (temperature in excess of 200° F), to force the fibers closer together and to flatten them out. This process determines the permeability.

Permeability:

Permeability is defined as the number of cubic feet of air which will pass through a square foot of cloth in one minute under .5" of water pressure. Nylon and Dacron threads are not relatively fuzzy and the fabric must be woven quite tightly to restrict the air flow.

Some plastics become brittle and crack in cold weather limiting their use to the warmer months.

Polyethylene is inexpensive, low strength, high stretch, is non-porous, easy to repair, has good sun resistance and fair tear resistance. It may be attached with pressure sensitive tape but should be well washed with detergent first to remove the lubricant applied during manufacture. 2 mil and 6 mil thicknesses are popular and some consider the black better than the clear. Rogallos require heavier coverings than built up wings. Color changes may indicate weakness and should be inspected closely. Polyethylene stretches when warm and, therefore, it should be applied to fixed wing forms in warm air. On Rogallo type gliders, old poly sails replaced with new poly or Dacron results in a sudden performance improvement because of the stretch in the old replaced sail.

Mylar is more stable in warm temperatures and will add some strength to the structure but it is expensive and tears once started, continue easily.

Tyvek is a calendered Dupont polyethylene mat of fibers which are welded together rather than woven. It is dimensionally stable, difficult to tear and the cost is lower than woven fabrics. For more information, write DuPont, Technical Services Section, Room P, Wilmington, Del 19898.

For samples of nonwoven fabrics, request Kendall's Introductory Nonwoven Fabric Brochure from The Kendall Co, Fiber Products Division, Room P, Walpole, MA 02081

Cotton and Linen are common wing covering materials but they have been displaced by synthetics with preferable qualities.

Rogallo sails are usually made of Dacron since it has outstanding characteristics such as low stretch, and high resistance to ultra-violet (sun) light. Normally 3.8 oz. Dacron is used though 2.2 oz. fabric can be found on some models. One supplier is Howe and Bainbridge, 220-P Commercial St., Boston, Mass. Dacron is also very expensive and is not available in a great variety of weights and permeabilities. Dacron sails become porous with use and glider performance is decreased.

Dacron is a popular covering for fixed wings. The Icarus II once had a 2 mil poly skin but now sports a 1.8 oz Dacron cover. Dacron is fairly easy to work with. Once installed, it may be shrunk to fit with a hot iron. Inexpensive polyester sheath (dress) lining may be purchased in fabric shops and coated once installed to reduce its air permeability. "Dacron" is polyester made by DuPont.

Nylon is not normally used for Rogallo sails. While it is available in a greater variety of colors and weights, it stretches more than Dacron and has poor sun light resistance.

Forbon is a laminated cellulose fiber which has half the weight of aluminum. For information on it and other interesting materials, write: NVF Co, Dev. Lab. and Tech. Serv. Room P., Yorklyn, Del 19736

Verticel is a paper honeycomb with a high strength to weight ratio. For more information, write: The Verticel Co, 3880P So. Klamath, Englewood, Colo 80110.

Many substances have been used to seal porous fabrics. It should be remembered that these coating have weight of their own and will add to the final product. Tests should be run on samples before being tried on the full wing. Two sealers which have been reported as successful are "Humicure" by Flecto and "Diatron". These substances fill the fabric and remain flexible once dry. They will "glue" Dacron to aluminum and it may be lightly ironed over to shrink the fabric in place. Always test a sample; some dopes create problems such as dissolving styrofoam.

For a refinishing manual, send .50ᶜ to Randolph Products Co, Dept P, Carlstadt, NJ 07072

For information on pressure sensitive tapes, write: Industrial Tape Division, Room P, 3 M Co, St Paul, Minn.

One way to monitor the weathering of the sail is to attach an extra piece to the top side such as around the king post. A periodic tear test will check the fabric condition without damaging the sail itself.

THREAD

A thread is a thin, continuous filament made by the spinning of fibers and the combining of strands so produced. Thread is used to join two or more pieces of fabric, tape or webbing or any combination of them.

Man made threads are made of continuous filaments rather than of short pieces (staples) as with natural materials. When twisted together, the man made fibers are far stronger and often a finer thread and smaller diameter needle may be used.

In sail manufacture and repair, thread of the same type as the fabric is used, hence we are concerned mainly with Dacron and Nylon.

Stitches per inch
MIL-G-6635 and MIL-P-7567 set forth the following acceptable number of stitches per inch for several sizes of thread:

Thread Size And Number of Stitches Per Inch

Thread size	Straight stitch	Zigzag stitch	
	Type 301	Type 304 Single throw	Type 308 Double throw
B	7-11		
E	7 to 11	12 to 16	8 to 12
F	7 to 11	12 to 14	7 to 10
FF	6 to 9	12 to 14	7 to 10
3-cord	5 to 8		4 to 6
5-cord	4 to 6		3 to 5

Generally the strength of the seam is greater as the number of stitches per inch progresses towards the upper end of the scale.

General Needle Size	Nylon Thread V-T-295 MIL-T-7807			Nylon Thread Commercial			Cotton thread V-T-276 MIL-T-5660			Dacron thread			Silk thread V-T-301		
	Size Thread	Tensile strength pounds (min.)	Yards per pound (min.)	Ticket number	Tensile strength pounds	Yards per pound	Ticket number	Tensile strength pounds	Yards per pound	Ticket number	Tensile strength pounds	Yards per pound	Ticket number	Tensile strength pounds	Yards per pound
10-12	A	2.75	16,900	23	3.0	19,500	30/3	3.0	7,275	23	2.4	20,500	A	3.0	14,400
12-14	AA	3.9	11,800	33	4.5	13,350	20/4	4.7	5,040	30	3	14,200	B	3.7	11,680
14-18	B	5.5	7,375	46	6.0	9,650	16/4	6.0	3,880	46	4.8	10,200	C	5.0	8,800
				46 A	6.3	9,650	16/4	6.0	3,880	46A	5.6	10,000	D	5.9	7,300
16-19	E	8.5	5,000	69	10.0	6,250	12/4	8.00	2,810	69	9.5	6,500	E	8.2	5,280
18-22	F	11.0	3,350	99	13.0	4,450	8/4	15.0	1,600	115	12.0	4,100	F	10.9	3,760
21-22	FF	16.	2,450	138	18.0	3,000	8/5	22.0	1,000	138	17	3,250	FF	12.8	3,360
24-26	Cord 3	24.	1,600	207	260	2,050	3	16.0	1,775	207	25	2,430			
26-28	4	32.	1,200	277	39.0	1,550	4	21.0	1,200	231 277	30 37	2,150 1,780			
28	5	40.	950	346	45.0	1,250	5	31.0	860	346	44.5	1,370			
28-30	6	50.	775	415	57.0	1,000	6	37.0	720	415	53	1,035			
	7	60.	650	485	66.0	900	7	41.0	625	462	61	1,045			
	8	68.	575	554	75.0	800	8	45.0	525	577	75	850			
	9	80.	500	623	84.0	715	9	57.0	500	623	79	760			
	10	90.	450	693	92.0	640	10	62.0	480	693	92	692			

ALUMINUM

Aluminum has a number of favorable characteristics but lightness and strength are the most important to the skysurfer. Aluminum weighs about 0.1 pound per cubic inch as compared with 0.28 for iron and 0.32 for copper; aluminum goes about three times as far.

Pure aluminum is very soft but it can be hardened by working it, making an alloy and/or heat treating it. Soft tempers bend easier than hard but at a sacrifice in strength; as usual there is a compromise.

Aluminum has high corrosion resistance, exposure to air forms a thin oxide skin: aluminum oxide. Direct contact with other metals in the presence of an electrolyte should be avoided as a galvanic corrosion may occur.

"Alclad" designates aluminum stock which has been coated with a purer aluminum to protect it since the alloyed piece would have less corrosion resistance.

Aluminum comes from the mill with a code printed on it and this code is very important since all aluminum looks the same. In the case of tubing, the code "ALCOA *** 6061-T6

ALCOA* 1.750 x .058 wall" indicates the manufacturer, the mill, the lot number, the alloy, temper, tubing outside diameter and the wall thickness.

Aluminum is easily worked. It may be cut, drilled, machined, riveted, bent etc.

There are two alloy categories: heat treatable and non-heat treatable and their classification depends upon the amounts and types of other elements in the alloy.

One must be careful not to use just any aluminum; get the correct *alloy* and *temper*. All alloys except cast are identified by a four digit designation. The first digit indicates the alloy group.

Designations for alloy groups	
99.00/ pure	1XXX
Major alloying element	
Copper	2XXX
Manganese	3XXX
Silicon	4XXX
Magnesium	5XXX
Magnesium/Silicon	6XXX
Zinc	7XXX
Other element	8XXX
Unused series	9XXX

The second digit indicates modifications to the original alloy or impurity limits. The last two digits identify the alloy or indicate the aluminum purity.

From this legend we can see that 2024 aluminum is a copper based alloy, unmodified, with a purity indication of 24.

The prefix "X" designates an experimental alloy.

A temper designation system is based on the sequence of basic treatments used to produce various strengths. The temper designation follows the alloy designation. They are as follows:

F: As fabricated (no control over thermal conditions or strain hardening).

O: Annealed wrought products to obtain lowest strength condition.

H: Strain hardened (wrought products). Strain hardened with or without heat treatments to reduce strength. The "H" is followed by two or more digits.

W: Solution heat treated. An unstable heat treatment; the alloy will age at room temperature.

T: Thermally treated to produce a stable temper with or without supplementary strain hardening. The "T" is followed by one or more digits.

There are subdivisions of the basic tempers but only the "T" temper is of importance to hang glider products.

H Numbers Indicate Hardness

H3 Strain hardened and stabilized. This is followed by numbers that show the degree of hardness.

2: ¼ Hard	4: ½ hard	6: ¾ hard
8: Full hard	9: Extra hard	0: Soft

T Numbers Indicate Thermal Tempering

T-1   Naturally aged at room temperature.
T-2   Annealed material
T-3   Solution heat treated then cold worked.
T-4   Solution H.T. then naturally aged.
T-5   Artificially aged at high temperatures.
T-6   Solution H.T. then artificially aged.
T-7   Solution H.T. then stabilized.
T-8   Sol. H.T., cold worked, artificially aged.
T-9   Sol. H.T., artificially aged, cold worked.
T-10 Artificially aged, then cold worked.

Thus, 2024-T3 is a copper based alloy, heat treated and strain hardened, and 6061-T6 is an alloy of magnesium and silicon, artificially aged after heat treating. These two alloys are the most common found in hang glider construction.

Tensile Strength Table

AMS No.	T or H	Max.	Yield
2014	0	25M	10M
	T-4	61M	37M
	T-6	68M	60M
2024	0	27M	11M
	T-3	70M	50M
	T-4	68M	47M
5052	0	28M	13M
	H32	33M	28M
	H34	38M	31M
	H36	40M	35M
	H38	42M	37M
5083	0	44M	22M
	H113	46M	33M
5086	0	38M	17M
	H32	42M	30M
	H34	47M	37M
	H112	39M	19M
6061	0	18M	8M
T4 or	T451	35M	21M
T6 or	T651	45M	40M
7075	0	33M	15M
	T6	83M	73M
	T651	83M	73M

M equals 1000 lbs./sq. in.

When aluminum must be bent to shape, formability becomes a consideration. Here, a trade-off presents itself: strength vs. formability.

GENERAL FORMABILITY CLASSIFICATION OF COMMERCIAL ALUMINUM TUBE ALLOYS

Non-Heat-Treatable Type	Heat-Treatable Type
1. 1060	
2. EC	1. 6063
3. 1100	2. 6061 & 6062
4. 3003	3. 2024
5. 5050	4. 2014
6. 5052	5. 7075
7. 3004 & 5154	
8. 5454	

Presented in the order of decreasing formability.

104

The Alloys of aluminum

1000: Commercially pure aluminum.Easy to work,hardens slowly,easy to weld. Very soft.

2000: Mechanical properties approach those of mild steel. Poor corrosion resistance,should be covered.

2011: High strength, easily machined

2017: Easily machined.

2024: High strength, excellent fatigue resistance, easily machined. Hard to weld. Poor corrosion resistance. Used in aircraft products. Conforms to Fed Spec. QQ-A-250/4. 2024-T3 is common. Alclad 2024 conforms to QQ -A-250/5. More expensive

3000: Moderate strength with good workability.

3003: Some 20% stronger than 1000. Not used in structural applications. Conforms QQ-A-250/2

4000: Has a lower melting point. Used in welding wire and brazing alloys.

5000: Good welding characteristics and corrosion resistant but subject to stress corrosion if over worked.

5005: Similar to 3003. Easily formed.

5052: Good forming, welding, strength and corrosion resistance. Slightly stronger that 1000 and 3003.

5083: High strength, corrosion resistance, weldability and good forming characteristics.

5086: Has mechanical properties almost as high as 5083. Conforms to QQ-A-250/7

5456: Highest strength alloy of the non heat treatable grades. Good corrosion resistance but not as weldable as 5086. conforms to QQ-A-250/9

6000: Not as strong as the 2000 or 7000 alloys but has good formability and corrosion resistance. May be tempered.

6061: Least expensive and most versatile of the heat treatable alloys.Good strength, easily worked and weldable. Common to hang gliders. Good price and availability.

7000: High strength is the most important characteristic.

7075: Very high strength and hardness with limited workability and good machining. Good for aircraft structural parts. Conforms to QQ-A-250/12

Those alloys and tempers most common to hang gliders are 6061-T6 and 2024-T3

2024-T3 BARE ALUMINUM FLAT SHEET
Mill Finish
Stenciled and Interleaved
Federal Specifications QQ-A-250/4d   AMS 4037H

Size in Inches	Approx. Wt. per Sq. Ft.	Approx. Wt. per Sheet
.020 x 36 x 144	.288	10.37
.025 x 48 x 144	.360	17.28
.032 x 48 x 144	.461	22.13
.040 x 48 x 144	.576	27.65
.050 x 48 x 144	.720	34.56
.063 x 48 x 144	.907	43.54
.071 x 48 x 144	1.020	48.96
.080 x 48 x 144	1.150	55.20
.090 x 48 x 144	1.300	62.40
.100 x 48 x 144	1.440	69.12
.125 x 36 x 96	1.800	43.20
.125 x 48 x 144	1.800	86.40
.160 x 48 x 144	2.300	110.40
.190 x 48 x 144	2.740	131.52

Sheets are cut to make nose plates, etc. though most manufacturers have switched to stainless steel. The most common alloys and tempers are 2024-T3 and 6061-T6. Often they are .125'' thick.

Tubing and pipe.

Tubing with tube sleeve.

Tubes and pipes are intermixed because there is more than one classification system and this makes the terminology confusing.Generally, pipe has a thicker wall. Be careful to check both the ID and the OD before purchasing. The most common tubing is 6061-T6 and the common pipe is Schedule 40.''Schedule'' indicates the wall thickness.

Tubing is used for main structures. Slightly larger ID tubing is used for main framework sleeving. Smaller diameter pipe is used for control frames and king posts.Drawn tubes are available in lighter wall thicknesses, smaller diameters, better finish and closer dimensional tolerance than extruded tube. Never use seamed tubing, it is very weak. Any tubing which will be touched by sweatty hands should be anodized or those hands will turn black from the oxidation of the aluminum.

6061-T6 DRAWN ALUMINUM TUBING

12 Foot Length   AMS 4082H
Federal Specifications WW-T-700/6d Amend 1

Size in Inches	Approx. Wt. per Lin. Ft.	Approx. Wt. per Length	Size in Inches	Approx. Wt. per Lin. Ft.	Approx. Wt. per Length
3/16 O.D. x .035	.0197	.236	7/8 O.D. x .058	.1750	2.100
3/16 O.D. x .049	.0251	.301	7/8 O.D. x .065	.1950	2.340
1/4 O.D. x .035	.0278	.334	1 O.D. x .035	.1250	1.500
1/4 O.D. x .049	.0364	.437	1 O.D. x .049	.1720	2.064
5/16 O.D. x .035	.0359	.431	1 O.D. x .058	.2020	2.424
5/16 O.D. x .049	.0477	.572	1 O.D. x .065	.2250	2.700
5/16 O.D. x .058	.0545	.654	1 O.D. x .083	.2810	3.372
3/8 O.D. x .035	.0440	.528	1 1/8 O.D. x .035	.1410	1.692
3/8 O.D. x .049	.0590	.708	1 1/8 O.D. x .058	.2290	2.748
3/8 O.D. x .058	.0679	.815	1 1/4 O.D. x .035	.1570	1.884
3/8 O.D. x .065	.0745	.894	1 1/4 O.D. x .049	.2170	2.604
7/16 O.D. x .035	.0521	.625	1 1/4 O.D. x .058	.2550	3.060
7/16 O.D. x .049	.0703	.844	1 1/4 O.D. x .065	.2840	3.420
7/16 O.D. x .065	.0895	1.074	1 1/4 O.D. x .083	.3580	4.296
1/2 O.D. x .035	.0601	.721	1 3/8 O.D. x .049	.2400	2.880
1/2 O.D. x .049	.0817	.980	1 3/8 O.D. x .058	.2820	3.384
1/2 O.D. x .058	.0947	1.136	1 3/8 O.D. x .083	.3960	4.752
1/2 O.D. x .065	.1040	1.248	1 1/2 O.D. x .035	.1890	2.268
1/2 O.D. x .083	.1280	1.536	1 1/2 O.D. x .049	.2630	3.156
5/8 O.D. x .035	.0763	.916	1 1/2 O.D. x .058	.3090	3.708
5/8 O.D. x .049	.1040	1.248	1 1/2 O.D. x .065	.3450	4.140
5/8 O.D. x .058	.1220	1.464	1 1/2 O.D. x .083	.4350	5.220
5/8 O.D. x .065	.1340	1.608	1 1/2 O.D. x .125	.6350	7.620
3/4 O.D. x .035	.0925	1.100	1 5/8 O.D. x .049	.2850	3.420
3/4 O.D. x .049	.1270	1.524	1 5/8 O.D. x .058	.3360	4.032
3/4 O.D. x .058	.1480	1.776	1 3/4 O.D. x .058	.3630	4.356
3/4 O.D. x .065	.1650	1.980	1 7/8 O.D. x .058	.3890	4.668
3/4 O.D. x .083	.2050	2.460	1 7/8 O.D. x .083	.5500	6.600
7/8 O.D. x .035	.1090	1.308	2 O.D. x .035	.2540	3.048
7/8 O.D. x .049	.1500	1.800			

6061-T6 ALUMINUM PIPE
Schedule 40
20 Foot Length

S.P.S.	O.D. Inches	I.D. Inches	Wall Thickness Inches	Weight per Ft. in Lbs.
⅛ *	.405	.269	.068	.084
¼ *	.540	.364	.088	.147
⅜ *	.675	.493	.091	.196
½	.840	.622	.109	.294
¾	1.050	.824	.113	.390
1	1.315	1.049	.133	.580
1¼	1.660	1.380	.140	.785
1½	1.900	1.610	.145	.939
2	2.375	2.067	.154	1.262
2½	2.875	2.469	203	2.002
3	3.500	3.068	.216	2.617
3½	4.000	3.548	.226	3.147
4	4.500	4.026	.237	3.729
5	5.563	5.047	.258	5.051
6	6.625	6.065	.280	6.556
8	8.625	7.981	.322	9.867
10	10.750	10.020	.365	14.00

*12 Ft. Lengths

Comparitive weights of metals	
	Density
1100 Aluminum	2.7
2017	2.8
Copper	8.89
Brass	8.46
Phosphor Bronze	8.66
Everdur	8.30
Nickel Silver	8.75
Monel	8.80
Nickel	8.85
Inconel	8.55
18/8Cr/Ni Steel	7.9
17%Cr Iron	7.6
14%Cr Iron	7.7
Zinc	7.14
Lead	11.38
Iron	7.7
Steel	7.9
Cast Iron	7.2
Silver	10.51
Platinum	21.5

EXTRUDED SHAPES are cut off and used in the hang glider structure. Usually conforms to 6061-T6 (QQ-A-200/8). Available in channels, angles, "I's", "T's", etc.

For more information, Write the Aluminum Association, 402P Lexington Ave., NYC, NY 10017

BUSHINGS

Most Bushings are made from ⅜" OD soft aluminum tubing. Copper is called out in some plans but it is not preferred as moisture, particularly salt water, may cause a galvanic action due to the adjacent dissimilar metals and a breakdown in the metals will occur.

GROMMETS, METALLIC

MIL-G-16491, MS20230 ss. AN 230. FSC 5325. Grommets, plain and spur are used to reinforce attachment areas of hang glider sails. They are available in several sizes and finishes.

#00 G & W
5/32″ HOLE

#0 G & W
1/4″ HOLE

#1 G & W
5/16″ HOLE

#2 G & W
3/8″ HOLE

#3 G & W
7/16″ HOLE

#4 G & W
1/2″ HOLE

Type I – Plain grommet with plain washer.
Type II – Plain grommet with toothed washer.
Type III – Rolled rim grommet with spur washer.
Type IV – Oblong grommet with flat washer.
Type V – Oblong grommet with raised washer.
Type VIII – Eyelet grommet with ring.
Class 1 – Brass, bright finish.
Class 2 – Brass, nickel plated.
Class 3 – Brass, black chemical finish.
Class 4A – Brass, bright finish, and steel or malleable iron.
Class 4B – Brass, black chemical finish, and steel or malleable iron ring, zinc coated.
Class 5 – Aluminum, natural finish.

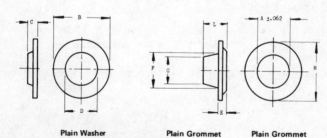

Plain Washer   Plain Grommet   Plain Grommet

Assy Dash No.			Detailed Part No.							Trade Size No.	A Dia After Insertion	B ±.005 Dia	C ±.005	D ±.005 Dia	E ±.005	F ±.005 OD	G ±.005 ID	H ±.005 OD	L ±.005	For use with material thickness (maximum) in inches	Chuck and Die Size
			Grommet			Washer															
AL	Brass		AL	Brass		AL	Brass														
	Plain	Plated		Plain	Plated		Plain	Plated													
A20	B20	BP20	GA20	GB20	GBP20	WA20	WB20	WBP20	00	.156	.460	.029	.218		.218	.176	.425	.170	.120		
A10	B10	BP10	GA10	GB10	GBP10	WA10	WB10	WBP10	0	.250	.546	.030	.286		.290	.240	.545	.210	.160		C-9191, D-9192
A1	B1	BP1	GA1	GB1	GBP1	WA1	WB1	WBP1	1	.312	.700	.041	.359	.035	.375	.286	.687	.220	.170		C-9193, D-9194
A2	B2	BP2	GA2	GB2	GBP2	WA2	WB2	WBP2	2	.375	.835	.045	.453		.475	.362	.815	.250	.200		C-9195, D-9196
A3	B3	BP3	GA3	GB3	GBP3	WA3	WB3	WBP3	3	.438	.955	.050	.530	.050	.545	.433	.970	.345	.280		C-9197, D-9198
A4	B4	BP4	GA4	GB4	GBP4	WA4	WB4	WBP4	4	.500	1.062		.585	.046	.630	.486	1.050	.420	.300		
A5	B5	BP5	GA5	GB5	GBP5	WA5	WB5	WBP5	5	.625	1.205	.055	.740	.045	.785	.594	1.220	.375	.300		
A6	B6	BP6	GA6	GB6	GBP6	WA6	WB6	WBP6	6		1.828	.070	.875	.080	.885	.810	1.750	.312			

Example of part number for ordering:
MS20230B20: No. 00 size, plain grommet and washer assembly, brass.

108

CABLE

Early aircraft used tinned steel wire for bracing and it may still be used today but one must be careful in choosing the source and grade. Later, the switch to cable was made and terminals were wrapped with copper wire and sweat soldered in place. This practise gave way to swaging in the 1940s.

The galvanized carbon steel cables are less expensive and stronger than the corrosion resistant stainless steel type for a given diameter and there is much discussion as to which is the better since the galvanized will rust if scratched and the stainless rusts slightly as is. A plastic coating will protect the cable from abrasion and rusting but it should be clear to facilitate inspection. Coated front rigging wires are recommended for facial safety in unexpected landings. Some manufacturers cover the cable with split tubing.

Most hang gliders use 3/32'' cable for structural bracing though some call out ⅛'' as an option and 1/16'' is commonly used for control cables.

"Non-flexible" cable has more metallic area and is stronger than the "flexible" and is, therefore, generally used for bracing rather than for controls. 7 X 7 has the best abrasion resistance.

In designing a hang glider, select the proper size cable to provide adequate strength at or below 60% of the breaking strength.

The cable is preformed; each individual wire or strand is formed to the shape it will eventually take. This removal of inner stresses prolongs the life of the cable, makes it easier to work with and lessens the tendency to fray.

Incidentally, the terms "wire rope" and "cable" are interchangeable though wire rope usually refers to size ¼'' and larger.

Cable should be drawn straight off the reel, not off the end as this will place an unnatural twist in the cable. A twist can result in a kink which will become a permanent weak spot and cannot be wholly removed.

Measuring the diameter

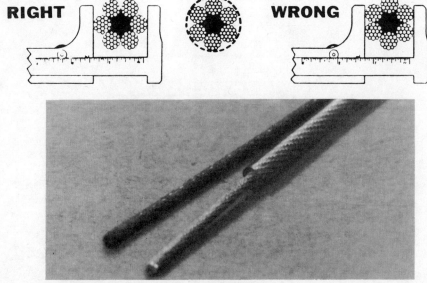

7 x 7, 3/32" cable with and without plastic coating.

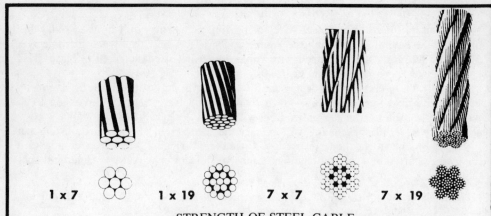

STRENGTH OF STEEL CABLE

Diameter in inches		1 x 7 and 1 x 19		7 x 7, 7 x 19, and 6 x 19 (1WRC)			
		Nonflexible, carbon MIL-C-6940		Flexible, carbon MIL-C-1511		Flexible, stainless steel MIL-C-5424	
		Weight in pounds per 100 feet	Breaking strength (pounds)	Weight in pounds per 100 feet	Breaking strength (pounds)	Weight in pounds per 100 feet	Breaking strength (pounds)
0.031	1/32	0.30	185	———	———	———	110
0.047	3/64	0.52	375	———	———	———	———
0.062	1/16	0.78	500	0.75	480	0.75	480
0.078	5/64	1.21	800				
0.094	3/32	1.75	1,200	1.53	920	1.53	920
0.109	7/64	2.60	1,600				
0.125	1/8	3.50	2,100	2.90	2,000	2.90	1,760
0.156	5/32	5.50	3,300	4.50	2,800	4.44	2,400
0.187	3/16	7.70	4,700	6.50	4,200	6.47	3,700
0.218	7/32	10.00	6,300	8.60	5,600	9.50	5,000
0.250	1/4	13.50	8,200	11.00	7,000	12.00	6,400

This graph shows the elongation of various diameters of MIL-C-5424, 7 X 19 stainless steel aircraft cable; the cables have been pre-stretched.

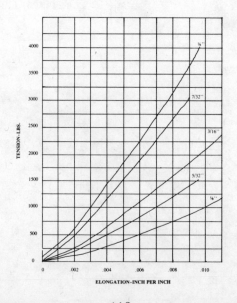

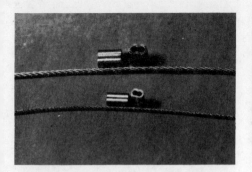
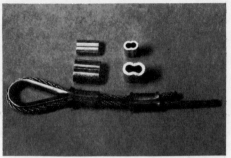

Nicopress fittings are available in oval sleeves and stops. The sleeves are used to fasten the cable to itself such as when making loops in rigging wires while the stops are used in terminal work or to prevent the cable from slipping through a hole such as on some king post rigging.

Fittings are available in different materials and each has a specific use. Tin or nickel plated copper fittings are recommended for use with stainless steel cables. Plain copper fittings are designed for use on carbon steel cable and they should be zinc coated if the cable is to be used near salt water. Aluminum fittings are designed to be compatible with carbon steel and should not be used on stainless particularly if subject to dampness. Aluminum oval sleeves hold nearly as well as the copper, are cheaper and are one third the weight. Oval sleeves hold at 100% of the cable strength while stops hold to 64%. Oval sleeves must be installed with a thimble to protect the cable.

NICOPRESS OVAL SLEEVES

Cable Size	Tin Plated copper for stainless steel cable Stock No.	Aluminum for carbon steel cable Stock No.	Plain copper for carbon steel cable Stock No.	Zinc plated copper for carbon steel cable Stock No.	Nicopress Hand Tool Stock No.
1/16"	428-2-VC	188-2-VC	18-1-C	28-1-C	51-C-887
3/32"	428-3-VG	188-3-VG	18-2-G	28-2-G	51-G-887
1/8"	428-4-VM	188-4-VM	18-3-M	28-3-M	51-M-850
5/32"	428-5-VP	188-5-VP	18-4-P	28-4-P	51-P-850
3/16"	428-6-VX	188-6-VX	18-6-X	28-6-X	51-X-850

NICOPRESS STOP SLEEVES

Size of Cable	Aluminum Stop Sleeves Stock No.	Copper Stop Sleeves Stock No.	Hand Tools Stock No.	Tested Strength of Copper Stop Sleeves Lbs.
1/16"	878-2-VC	871-1-C	51-C-887	525
3/32"	878-3-J	871-17-J	51-MJ	600
1/8"	878-4-J	871-18-J	51-MJ	800
5/32"	878-5-M	871-19-M	51-MJ	1,200
3/16"	878-6-M	871-20-M	51-MJ	1,600
1/4"	878-8-VF6	871-23-F6	3-F6-950	3,500
5/16"	878-10-VF6	871-26-F6	3-F6-950	3,800

THIMBLES

Thimbles protect the cable and increase the strength of the joint by providing a large firm radius. The use of thimbles in cable connections is mandatory. If the sharp tips are clipped off, the Nico sleeve will seat tighter and lessen the chance that the thimble will fall out later in use.

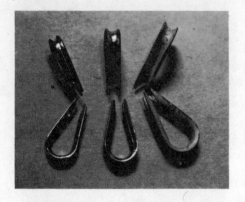

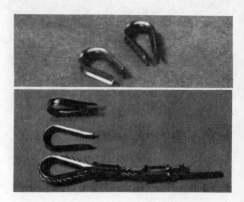

| AN PART NO. | | | CABLE DIA | A | B | F MIN | L APPROX | S +1/64 -0 | T | W +1/64 -0 |
LOW CARBON STEEL	CORROSION RESISTING STEEL	PHOSPHOR BRONZE								
(a) AN100-20			5/8	1.750 MIN	3-1/4 MIN		5-1/8		.168±.019	41/64
(a) AN100-18			9/16	1.500 MIN	2-3/4 (MIN)		4		.156±.016	37/64
AN100-16	AN100C-16	AN100B-16	1/2	1.250	2-1/2	1	33/64		.080±.004	13/32
AN100-14	AN100C-14	AN100B-14	7/16	1.250	2-1/4	1	29/64		.080±.004	13/32
AN100-12	AN100C-12	AN100B-12	3/8	1.125	2	5/8	25/64		.060±.004	5/16
AN100-10	AN100C-10	AN100B-10	5/16	1.000	1-51/64	7/16	21/64		.040±.003	7/32
AN100-9	AN100C-9	AN100B-9	9/32	.900	1-39/64	13/32	19/64		.040±.003	7/32
AN100-8	AN100C-8	AN100B-8	1/4	.800	1-39/64	13/32	17/64		.040±.003	5/32
AN100-7	AN100C-7	AN100B-7	7/32	.700	1-13/32	3/8	15/64		.032±.003	5/32
AN100-6	AN100C-6	AN100B-6	3/16	.600	1-13/64	3/8	13/64		.032±.003	9/64
AN100-5	AN100C-5	AN100B-5	5/32	.500	51/64	5/16	11/64		.032±.003	7/64
AN100-4	AN100C-4	AN100B-4	3/32, 7/64, 1/8	.350	51/64	7/32	3/16		.032±.003	5/64
AN100-3	AN100C-3	AN100B-3	1/16, 5/64	.350	45/64	7/32	5/32		.032±.003	5/64

(a) FOR -18 AND -20, THE FINISH REQUIREMENT ONLY, OF THE PROCUREMENT SPECIFICATION SHALL APPLY. THE MATERIAL SHALL BE OF COMMERCIAL WROUGHT STEEL SUITABLE FOR THE PURPOSE.

MATERIAL: SEE PROCUREMENT SPECIFICATION.
FINISH: SEE PROCUREMENT SPECIFICATION.
DIMENSIONS IN INCHES. UNLESS OTHERWISE SPECIFIED, TOLERANCES: FRACTIONS ±1/64, DECIMALS ±.010.

PROCUREMENT SPECIFICATION MIL-T-5677

AIR FORCE-NAVY AERONAUTICAL STANDARD

THIMBLE - WIRE CABLE

AN100

APPROVED 12 Nov 42   REVISED ① 20 Mar 51

CLEVIS PINS

Clevis pins may be used to make simple attachments such as between turnbuckles and tangs. They are available in numerous diameters and grip lengths; the entire MS drawing should be consulted.

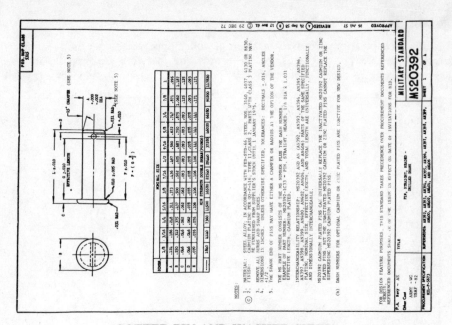

COTTER PIN AND WASHER SIZES
To Use With Clevis Pins

MS NUMBER	USE COTTER PIN NUMBER:		USE FLAT WASHER NUMBER
	CORROSION RESISTING STEEL	CARBON STEEL	
MS20392-1	AN381-2-8	AN380-2-2	AN960-6
MS20392-2	AN381-2-8	AN380-2-2	AN960-10
MS20392-3	AN381-2-8	AN380-2-2	AN960-416
MS20392-4	AN381-3-12	AN380-3-3	AN960-516

COTTER PINS

Cotter pins may be used to secure fasteners such as clevis pins, nut/bolt combinations, etc. but they should be used on semi-permanent installations since they are not easy to deal with under field conditions.

Pins

COWLING LOCK PINS

Cowling lock pins may be used in place of cotter pins where easy installation and removal are desired but care must be taken to insure that they are properly fastened and installed prior to each flight. They may be knocked out or, if bent, may fall out.

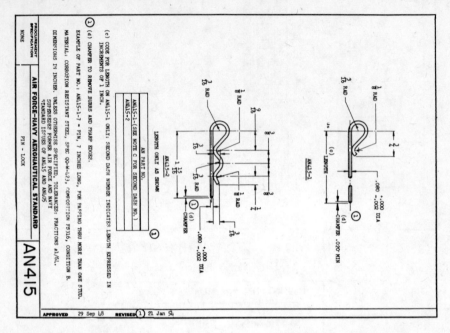

COWLING SAFETY PINS

Cowling safety pins may be used in place of cotter pins where easy installation and removal are desired. Their security should be double checked prior to flight.

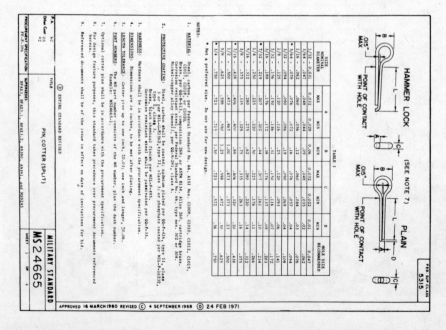

114

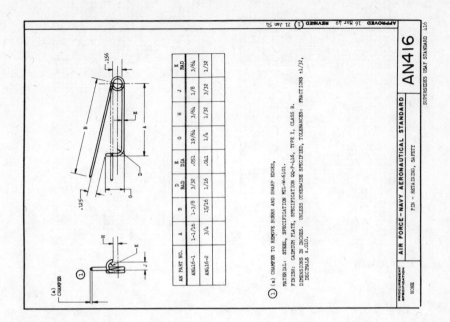

AN PART NO.	A	B	D RAD	E DIA	G	H	J	K RAD
AN416-1	1-1/16	1-3/8	3/32	.051	19/64	3/64	1/8	3/64
AN416-2	3/4	15/16	1/16	.041	1/4	1/32	3/32	1/32

(a) CHAMFER TO REMOVE BURRS AND SHARP EDGES.

MATERIAL: STEEL, SPECIFICATION MIL-W-6101.

FINISH: CADMIUM PLATE, SPECIFICATION QQ-P-416, TYPE I, CLASS B.

DIMENSIONS IN INCHES. UNLESS OTHERWISE SPECIFIED, TOLERANCES: FRACTIONS ±1/32, DECIMALS ±.010.

APPROVED 16 Mar 49 REVISED (1) 21 Jan 54

AIR FORCE-NAVY AERONAUTICAL STANDARD

AN416

PIN - RETAINING, SAFETY

PROCUREMENT SPECIFICATION: NONE

SUPERSEDES USAF STANDARD 4716

LOCKING PINS, QUICK RELEASE

A positive locking pin which requires a push of the button to retract the balls at the other end. They are available in four handle styles; the T and L styles are recommended on large assemblies where lever action may cause pinching and a good grip on the pin is desired. When used to join aluminum, a steel washer should be used or the steel ball of the pin will soon work its way through the softer metal. They are available in a variety of diameters and grip lengths and some conform to MS17984-MS17987. In use, buttons should be "clicked" to assure that sand is not present.

The shear strength for a ¼" pin is 8,200 lbs. These locking pins require the push of a button to release and should not be confused with the spring loaded ball type which are not recommended. The installation of the locking pin should be carefully inspected prior to each flight. These locking pins are available from: Lockwell Products Co., 701P W. Foothill Blvd., Azusa, Ca 91702, Carr Lane Mfg. Co., 4200P Krause Ct., St. Louis, Mo. 63119 and Avibank, PO Box 391-P, Burbank, CA 91503.

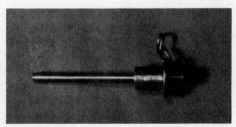

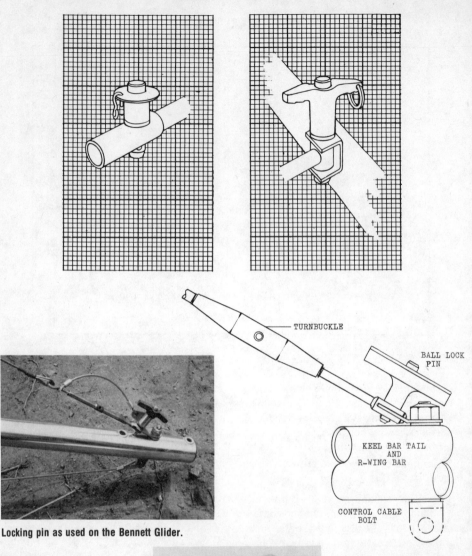

TURNBUCKLE

BALL LOCK
PIN

KEEL BAR TAIL
AND
R-WING BAR

CONTROL CABLE
BOLT

Locking pin as used on the Bennett Glider.

Locking pin as installed by Ultralite Products.

RAPID LINKS

French made and distributed in the U.S. by: Peerless Chain Co.,1416P East 8th St., Winona, Minn. 55987.

Rapid links are oval screw together rings used to connect cables, turnbuckles, tangs, eyebolts, etc. They are available in five sizes to 4,400 lbs; those shown are:

¾" X 1⅜" with ⅛" dia bar (Distorts at 1000 lbs but does not separate.)

1" X 2" with 3/16" dia. bar. (Breaks at 2,900 lbs.)

Care should be taken to insure that they are screwed completely together. When left unthreaded they fail under light loads.

RIPSTOP TAPE

Ripstop nylon repair tape is a sail fabric with an adhesive backing designed for in the field repairs; simply peal off the paper backing and press over the tear. Conforms to MIL-T-43618. Caution, ripstop tape may lose its adhering qualities in very cold weather and it may degrade the fabric after a long period of time. Available in white, blue, red, black, gold and green in rolls 2" X 25' and sheets 36" wide. Many use it to decorate sails.

SHACKLES

Shackles are often used as cable termination points when attached with a nut and bolt combination, particularly where several cables converge such as at the lower corners of the trapeze bar.

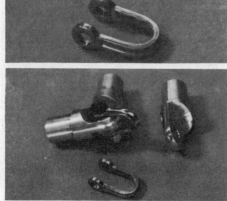

Shackle as installed on a rounded triangle bar by Ultralite Products.

Shackle as installed on a hinged triangle bar by Eipper-Formance and Sky Sports.

SPEED - RAIL TYPE FITTINGS

Speed - Rail, Nu - Rail and Rackmaster slip on fittings make hang glider framework assembly quite simple. The fittings are made from an aluminum/magnesium alloy which offers good corrosion resistance, strength of 30,000 - 45,000 psi, and is one-third the weight of iron. The set screws must be removed and the hole drilled out so that a bolt and nut may be used for a more positive connection. The fittings are generally available in ¾'', 1'', 1¼'' and 2'' ID sizes.

The following data based on laboratory tests with 100% SAFETY FACTOR, indicate the loads Nu-RAIL FITTINGS can support.

TEST: Forcing standard steel pipe through the fitting by a direct load on the pipe.

Maximum Load in Pounds 100% Safety Factor	
¾ In.	1900 lbs.
1 in.	1800 lbs.
1¼ in.	3100 lbs.
1½ in.	2350 lbs.
2 in.	3200 lbs.

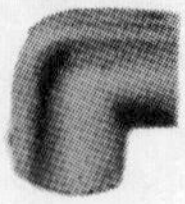

No. 3
ELL

No. 5
TEE

No. 5-AT
55° ANGLE TEE

No. 7
CROSS

No. 9
SIDE-OUTLET ELL

No. 11
SIDE-OUTLET TEE

No. 13
SIDE-OUTLET CROSS

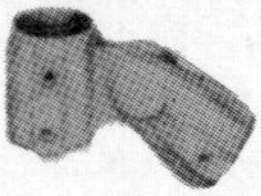

No. 17
ADJ. ELL or TEE

No. 19
ADJ. CROSS

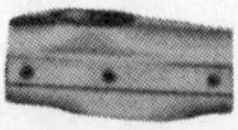

No. 21 - 35°
ADJ. CROSS
(10° to 35°)

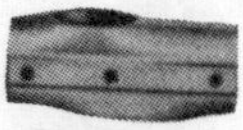

No. 21 - 45°
ADJ. CROSS
(30° to 45°)

No. 23
ADJ. TEE or CROSS

No. 25
ADJ. SIDE-OUTLET
ELL or TEE

No. 27
DBL. ADJ. SIDE-OUTLET
ELL or TEE

No. 41
ADJ. FLANGE

No. 43
FLANGE

No. 46
FLANGE

For further information, write: Hollaender Mfg Co, 3841P Spring Grove Ave, Cincinnati, Ohio 45223

TURNBUCKLES

Commercial type should never be used as the incomplete eye will open up in use.

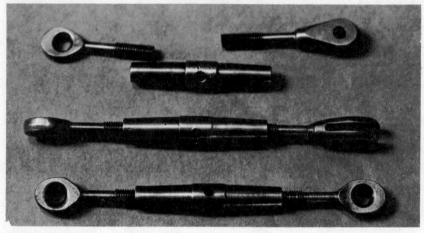

Aircraft type.

Turnbuckles are used to attach and tension upper cables. They should not be used in rigging the lower "flying wires".

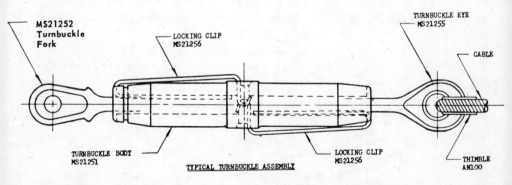

MS21252
Turnbuckle
Fork

LOCKING CLIP
MS21256

TURNBUCKLE EYE
MS21255

CABLE

TURNBUCKLE BODY
MS21251

TYPICAL TURNBUCKLE ASSEMBLY

LOCKING CLIP
MS21256

THIMBLE
AN100

Turnbuckles consist of a brass barrel, and two steel ends, one having a right-hand thread and the other a left-hand thread. Types of turnbuckle ends are cable eye, pin eye, and fork.

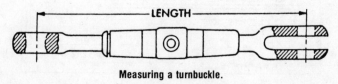

|←————————— LENGTH —————————→|

Measuring a turnbuckle.

119

This addition facilitates tightening and removal.

Old (AN) and new (MS), turnbuckle barrels are not interchangeable since the old were designed for locking safety wire and the new are compatible with the locking clips.

The MS Drawing lists a 1,600 lb. minimum breaking strength for the turnbuckle sized for the common 3/32" cable. Tensile tests show, however, that it will go almost 2,500 lbs. and the break is in the shank just below the eye; the threads do not strip out.

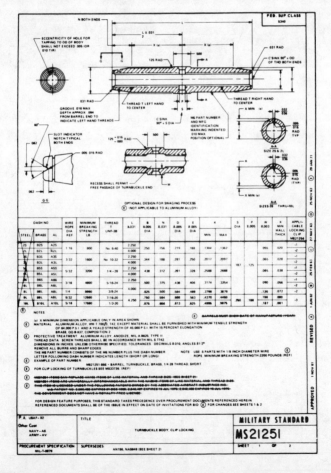

MILITARY STANDARD

MS21251

TURNBUCKLE BODY, CLIP LOCKING

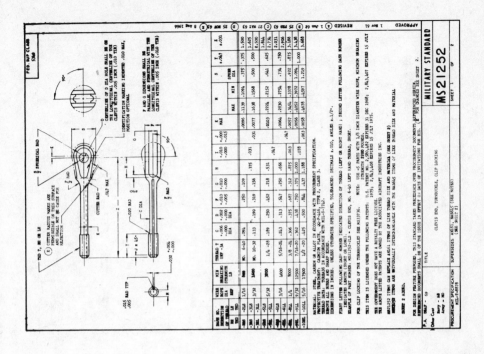

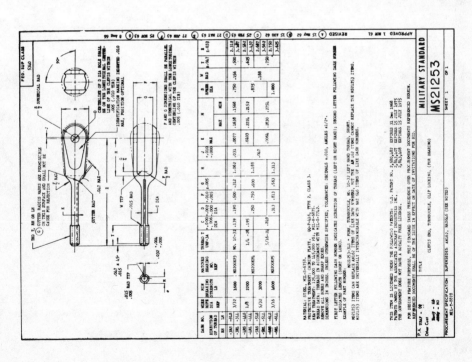

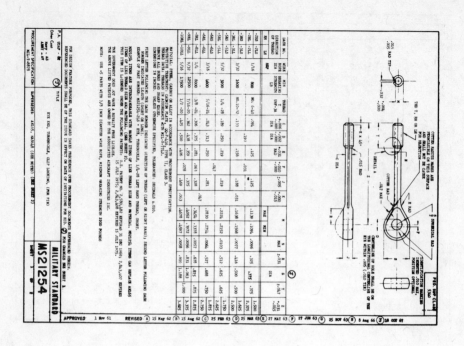

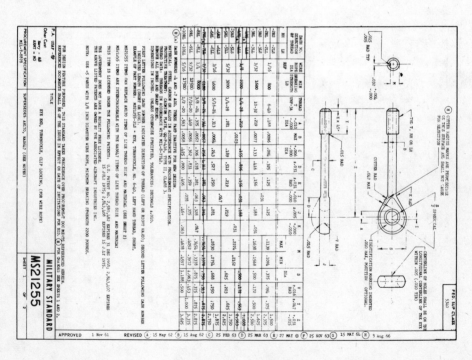

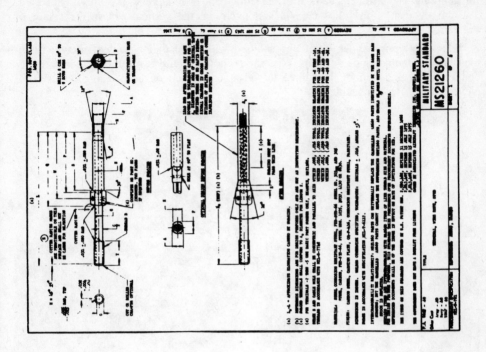

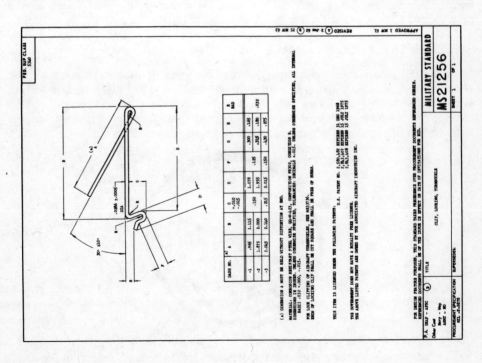

TITLE: CLIP, LOCKING, TURNBUCKLE

DASH NO.	A	B	C +.010 -.015	D	F	G	H	R RAD
-1	.945	1.115	.150	1.078	.125	.300	.165	.032
-2	1.875	2.000	.150	1.955	.150	.325	.180	.075
-3	2.015	2.140	.215	2.015	.150	.430	.075	

(a) DIMENSION A MUST BE HELD WITHOUT DISTORTION AT END.

MATERIAL: CORROSION RESISTANT STEEL WIRE, QQ-W-423, COMPOSITION FE302, CONDITION B. DIMENSIONS IN INCHES. UNLESS OTHERWISE SPECIFIED, TOLERANCES: DECIMALS ±.015. UNLESS OTHERWISE SPECIFIED, ALL INTERNAL RADIUS .032 -.000, -.015.

FOR LOCK CLIPPING OF AIRCRAFT TURNBUCKLES, SEE MS33736.
ENDS OF LOCKING CLIP SHALL BE CUT SQUARE AND SHALL BE FREE OF BURRS.

THIS ITEM IS LICENSED UNDER THE FOLLOWING PATENTS: U.S. PATENT NO. 2,560,442 EXPIRES 31 DEC 1968
2,813,407 EXPIRES 15 JULY 1975
2,813,408 EXPIRES 15 JULY 1975

THE GOVERNMENT DOES NOT HAVE A ROYALTY FREE LICENSE.
THE ABOVE LISTED PATENTS ARE OWNED BY THE ASSOCIATED AIRCRAFT INDUSTRIES INC.

FOR DESIGN FEATURE PURPOSES, THIS STANDARD TAKES PRECEDENCE OVER PROCUREMENT DOCUMENTS REFERENCED HEREIN. REFERENCED DOCUMENTS SHALL BE OF THE ISSUE IN EFFECT ON DATE OF INVITATION FOR BID.

The new (MS) clip-locking turnbuckles use two locking clips instead of safety wire for safetying.The terminals and barrel are slotted and once aligned, the clips are inserted. The curved end of the clips expand and latch in the vertical slot in the center of the barrel.

Older (AN) turnbuckles should be safetied with .040 dia. annealed safety wire in the standard double or single wrap. Wire should not be reused. A turnbuckle is correctly connected when no more than three threads are exposed on each side of the barrel. Never lubricate a turnbuckle.

Quick attaching and instant lever action tensioning turnbuckle as found on the Wills Wing by Sport Kites.

FASTENER TAPE, HOOK AND PILE, NYLON MIL-F-21840

Velcro (R) is a woven nylon tape fastener consisting of two mating strips. The Hook or male section is covered with stiff little hooks. The Pile or female section is covered with tiny, soft loops. When pressed together the hooks and loops engage creating an adjustable, highly versatile and secure closure. To open, it is simply peeled apart. Velcro (R) tapes can be opened and closed many thousands of times.

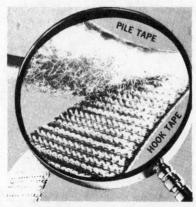

Velcro's applications to hang gliders and accessories are limited only by the imagination. For complete technical data, write: Velcro Corporation, 681P Fifth Ave, NYC, NY 10022

WASHERS

Washers should always be used with nut and bolt fastener combinations and while there are many types, the regular flat type is most common to hang glider assembly. Some of the others are:

Split spring lock: AN 935, MS35388
Tooth lock: AN936 (internal MS35333, external MS35335)
Flat electrical: An 961
Flat for wood: AN970
Plain steel: AN 122576-AN 122600
Countersunk and plain, high strength: MS20002
And numerous ornamental commercial models

AN960

WASHER, FLAT

AIR FORCE-NAVY AERONAUTICAL STANDARD

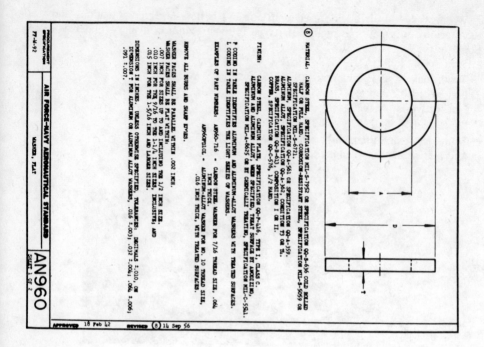

CHAPTER VI

MODEL LIST

Listed in the following pages are all of the currently available plans, kits and complete hang gliders with complete descriptions of each model. This will aid the purchaser in choosing the best one for his use considering cost, construction time, portability, performance, etc.

Most of the Rogallo wing type hang gliders are essentially the same. They all glide at about 4:1, nearly all are made with 6061-T6 aluminum tubing, aircraft quality hardware, 3/32" 7x7 stainless steel cable with double Nico press swages, Dacron sails of 3.8 oz. stabilized cloth, etc. Models having certain special qualities will have them pointed out in the text.

All models are constantly being improved and space does not permit a full description of each one. Readers are urged to write directly to the manufacturers for the latest information and the name of their nearest dealer.

Manufacturers receive scores of inquiries each day and they will greatly appreciate a stamped, self addressed envelope with your request for more information.

During the last century, many hang gliders have been built, many have been described and many have stayed on the drawing board. The models listed here are those for whom plans are CURRENTLY AVAILABLE. Gliders still in the developmental stages and some designer's dream are not listed.

The performance specifications are SUPPLIED BY THE MANUFACTURER and the reader/purchaser should be wary, particularly of the glide ratio claims; Caveat Emptor!

A glider must be properly sized for a pilot's given weight. If it is too small, it will fly too fast and the sink rate will be high. If it is too large, it will be difficult to control and, therefore, dangerous. Consult the sizing diagrams and discussion in the design chapter.

AIRCRAFT UNLIMITED ROGALLO
A Rogallo type hang glider with trapeze bar control.

Zero permeability ripstop nylon sail, parachute type harness and tow release for kiting. 18' KL, 8.5' high, weight 39 lbs.

Complete gliders, kits, replacement parts and plans available from:

Aircraft Unlimited, Inc.
Box 1616p
Mpls. International Airport, Minn. 55111
(612) 483-3765
T. Carlson, General Manager

ARION
A Rogallo type hang glider with trapeze bar control.

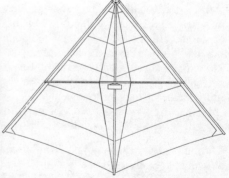

16' 9" KL, 2" OD tubing, 2 oz. proofed ripstop nylon sail, weight 37 lbs.

Plans, flying handbook, complete units and parts are available from:

McBroom Sailwings Ltd.
12P Manor Court Drive
Horfield Common
Bristol BS7 OXF
ENGLAND
Bristol (0272) 44350
Geoff McBroom

SUNDANCE WING

A flying wing with drag rudder control.

A swept, washed out flying wing with a span of 27'3" and an area of 134 sq. feet. Made of aluminum and Dacron, it weighs 45 lbs. and is completely collapsable. A new and particularly interesting design.

Complete units available from:

Magnan Manufacturing
23011 Moulton Parkway # B-3/P
Laguna Hills, CA 92653
(714) 581-8370

WATERMAN & SEAGULL FLYER

A biplane with three axis control.

 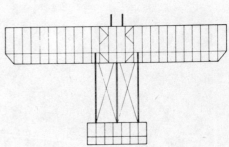

Control: Three Axis.

Construction: A real classic made of wood and bicycle parts, well engineered.

Dimensions: 26' span, 14' length weight 60 lbs.

Plans kits and parts available from:

Seagull Aircraft
3021-P Airport Ave.
Santa Monica, CA 90401
(213) 394-1151
Mike Riggs

CONQUEST

A monoplane type hang glider with trapeze bar and rudder control

Adapted from the Quicksilver, the Conquest offers a number of design improvements and is exceptionally clean in detail. The wing measures 32' by 52'' and total weight is 57 lbs. The steerable rudder is linked to the seat.

Complete units are available from:

Conquest Glider
323 North Euclid #140-P
Santa Ana, CA 92703
(714) 554-0877
Earl Manning

manta wings

Rogallo type hang gliders with trapeze bar control.

80° frame, 88° sail, uniquely designed hardware and specially cut sail. No tools needed for set up or break down. Cushioned control bar swings apart for dismantling. Six sizes from 15' - 20'. Optional takedown model breaks down to 6.5'.

Complete units, kits, parts and accessories available from:

Manta Wings
1647p East 14th Street
Oakland, CA 94606
(415) 536-1500
Kent Trimble

Above all, fly a Manta Wing

ARROW WING
A Rogallo type hang glider with trapeze bar control.

A well designed, fine performing glider with vinyl coated cable, 1.5" tubing and a variety of sail patterns. Many of the fine hardware items from Ultralite are used. Available in 16' through 19' models and a short keel, high performance 19 X 16 designated the "Arrow Wing II." Solo Flight also runs a flight school.

Complete units and replacement parts available from:

Solo Flight
1141-P North Citrus Ave.
Orange, CA 92667
(714) 538-9768

CAL-GLIDERS
Rogallo type hang gliders with trapeze bar control

Cal-Gliders offers a fine line of standard and short keel kites but specializes in custom-adjustable units. Sail billow, keel length and nose angle are varied according to pilot weight and level of skill.

Complete units, kits and parts are available from:

California Hang-Gliders
11545 Sorrento Valley Rd #3-303P
Sorrento Business Complex
San Diego, CA 92121
(714) 452-0351
Dick Messina

EAGLE
A sailwing monoplane with three axis control.

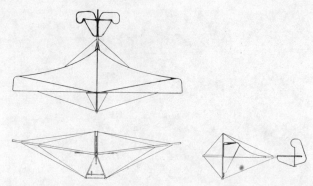

34' span, 19' long, 8' high, 158.5 sq ft wing area with an aspect ratio of 7.3. Aluminum frame, steel cable and Dacron covering. Weight 75 lbs. Control is through elevator, rudder and warperons. The unique cable trailing edge Sailwing principle allows this monoplane to fold like a Rogallo kite.

Available from:

Man-Flight Systems, Inc.
P.O. Box 872-P
Worcester, MA 01613
(617) 756-3000
Michael A. Markowski

PACIFIC GULL
A Rogallo type hang glider with trapeze bar control

 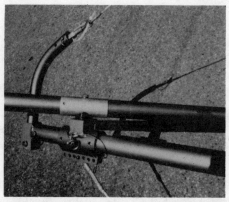

The Pacific Gull features the "sliding wing" system; the nine quick pins allow instant set-up and the ultimate in fine tuning adjustment. A particularly clean glider, it has a number of specially designed parts, all exposed parts are anodized and the cables are vinyl covered.

Complete units and replacement parts are available from:

Pacific Gull
1321 Calle Valle #F/P
San Clemente, CA 92672
(714) 492-0670
Steve Murray

FLANNIGAN SAILWING

A swept flying wing monoplane.

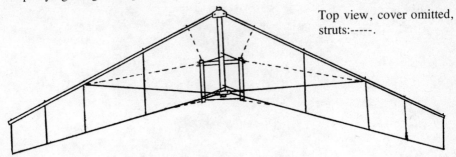

Top view, cover omitted, struts:-----.

32' span wing area, 136 sq. ft., weight 45 lbs. Aluminum tubing covered with plastic. Has parallel bars; guided by weight shift; not intended for high flight. Moderate performance. Folds for transport.

N-4678 was built in 1971 for about $75. Current materials cost about $100, depending upon source of supply. No material kits or complete aircraft available at this time. Drawings and description of how prototype was built are available from:

Mike Flannigan
20560-P Summerville
Excelsior, Minn. 55331
(612) 474-3513

FLYING CIRCUS ROGALLO

A Rogallo type hang glider with trapeze bar control.

88° frame, Dacron sail with battens, spring loaded king post. Available in 15' to 20' models.

Plans, kits, complete units and replacement parts available from:

High Perspective
RR #2, Box P
Claremont, Ontario
CANADA
(416) 294-2536
Michael Robertson

and The Flying Circus Flying School
Tod Mountain
Rt #P
Kamloops, BC
CANADA
(604) 578-7461
Neil Smith

FREE-FLIGHT
Rogallo type hang glider with trapeze bar control.

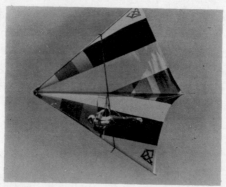

Nose has skid plate, harness sports leg support straps and kite has a variable C.G. plate. A well made glider available in 15' through 20' KL with weight about 35 lbs. Control bars are available in 36", 38" and 48" widths. Also available in the new high performance "Sierra" model.

Plans, kits, complete units and replacement parts available from:

Free-Flight Systems
12424 Gladstone Ave., Plant P
Sylmar, CA 91342
(213) 365-5607
Gerald B. Albiston

ZEPHYR ROGALLO
A Rogallo type hang glider with trapeze bar control.

Vinyl covered lower wires, Dacron sail and anodized tubing. Available in 15' through 22' models. A clean and well designed glider.

Complete units, parts and accessories available from:

Zephyr Aircraft Corp.
25-P Mill St.
Glastonbury, Conn. 06033
(203) 633-9074
Al Mulazzi

FREEDOM I & II

A Rogallo type hang glider with trapeze bar control.

The Freedom I is the less expensive model intended for low flight. The king post and upper rigging are an optional extra and it has a Tyvek sail. Freedom II is the deluxe model; it has higher quality components, upper rigging, Dacron sail and is designed for the more advanced flier.

Made with single pieces of aluminum tubing and available in 16', 17' and 20' models.

Foot Launched Flyers
11411-P Hyne
Brighton, Michigan 48116
(313) 229-8328
David E. Wood

THE GULL

A Rogallo type hang glider with trapeze bar control

Made with 7 x 19 cable, has shrink tubing over the bitter ends, sail is a urethane coated ripstop nylon in a delta ray pattern. 17.5' KL, 92° frame, 100° sail, weight 36 lbs.

Plans, kits and parts are available from:

Delta Ray Kites
1704P N. Valley View Drive
Layton, Utah 84041
(801) 376-9524
Leo Chidester

or: Mark Chidester
16603P Covello
Van Nuys, Calif. 91406
(213) 994-5834

HALL'S HAWK

A Rogallo type hang glider with trapeze bar control.

Dimensions: 18' KL, 83° frame, 90° sail, weight 40 lbs. sail area 222 sq. ft. Has wheels and polyethelene or Dacron sail. Prone harness plans are also available.

Plans available from:

Hall's Hawk Plans
12561-P Pearce St.
Garden Grove, CA 92643
(714) 636-1425
Jack Hall

HANG LOOSE

A Chanute type biplane hang glider

Construction: Wood, wire and plastic; a great looking craft with many wires and struts.

Dimensions: 27' span, 4.5' chord, 15.5 long.

Old model used weight shift for control; new one uses ailerons, rudder and weight shift. Costs about $35. to build

Plans with an entertaining description and kits are available from:

Aerodyne Co
115-B/P Merrimac
Anaheim, CA 92807
(213) 925-6040
Jack Lambie

ICARUS II

A swept biplane with high dihedral and three axis control.

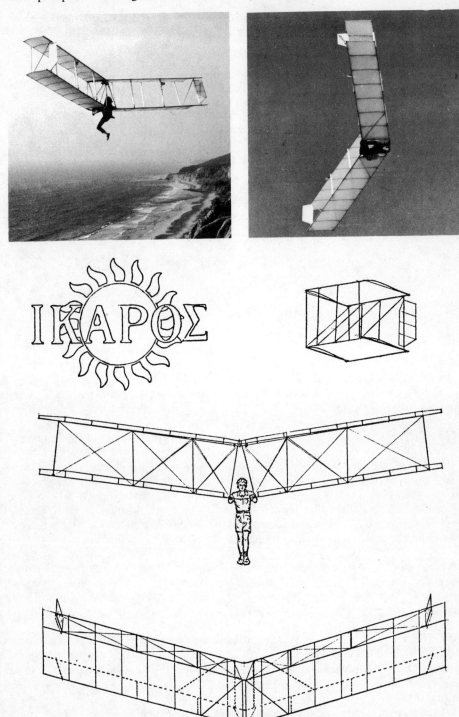

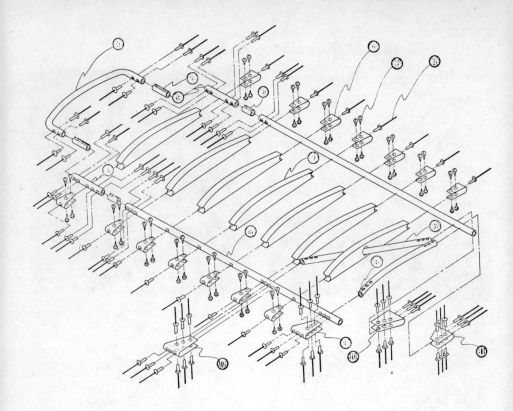

The Icarus II is a swept wing,tailless biplane with pronounced sweep, washout, stagger and dihedral. It has a reflex airfoil (up turned trailing edge) and a positive decalage of approximately 2 degrees.

Controls: Twist controls on the hand grips connect to wing tip mounted drag rudders.

The rudders are turned outward only so that the drag of the rudder is as important as side force in producing yawing moment. Dihedral and sweepback produce a brisk roll as soon as the craft is yawed. If a wing drops, the opposite twist grip is given a turn outward to deflect that rudder, the craft yaws and dihedral action levels the wings. The sweep back, twist and decalage of the wings makes the craft fly at a constant angle of attack according to the position of the body on the parallel bars.

Performance: 18-40 mph speed range, stall speed 18 mph, takeoff speed 20 mph, best glide speed 25 mph, glide ratio 8:1. Has soared for 2½ hours and has gained over 1000'. Sink rate 3.5 fps. Provides ''hand-off'' stability and is capable of tight spiral turns.

Construction: The main spars (leading and trailing edges)are of 1'' diameter aluminum tube. Pop riveted sheet aluminum gussets tie the primary structure together. Wing ribs are made of .5'' styrofoam and spruce. Aluminum tubing is used for interplane struts. Cable braces are of 1/16'' material. The covering consists of 1.8 oz dacron, heat shrunk and doped.

Kits can be assembled with a Pop rivet tool and a swaging tool and some simple, common hand tools. May be built in 150-200 man hours at a cost of $100.-$350.

Dimensions: 30' span, 200 sq ft wing area, aspect ratio 9, weight 55 lbs, stressed for 3 Gs. Designed for pilots weighing up to 205 lbs.

Plans available from:

Icarus
Box P
Palomar Mountain, CA 92060
(714) 742-3933
Taras Kiceniuk, Jr.

Kits and replacement parts available from:

Ultralight Flying Machines
Box 59P
Cupertino, CA 95014
(408) 732-5463
Larry Mauro

ICARUS V

A swept flying wing with a high dihedral and three axis control.

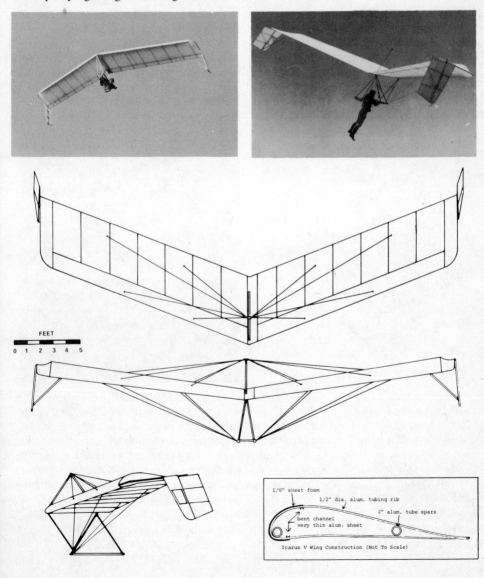

FEET
0 1 2 3 4 5

1/8" sheet foam
1/2" dia. alum. tubing rib
2" alum. tube spars
bent channel
very thin alum. sheet

Icarus V Wing Construction (Not To Scale)

The Icarus V is a flying wing with pronounced sweep, washout, dihedral, and a reflexed high lift, low moment airfoil.

Controls: Twist controls on the hand grips connect to wing tip mounted drag rudders.

Performance: 16mph stall speed, maximum glide ratio: 10:1 at 22-24 mph, minimum sink speed is 3 fps at 18-20 mph, maximum speed is over 40 mph. Very stable with gentle stall.

Construction: Aluminum tube frame, foam sheet leading edge with doped fabric covering.

Dimensions: 32' span, 160 sq. ft. wing area, 5' chord, aspect ratio of 6.4, stressed for 6.5 Gs, weight 65 lbs.

Plans are available from:
Icarus
Box P
Palomar Mountain, CA 92060
(714) 742-3933
Taras Kiceniuk, Jr.

Kits, complete units
and replacement parts
are available from:
Free-Flight Systems
12424 Gladstone Ave., Plant P
Sylmar, CA 91342
(213) 365-5607
Gerald B. Albiston

LARK (Low Aspect Ratio Kite) Bob Cat and Peregrine.
Rogallo type hang gliders with trapeze bar control

90° frame with 98° sail in 14' through 20' KL models. Standard LARK has leading edge tubes equal to the keel while the Bob Cat has a keel length which is two feet shorter than the leading edges. Hinged control bar allows it to fold along the main tube for carrying, angled nose plate avoids digging in while palm nuts and rapid links provide no tool set up and break down. Unique chain link assembly allows rapid change from seated to prone configurations. Clear vinyl covered lower wires and tubing caps round out the fine detail in this well designed glider. The all new high performance Peregrine is also available. Complete units, kits, parts and personal accessories are available from:

Sky Sports Inc.
Pine/High Streets
Whitman, MA 02382
(617) 447-3773
Ed Vickery

Sky Sports, Inc.
Ellington Airport, Bldg. P
Ellington, Conn. 06029
(203) 872-7317

LIGHTER THAN AIR PRODUCTS ROGALLO

A Rogallo type hang glider with trapeze bar control.

Anodized aluminum frame, Ultralite Products hardware and Dacron sail. Special swing seat,. School for tow kiting and foot launching.

Complete units and parts available from:

Lighter Than Air Products
40-P Center Street
Springfield, NJ 07081
(201) 467-3562
Michael Lyons

MONTGOMERY CLASSICS

1883 monoplane hang glider
1905 tandem monoplane hang glider Santa Clara

(See photos and drawings in the history chapter).

Plans are available from:

Jim Spurgeon
5590P Morro Way
La Mesa, Ca 92041

Muller Kites

Rogallo type hang gliders with trapeze bar control.

Three models:
Model 1616 - 16 ft. keel - 16 ft. wing, 180 sq. ft.
Model 1718 - 17 ft. keel - 18 ft. wing, 210 sq. ft.
Model 1820 - 18 ft. keel - 20 ft. wing, 245 sq. ft.

Plans, kits, complete units and materials are available from:

Muller Kites Ltd.
PO Box 4063-P, Postal Station C
Calgary, Alberta T2T 5M9
CANADA
(403) 266-1446
Willi Muller

QUICKSILVER C

(Supersedes the Hightailer) A monoplane type hang glider with trapeze bar and rudder control designed by Bob Lovejoy.

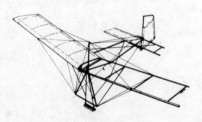 

Additional dimensions: 5' chord, length 13', height 9.5'.
Construction: Anodized aluminum tubing, aircraft hardware, and Dacron covering.
Control: A Steerable rudder is linked to the seat.

The Quicksilver sets up without tools in 15 minutes and can easily carried on a roof rack. Numerous long soaring flights have been made in this well designed craft.

Plans, complete units and replacement parts are available from:

Eipper-Formance, Inc.
PO Box 246-47
Lomita, CA 90717
(213) 328-9100
Steve Wilson

BAT GLIDER

Originally produced in 1967, Bat Glider Plans were the first available to the sport. The plans call out bamboo and polyethylene film in the construction but the drawings can be used for aluminum tube and dacron construction. Materials for building the Bat Glider from bamboo and polyethylene costs about $20.00. A quick flying lesson is included in the plans.

Dimensional specifications: Leading edges 16', Keel 23', weight is 30 to 40 pounds, designed for pilots to 160 pounds.

Plans and information available from:

Bat Glider Plans
P.O. Box 7115-P
Amarillo, Texas 79109
(806) 352-8546
Jim Foreman

BATSO
A Rogallo type hang glider with parallel bars.

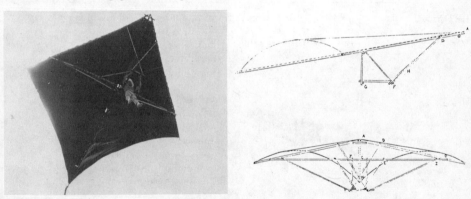

Batso evolved from Richard Miller's bamboo butterfly. Designed by Taras, it was built by four high school students in two days. Taras later went on to design and build the Icarus , the Icarus II and the Icarus V.

Construction: Bamboo and 4 mil polyethylene

Dimensional specifications: 16' leading edges and 23' keel length (for stability), weight 40 lbs, designed for 150 lb pilot

Plans available from:

Batso
Box P
Palomar Mountain, CA 92060
(714) 742-3933
Taras Kiceniuk, Jr

SUPER FLOATER

A monoplane hang glider with three axis control.

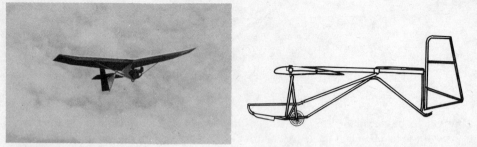

Dimensions: 32' span, 132' wing area, aspect ratio 7.35, length 16', height 5'6'', airfoil 12% & weight 90 lbs.
Performance: Foot launched but can be landed on wheel and skid. After takeoff, pilot rests his feet on tubing in front.
Control: Rudder and elevator
Construction: Aluminum tubing, sheet aluminum, styrofoam; Dacron covered.

Plans are available from:

Mountain Green Sailwing
Box 771-P
Morgan, Utah 84050
(801) 829-6590
Klaus Hill and Larry Hall

BIRDMAN

A Rogallo type hang glider with trapeze bar control

Aluminum frame, Ultralite Products hardware and Dacron Sail. 14'-20' models
Kits, complete units and materials available from:

Birdman Enterprises
8011 Argyll Rd., Suite P
Edmonton, Alberta T6C 4A9
CANADA
(403) 466-5370, 439-4276
Terry Jones

144

PLIABLE MOOSE

A Rogallo type hang glider with trapeze bar control.

Pliable Moose Delta Wings are designed particularly for thermaling in the flat lands. The unique design allows fine tuning adjustment, easy breakdown and a very low weight.

Complete units are available from:

Pliable Moose Delta Wings
243-P Matthewson
Wichita, KS 67214
(316) 262-2664
Gary Osoba

STREAKER

A Rogallo type hang glider with trapeze bar control.

The Streaker is a unique design which quickly breaks down to fit in a five foot long carrying bag. It features steel rings instead of shackles, captive heart bolt and a threaded kingpost bracket. Weight is 35 lbs.

Complete units and replacement parts are available from:

AA Flight Systems, Inc.
10-P North Barton
New Buffalo, MI 49117
(616) 469-1643 (219) 879-6756
Tom Arbanas and Peter Arp

FLIGHT SYSTEMS, Inc.
Custom Construction   Personalized Training

THE SKYSURFER
A Rogallo type hang glider with trapeze bar control.

Plug in cross tubes, double side flying wires, integrated trapeze bar/king post, 90° nose. Larger diameter, thicker wall tubing. Available in 13' to 18' models.

Plans, kits, complete units and replacement parts are available from:

Man-Flight Systems, Inc.
PO Box 872-P
Worcester, Mass. 01613
(617) 756-3000
Michael A. Markowski

PERFORMER
Rogallo type hang gliders with trapeze bar control

Sunbird gliders feature exceptionally attractive sail patters on a clean, well designed frame. The Sailfeather, a horizontal stabilizer which provides dynamic stability in pitch is offered as standard equipment.

Plans, complete units and parts are available from:

Sunbird Ultralight Gliders
21420 Chase Street #7-P
Canoga Park, CA 91304
(213) 882-3177
Gary Vallè

BROCK 82, RED TAIL AND DRAGON FLY
Rogallo type hang gliders with trapeze bar control.

A fine quality line of gliders with all of Brock's fancy hardware (see Chapter three). Available in 16' - 19' KL standard models, the short keel "Red Tails" and the new high aspect ratio Dragon Fly.

Plans, kits, complete units, replacement parts and tools available from:

Ultralite Products
137-P Oregon St.
El Segundo, CA 90245
(213) 322-7171
Pete Brock

DELTA WING KITES
Rogallo type tow kites and hang gliders with trapeze bar control.

The Phoenix   **Duo Delta under tow.**

Several models available for kiting and hang gliding; the kite model has a stainless steel trapeze bar with a release mechanism for the tow rope and three floats while the glider has an aluminum trapeze. Bill Bennett, the Australian kiteman with over 19 years of experience first introduced the water ski kite to the U.S. in 1969. His free flights demonstrated better control than the parallel bar arrangement and the Bennett hang glider soon evolved. Kites and gliders are available in standard and deluxe models including the short keel "Skytrek" and the all new "Phoenix."

80° frame with unique slip together/lock fittings, grit tape on the control bar and battens in the sail.

Plans, kits, complete units and replacement parts available from:

Delta Wing Kites
PO Box 483-P
Van Nuys, CA 91408
(213) 785-2474
Bill Bennett

DOVE
A Rogallo type hang glider with trapeze bar control.

A well balanced glider designed for the strong, soaring winds of Hawaii. Aluminum tubing, Dacron sail. Collapsible model.

Complete units available from:

Dove Hang Gliders of Hawaii
2445 Ala Wai #5-P
Honolulu, Hawaii 96815
(808) 923-2767
Michael H. Baumgartner

FLEXI FLIER.

A Rogallo type hang glider with trapeze bar control.

The Flexi Flier was originally designed by Dick Eipper and has been continually refined through the years; it is probably the largest seller. The hinged trapeze bar folds flat against the main tubes for transportation. 3/32'' cable and 1.5'' tubing.

The 19' and 20' KL models are called ''Flexi Floaters'' and have ⅛'' cable and 1.75'' tubing. The larger models are designed for use by heavier pilots but are also very helpful in training due to the light wing loadings, stability, slower speed and low sink rate. A 19' x 17' model offers improved performance.

Plans, manuals, complete units, complete kits, partial kits and replacement parts available from:

Eipper-Formance, Inc.
PO Box 246-47
Lomita, CA 90717
(213) 328-9100
Steve Wilson

RIDGEMASTER AND PATHFINDER
Rogallo type hang gliders with trapeze bar control

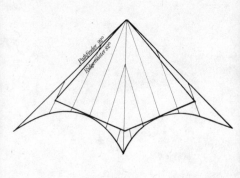

Standard and high performance gliders of exceptional quality and performance with particularly attractive sails. Available in a variety of sizes and colors. Electra Flyer also runs a flight school.

Complete units and parts available from:

Electra Flyer Corporation
3119-P San Mateo N.E.
Albuquerque, NM 87110
(505) 344-5789, 883-9339
Larry Newman

Electra Flyer Corporation

SKY HAWK, SKY-HIGH HAWK AND HALCYON HAWK
Rogallo type hang gliders with trapeze bar control

Three designs in a variety of sizes provide a glider for every level of weight and experience. The Sky-HAWK is a standard model while the Sky-High HAWK has a short keel and the Halcyon HAWK has a very short keel. HAWK is well known for their individually painted sails representing moths, butterflys and birds.

Complete units and replacement parts are available from:

HAWK Industries
8566-P Sugarman Drive
La Jolla, CA 92037
(714) 453-4443, 582-8039
Burke Ewing

SAILBIRD

A Rogallo type hang glider with trapeze bar control.

18' KL, area of 224 sq. ft., three piece trapeze bar, aluminum frame, Dacron sail, five minute assembly time.

Complete units, kits and replacement parts available from:

Sailbird Flying Machines
PO Box 9990-P
Colorado Springs, CO 80932
(303) 475-8639
Joe Sullivan

SKYSPRITE

A monoplane hang glider.

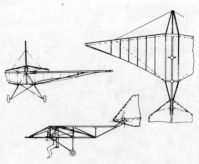

Dimensions: 30' span, 19.5' long, 8' high, weight 75 lbs.

Performance: 20 mph stall speed, 30 mph cruise speed. Stick control of ailerons and elevator.

Construction: Bolted aluminum structure, safety landing gear, may be folded for car top transport.

Plans available from:

Flight Dynamics Incorporated
PO Box 5070-P, State College Station
Raleigh, NC 27607
(919) 834-6806
Thomas H. Purcell, Jr.

SEAGULL I, SEAGULL II and SEAGULL III

Rogallo type hang gliders with trapeze bar control.

Seagull II

Seagull III. Note the shape of the nose.

Seagull V. Note the rudder.

   Construction: Larger diameter, larger wall (.058) aluminum tubing for strength and to combat sail distortion through tubing flex. Vinyl covered wires offer protection to the rigging, pilot and spectators. Control bar is padded with rubber tubing to protect the shoulders while launching and carrying. Dacron sail. Tubing caps. All the latest and finest hardware items from Ultralite Products are used. Well engineered and well made.

   Dimensions:

Seagull I: 82 degree nose, 16.5' leading edges and keel.

Seagull II. 82 degree nose, 18.5' leading edges and keel and 225 sq. ft. wing area.

Seagull III. 102 degree nose, 19' leading edges and 16' keel length. Has   "camber control" leading edge.

Seagull V. 30' span, aspect ratio 5.56, rudder control.

Complete gliders and parts available from:

Seagull Aircraft
3021-P Airport Ave.
Santa Monica, CA 90401
(213) 394-1151
Mike Riggs

and Pacific Kites Ltd.
PO Box 45-087-P
Te Atatu
Auckland 8,
NEW ZEALAND
Ph: 66-337 HSN
Rick Poynter

SEAGULL
AIRCRAFT

151

"SO-LO" VOLMER VJ-11

A biplane hang glider with three axis control.

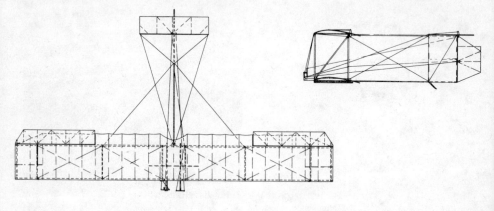

Originally designed and built in 1940 by Volmer Jensen, designer, builder and pilot of a dozen gliders, sailplanes and two airplanes, Can be built in six weeks with a material cost of about $200. Well engineered.

Controls: Ailerons, Elevators, Rudder

Performance: 15 mph stall speed, 20 mph cruise speed, glide ratio 7:1

Construction: Spruce, fir and mahogany plywood. Wire braced and fabric covered.

Dimensional specifications: Span 28', wing area 225 sq feet, length 15'5'', height 5', weight 100 lbs, useful load 180 lbs

Information kit ($2.) and complete plans available from:

Volmer Aircraft
Box 5222P
Glendale, CA 91201
(213) 247-8718
Volmer Jensen.

SWINGWING VJ-23

A cantilever monoplane hang glider with three axis control.

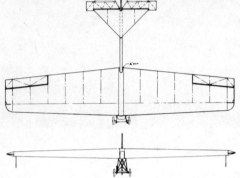
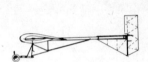

Construction of the original VJ-23 began in July 1972, it flew 3½ months later. It is probably the most advanced designed hang glider to date; it is the first high performance, fully controllable, monoplane cantilevered hang glider. The full controls and the glide angle of 9:1 allow tight turns at low altitudes without loss of stability allowing a positive return to level flight.

About 30 minutes are required to assemble and breakdown the glider. It will fit on any normal trailer for transporting to and from the launch site. If the 30 lb wings were crisscrossed, they could be stacked for car top carrying.

Controls: Ailerons, elevators, rudder.

Performance: 15 mph stall speed, 20 mph cruise speed, 25 mph top speed, glide ratio 9:1

Construction: The wing's leading edge is constructed of 1/32'' poplar plywood while the rest of the wing is covered with aircraft fabric and doped. The two wings are joined together with three bolts. The 15' tail boom is constructed of 4'' aluminum tubing. Wheels aid the return to the top of the hill. For the safety of the pilot, there is no structure behind him.

Dimensional specifications: Span 32'7'', wing area 179 sq feet, length 17'5'', height 6',16'' deep airfoil at the root.

Cost of materials: Approximately $400.00

Information kit ($2.00) and complete plans available from:

Volmer Aircraft
Box 5222P
Glendale, CA 91201
(213) 247-8718
Volmer Jensen

SUN FUN, VJ-24

A monoplane hang glider with three axis control.

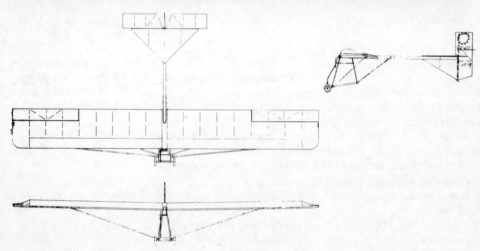

Dimensions: 18' long, 4.5' high, 36' span, wing area 160 sq. ft., weight 100 lbs.
Performance: 16 mph stall speed, 18 mph cruising speed.
Control: Ailerons, elevators and rudder.
Construction: All metal covered with fabric. Easier to build than the VJ-23; hacksaw the tubing and pop rivet it together.

Information kit ($2.00) and plans available from:

Volmer Aircraft
Box 5222p
Glendale, CA 91201
(213) 247-8718
Volmer Jensen

SUN SAIL
A Rogallo type hang glider with trapeze bar control.

SPECIFICATIONS

keel length	area	wgt.	height	span	l/d
16'	184	36	8'-4"	2'-6"	4:1
17'	204	37	10'-2"	24'-0"	4:1
18'	234	38	10'-2"	5'-6"	4:1
19'	256	39	11'-2"	7'-0"	4:1

More dimensions: 82° frame with 90° sail.
Construction: Anodized aluminum tubing, Dacron sail and some of the finer hardware parts.

Complete units, part and accessories are available from:

Sun Sail Corporation
Airport Business Center
6753 E. 47th Avenue Drive, Suite D/P
Denver, Colorado 80216
(303) 321-8482
Brian Jensen and Ted Schmiedeke

SWOOPER TOO (Supersedes the Swooper I)
A Rogallo type hang glider with trapeze bar control.

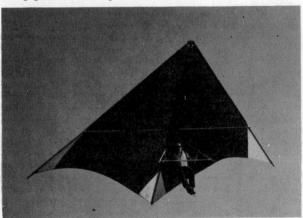

80° frame, 86° poly or Dacron sail and available in 15' - 20' KL models.

Plans, kits, materials and replacement parts available from:

Chuck's Glider Supplies
4200P Royalton Rd
Brecksville, Ohio 44141
(216) 526-5436
Chuck Slusarczyk

860 Jefferson Ave.
Cleveland, OH 44113
(216) 236-8440

True Flight

Rogallo type hang gliders with trapeze bar control.

Four models - 16' - 17' - 18' x 16' and 19' x 17' - 80 degree frame angle, weight 40 to 45 lbs.

Plans, complete units, complete kits, Dacron sails and related products are available from:

True Flight
1719-P Hillsdale Avenue
San Jose, Calif. 95124
Phone: (408) 267-0692
Herman Rice

VELDERRAIN KITES

Rogallo type hang gliders with trapeze bar control.

Velderrain's are characterized by a leading edge which is shorter than the keel length which results in greater stability. Choice of Dacron or poly sail. Available in 16' - 20' KL models.

Plans, complete gliders, kits and replacement parts available from:

Velderrain Kite Co.
P.O. Box 314-P
Lomita, Calif. 90717
(213) 325-2960
Red Miller

Valkyrie

A flying wing with drag rudder control

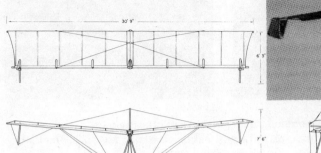

A single surface, cable stressed tailless monoplane of constant chord and straight planform employing wing tip drag rudders for directional and lateral control with pitch control achieved through weight displacement. 138 sq. ft., 54'' chord, aspect ratio 6.8, weight 48 lbs. Construction time is 50-60 hours.

Plans are available from:

Bill Wolf
3420-P Waycross Drive
Columbus, IN 47201

WINGS
A Rogallo type hang glider with trapeze bar control.

A well built, finely designed glider made of aluminum and Dacron. It features coated cable, aircraft quality materials and many specially designed fittings. Every Wings glider is accompanied by an operations manual.

Complete units are available from:

Sport Wings, Inc.
P.O. Box 1647-P
Lafayette, IN 47902
(317) 423-2646
Roger Circle, Jr.

WILLS WING AND SWALLOWTAIL
Rogallo type hang gliders with trapeze bar control

Wills Wing.   **Swallowtail.**

Special grade of 6061-T6 aluminum tubing with a uniform thickness. Stainless steel cable with shrink tubing over the ends. Kingpost has quick release turnbuckle on trailing edge keel cable. Wing nuts, nose skid plate, tube plugs, etc.

Available in 16' - 20' KL, control bar may be 4' or 5' wide with grip surfaces. Tandem seat available for flying dual. There is a lot of flying knowledge in the Wills Wing.

The all new swallowtail offers large kite performance with small kite response; it has proven to be a consistant winner in hang gliding competitions.

Complete wings, replacement parts and custom sails available from:

Sport Kites, Inc.
1202-H/P East Walnut
Santa Ana, CA 92701
(714) 547-1344
(714) 544-0445
Bob Wills and Chris Wills

OTHER MANUFACTURERS:

Phantom Wing, Inc.
PO Box 6044-P
Concord, CA 94524

Aerolab
PO Box 4168-P
Milwaukee, WI 53210

Trailwinds Glider, Inc.
PO Box 275-P
Wichita, KS 67201

New York Hang Gliders
144-45-P 35th Avenue
Flushing, NY 11354

Butterfly Industries
1191-P West Cumberland Ave.
Knoxville, TN 37916

Dyna-Sour
PO Box 236-P
Carmel, IN 46032

Cloudmen Glidercraft
905-P Church Street
Nashville, TN 37203

Hiway Hang Gliders
27/35-P Bernard Road
Brighton BN2 3ER
England

Breen Hang Gliders
New Road P
Crickhowell, Powys
Wales

Waspair Ltd
Melfort Road P
Thornton, Heath, Surrey
England

Birdman Sports Ltd.
#P Mildenhall, Marlborough, Wiltshire
England

Sailwings (Scotland) Ltd.
8-P Comely Bank Lane
Dumbarton G82 4JA
Scotland

Societe Delta SaRL
28-P, Avenue Houche
75008 Paris
France

Delta Manta
Bernard Danis
2-30-P, Square Hector-Berlioz
F-94 Maisons-Alfort
France

Savoie Delta
B.P. 25-P
F-74370 Pringy (Annecy)
France

Wind Wings
J.P. Aubert
4-P, rue des Mesanges
F-74240 Gaillard
France

Ikarus
Fred Michel
Postfach 98-P
CH-3800 Interlaken
Switzerland

Etienne Rithner
Outre-Vieze (Postfach 73-P)
CH-1870 Monthey
Switzerland

Arnaud Tavelli
CH-3960-P Sierre
Switzerland

Swiss Delta
Flug-und Fahrzeugwerke AG
Altenrhein
CH-9422-P Staad
Switzerland

CHAPTER VII

HANG GLIDER DESIGN

Man has tried to follow the birds by copying their design but the greatest problem is one of control; man cannot warp the surfaces the way a bird can. The wing of the bird takes on an endless number of shapes. Each individual feather flexes with every wing movement taking just the proper shape required for each movement and rush of wind. Man is able to control his movements under water about as effectively and in much the same way as bird can in the air but he cannot operate in the thinner medium. He can tread water with just the movement of his hands by tilting his palms as he moves them back and forth; the hummingbird uses the same technique in the air. Much may be learned from the birds; their better parts may be emphasized in a man made design and we have the advantage of substituting man made materials for nature's. A good reference to birds and their flight is: *The Miracle of Flight* By Richard Cromer, $4.95, Doubleday and Co, Garden City, NY.

There is a great technical void in the area of ultra-light, ultra-slow flight, in fact, man probably knows more about supersonic flight than about remaining airborne under 25 mph.

So little is known about hang gliders and the amateur designer doesn't have the test equipment normally available to the aerodynamicist working for a large aircraft company. And even if the data and equipment were available and formulas possible, the average hang glider builder is not an aeronautical engineer and wouldn't know how to use them. As a result, design is usually by trial and error. A very basic understanding of the problems is still necessary.

There are many good books on the various aspects of aircraft design and this text is not meant to replace them. The reader will want to "graduate" to these more sophisticated treatments of aerodynamics after getting his feet wet here. This simple, easy to digest presentation of some of the design problems may aid the neophyte in understanding why some hang gliders have evolved as they have, guide him in modifying an existing model or guide him to a proper choice of plans.

This basic text deals specifically with hang glider problems. Other publications recommended to the readers are available from the Experimental Aircraft Assn, PO Box 229P, Hales Corners, Wis 53130. Write for a publications list.

"These guys are amazing! Before you know it, they're gonna invent the airplane" - Keith Nichols

---

U.S. Government Printing Office
Public Documents Department
Washington DC 20402

Basic Glider Criteria Handbook ($1.00)
FAA No. 5.8/2:G49/962-P

A bibliography of over 100 reports and papers on the Rogallo wing is available from the Author for $2.00 Postpaid, P.O. Box 4232-P Santa Barbara, CA 93103.

Many are of the opinion that though Rogallos make up some 95% of all the hang gliders flying, the sport will change to the monoplane. The Rogallo type is simple, lightweight, portable, inexpensive, easy to build and it flys very well. In the battles for the duration record, Rogallos are often even or in front of the mono and biplanes It is no surprise to find the Rogallo the most popular despite its slightly reduced performance. Its flight characteristics are good and sometimes forgiving; a well balanced one will usually level in a stall and "parachute" the pilot back to earth as a full drag device. It is very strong particularly when constructed of the proper materials. But portability is its biggest selling point. One simply disconnects and rotates the cross bar, brings the leading edge bars to the center along side the keel, rolls the sail, coils the cables and stows it all in a long, small diameter bag. It is ideal for cliff launches as one may fly to the bottom of the hill, collapse it for car top carry and drive back to the top for another flight.

In aircraft design and particularly in this new sport of hang gliding, there are many widely spread schools of thought. The new designer should surround himself with all the information possible and seek advice whenever he is in doubt.

Be careful. In the design of an aircraft many items must be considered and developed into a smooth total mechanical flying device. Many parts are of major importance and must be given great consideration. And there are many little things, not so obvious, which the designer put there for a specific reason. The builder who deviates from the plans may be taking a chance. If only performance is affected, that's not too serious but if it affects the integrity of the design, there is a potentially great problem. Remember: Every single design feature must be considered properly.

BODY ENGLISH vs CONTROL SURFACES

A low, slow flying kite can be adequately guided by body movements or center of gravity changes but at higher altitudes, greater air speeds or more turbulent wind conditions, some positive method of control is a must. It is a basic law of physics that one just cannot move his weight far enough off center to lift a wing of adequate span for soaring once it has gone down to any appreciable degree; the shifting body just doesn't exert enough leverage. Few Rogallo's are seen with parallel bars these days.

Without controls, steep turns cannot be made without inviting spiral instability and a quick, unrecoverable return to earth. So machines to be controlled only by weight shifting should be limited to activities which are low, slow and in smooth air. Lilienthal suffered a gust induced stall and fell to his death; it could not be countered by any amount of frantic leg waiving. The control system of the Wrights, coordinated wing warping and aft rudders, provided at least some mastery of unpredictable gusts. Aerodynamic controls were *the* critical advance in heavier-than-air flight.

Self-soaring takes a good kite with three-axis control (yaw, pitch, and roll) - and a pilot with skill and guts (in that order).

In the design of flying machines, there are many trade-offs.

The hang glider must be designed to fly at a very slow speed, say 20 mph, which produces a dynamic pressure of less than 1 lb./sq. ft. Good, low drag aerodynamics are necessary. Induced drag must be minimized and this requires a span of some 28' for a biplane and 30' for a monoplane. Tight turns are required to remain in updrafts and the problem is that the craft is flying at the same speed as the seagull but has ten times his wing span. In a turn, lift decreases on the lower wing and increases on the upper one due to the difference in the air velocity over them. Lift varies with the square of the velocity and the rolling moment generated is aggravated; the wing can roll into a steep bank from which the only method of recovery is a steep dive; impossible unless roll and yaw control is available.

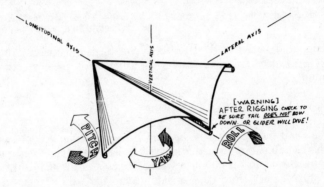

Aircraft stability is a complex subject involving both static and dynamic stability about three axes.

PITCH (nose up-down) INSTABILITY may be corrected with reflex airfoils, negative incidence tails, sweep, washout, etc.

ROLL (Wings up-down) INSTABILITY may be corrected with dihedral, with sweep, ailerons or spoilers (with a penalty of drag).

YAW(turning) INSTABILITY may be corrected with spoilers, ailerons, rudder (alone if the wings have enough dihedral).

Elevators while helpful during the launch are not a significant improvement over fore/aft movement of the feet during flight and probably aren't worth the extra weight and cabling complications involved.

On gliders with long spans, weight shifting is not adequate or recommended. At slow speeds, down ailerons cause the gliders to pivot in that direction due to the drag. Consequently, ailerons may be designed to go up on one side some 40 degrees while going down on the other only 10 degrees.

Any of these systems require a lot of cable, pulleys and so on and the biggest problem of all is making the system available to the pilot; his hands must be sufficiently free to carefully manipulate the controls.

"In the old days, aircraft flew very slow and control was very poor. As speed increased, control improved - due to the speed and there was no further research in this area. In hang gliding, we had to go back and begin again where they left off" - Volmer Jensen.

Note the stick in the cockpit of the VJ-23 Swingwing.

The Icarus II has twist controls on the hand grips which operate tip-mounted drag rudders.

In conclusion, the trapeze bar gives far more control than the parallel bar arrangement and while this amount of control is probably sufficient, it doesn't come close to full three axis control.

AIRFOILS AND COEFFICIENTS OF LIFT

Early aircraft had flat surfaced wings and depended upon the pressure underneath to remain airborne. This also created a lot of drag and was, therefore, quite inefficient. A good double surfaced airfoil minimizes drag and creates lift and, in fact, some 2/3rds of the lifting force comes from the top side due to the reduced pressure as the wing moves through the air (Bernoulli).

Now the total lift on a wing can be obtained by adding the low and high pressure regions together and multiplying this sum by the wing area. The coefficient of lift for a given wing section is obtainable from its lift-angle of attack graph. (See *Theory of Wing Sections* by Abbott and von Doenhoff). Here are some major airfoil types:

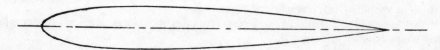

Symmetrical: use this section type for horizontal and vertical stabilizers. NACA 0012 shown. Type does not develop lift until angle of attack is presented.

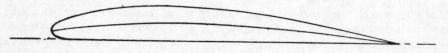

Flat Bottomed: good "all around" section. Can be used for wings. Clark-Y shown. This airfoil was used quite extensively on private aircraft of the 30's and 40's. (eg. Piper Cub). It has good lift characteristics and a gentle stall. Has small lift at zero angle of attack.

Under Cambered: Typical for biplane types with tails. Was used on aircraft from the Wright Brothers into the 20's. U.S.A. 2 shown. Has high lift at low angles of attack. Never used on high speed airplanes.

The wings of Dave Cronk's experimental flying wing, the Cronksail.

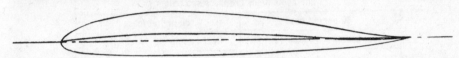

Reflexed: mean line is positively cambered until approximately the 75% chord position where it is seen to dip below the datum line and reverse its curve to meet the tail. Characterized by a turned up trailing edge. Use this type on flying wing, tailless airplanes. NACA M-6 shown. Up turned tail cancels tendency for airfoil to tuck under and dive. Is stable without a tail.

The wing of the Icarus V

NOTE: These airfoils are not to be traced as shown. All airfoils to be drawn from "airfoil table of ordinates" as published by NACA and others.

ROGALLO SAILS

Even after years of Government research into the Rogallo wing, there are many unanswered questions but the following generalities should be some help.

The sail should be about 4 degrees wider than the frame on each side; i.e. an 88 degree sail for an 80 degree frame. Making the sail too taut improves the glide angle while decreasing stability.

Most Rogallos have equal leading edge and keel tubes but some are unequal. If the keel tube is longer by a couple of feet, stability is improved. If the keel is shorter such as on a 19'/17' model, the glide angle improves, drag is reduced, pitch control is more sensitive, turns are tighter and the response is better. But it is somewhat more difficult to fly, the stall speed is higher and it is more likely to fall off to one side in a stall.

163

The trailing edge of the sail should reflex slightly, never cup; don't sew tape to it.

Battens reduce the flapping of the sail's trailing edge and this decrease in drag, increases efficiency. The flapping also knocks out the resin treatment and therefore makes the fabric more porous so battens can be a help here in reducing wear. They may also be used to correct a poorly contoured sail and can be an advantage at high speeds. The sail will pull the aft end of the leading edge tubes up and in while bending the part between the cross tube and the nose slightly out and down; the sail should be designed to take this into consideration. Other alternatives are larger diameter tubing or "wing posts", cabled outriggers.

WING AREA

Area* of Rogallo sails on those designs where the leading edge and keels tubes are the same length.			
80 degree nose		90 degree nose	
Keel Length	Area (Sq. Ft.)	Keel Length	Area (Sq. Ft.)
15'	143	14'	139
16'	168	15'	168
17'	187	16'	180
18'	207	17'	204
19'	233	18'	229
20'	260	19'	256
		20'	284

*This is really the planform or projected area as no allowance is made for the extra square feet of billow in the sail.

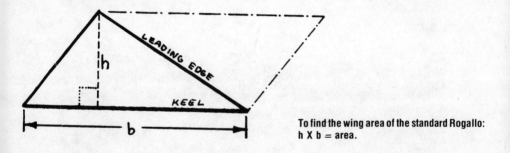

To find the wing area of the standard Rogallo:
h X b = area.

WING LOADING is the wing area in square feet divided by the gross (pilot and machine) weight. Wing area is the length times the width for rectangular wings and a little more difficult to figure out for other shapes.

For biplanes, figure total wing area and then deduct the portions blanketed by the pilot's body etc, and otherwise cut out portions. "Biplane theory" dictates that more must be subtracted due to interference if the gap between the wings is less than their chord.

For Rogallos, wing loadings of one pound are about right for light conditions but for windier days, say over 10 mph, 1.25 and better are recommended. Ballast such as water or skin diver weight belts might be used to extend a craft's versatility. Remember that high speed aircraft have small wings and, therefore, a high wing loading.

"In the beginning the height should be moderate and the wings not too large, or the wind will soon show that it is not to be trifled with" - Otto Lilienthal

164

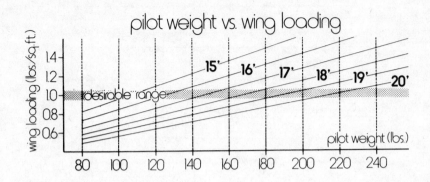

Eipper-Formance chart for the 80 degree nose Rogallo

More accurately, sizing depends upon the square feet of wing area as compared to the *gross* weight (both man and machine). It is assumed here that the glider weighs in at 30-40 lbs. depending on the keel length.

It should be mentioned that there has been a tendency to go larger recently (lighter wing loading) to decrease the sink rate and increase soaring possibilities. Older men with a lot of common sense who can resist the urge to fly unless conditions are very good, may consider an oversize wing.

An increase in wing area or a reduction in the load will lower the "wing loading" and this results in slower forward speed and slower rate of descent.

If the wing is too big (area) for the gross load (you and the craft) (called "low wing loading"), it will fly too slow. This is acceptable IF you are flying straight and level but in a turn, the inboard wing will slow down and may stall (Not much of a problem with the short spanned Rogallo).

The longer the wing, the worse the problem because the slower the tip will be going in the turn; once it goes below the flying speed, it stalls and drops. Keep the speed up for turns!

If the wing is too small for the load, the craft will be too fast both forward and down. The pilot won't be able to run fast enough to get under it and if he does manage to get airborne, he'll find the landing rather snappy. The answer is to choose the right size wing for the gross load.

Small kites are easier to carry. The very small ones (13' - 14') are built for kiting only and are not in any way suitable for foot launch. The extra large Rogallos are often used for training because of their increased stability, slower speeds and rate of sink. But their use must be restricted to very steady winds of less than 10 mph. A kite which is too large will be harder to maneuver; slower to respond. It will be difficult to handle on the ground but once up it will provide a longer flight.

"The most dangerous part of hang gliding is the male ego" – Donnita Holland

---

Flying speed is affected by the wing loading.

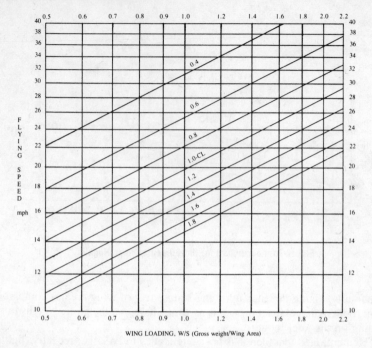

WING LOADING, W/S (Gross weight/Wing Area)

The slant lines represent the lift coefficient (from the airfoil tables); crude wings will give at least .8 and refined wings without flaps may reach 1.4 at these low speeds. Once the flying speed is found, a red "stall" line may be made on the wind speed indicator. And subtracting the wind speed gives the ground speed the pilot must run for a good launch.

Figure on a launch speed of 15-20 mph and then hope for a 10-15 mph wind.

PLANFORM is the profile of the wing as seen directly from above. There are many shapes in hang gliders some of which are dictated by structural considerations. On many light planes, the wings are straight and have square tips. There is much air leakage around the tip and therefore the tips are working as though they were set at a lower angle of attack. The result is that the stall comes first some distance from the tips. With a tapered wing the tips do not lose so much lift and therefore will stall first. On the square wing, aileron control can be maintained longer in a stall.

Pressure leaks occur at the ends of the wings. Droop tips or flat plates at the wing tips reduce "wing tip vorticies" and wing tip loss of lift by decreasing the amount of high pressure air escaping around and up to the top side low pressure area. Similarly, gaps in the center where the wings join at the root should be closed with a gap cover.

Wing tip vorticies=Drag

166

WING SLOTS may be used, particularly near the wing tips to prevent tip stalls and the resultant loss of aileron control and possible spin. An extra flap near the leading edge or a slot in the wing redirects the flow of air so that higher angles of attack are possible before the wing stalls.

SWEEPBACK is when the center of the tips of the wings are farther back than the center of the chord at the midpoint of the wing. Sweepback is similar to dihedral in that it corrects for roll indirectly through the slip that is produced by the roll. But sweepback is only 10-15%as effective as dihedral. As the sweptback wing approaches the stall,the corrective forces increase and the tips stall first.

CANTILEVER: No external bracing, as in a wing without wires. A good example is the VJ-23. The alternative is strut and cable bracing which is much lighter but adds some drag.

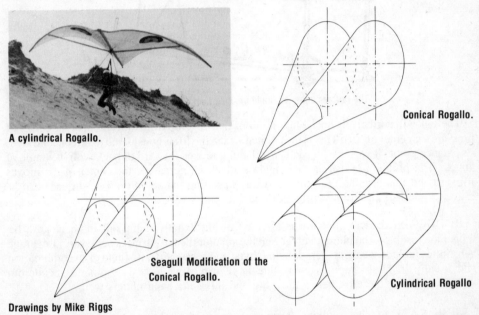

A cylindrical Rogallo.

Conical Rogallo.

Seagull Modification of the
Conical Rogallo.

Cylindrical Rogallo

Drawings by Mike Riggs

CYLINDRICAL AND CONICAL refer to the affect of the leading edge on the common Rogallo sail. A straight leading edge tube produces a conical parawing while a helical leading edge makes the Rogallo cylindrical.Wind tunnel tests show a great glide ratio improvement for the cylindrical but it stalls easily and is harder to fly. Most authorities agree that the cylindrical Rogallo needs controls.

Note the dihedral on the Quicksilver.

167

DIHEDRAL refers to the upward angling of the wings. It creates stability and permits maneuverability with greater safety. It is the angle between the wing and a line normal to the plane of symmetry. Increasing dihedral, increases the tendency to return to level flight if a gust, for example, should force one wing down. This tendency to right results from the increase in angle of attack (and therefore lift) on the low wing as a result of a side slip in the direction of the low wing.

A TAIL on the glider will contribute greatly to control. The Wright Brothers placed it in front of the craft (canard type) where it afforded them some energy absorbing protection in case of a crash but cluttered the view. Placing it in the rear, however, invites breaking it off in a crash during a pilot error stall on takeoff or a spiral dive into the hillside on account of insufficient lateral stability in the presence of excessive directional stability.

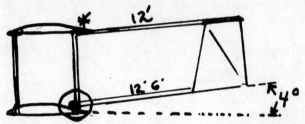

The tail assembly as found on Jack Lambie's Hang Loose.

The tail will correct any unstable conditions that develop from movement of the center of pressure (or center of lift). This is the point at which the lift is considered to be concentrated, its balance point. It varies with each airfoil and it moves forward or back with the angle of attack. The problem is that as the angle of attack is increased, the center of lift moves forward and this lifts the nose more, further upsetting the stability. Tail surfaces can be moved to deflect air and lever the craft back to the level.

RUDDER SIZE determination is affected by the length of the tail moment arm(the longer the fuselage, the more leverage and the smaller the tail surfaces necessary).Leverage substitutes include washout, aerodynamic twist and reflex airfoils single or in combination and usually in large amounts contribute large trim-drag losses. Another is pendulum stability, placing the pilot below the wing and this suits hang gliders well.

SINK RATE is what a glider depends upon for its ability to soar. Glide angle and speed are not so important in hang gliding but rather attention should be paid to sink rate and maneuverability. One must be able to sustain in slow updrafts and have the ability to turn sharply enough to remain in them. A sink rate below 4 fps should be sufficient. One way to decreased the sink rate is to increase the span of the wing but this contributes other problems.

ASPECT RATIO is the square of the span divided by the area and is expressed as a ratio such as 4:1. On a rectangular wing it is easier to figure as it is simply the span divided by the chord. Most of the lift comes from the top of the wing just back from the leading edge so it stands to reason that to increase the lift, this surface should be enlarged; the result is a long narrow wing. The trade off for the low, slow hang glider is that the wing tip may stall in a turn and drop to the ground or may catch on the ground or a bush in a turn and provide the same disasterous results. And, of course, a long wing requires more bracing which adds weight.

GLIDE ANGLE is one of the most important considerations in selecting a hang glider kit or design. Glide angle is expressed as L/D or lift to drag ratio and means the distance

168

the craft will move forward for the altitude it drops. eg, 4:1 means it will travel four feet forward for every foot it descends.

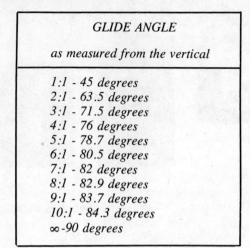

GLIDE ANGLE

as measured from the vertical

1:1 - 45 degrees
2:1 - 63.5 degrees
3:1 - 71.5 degrees
4:1 - 76 degrees
5:1 - 78.7 degrees
6:1 - 80.5 degrees
7:1 - 82 degrees
8:1 - 82.9 degrees
9:1 - 83.7 degrees
10:1 - 84.3 degrees
∞ -90 degrees

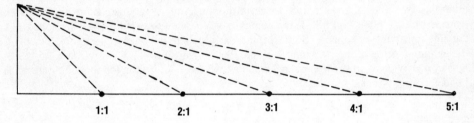

So it can be seen that over around 5:1, sink rate becomes more important than glide ratio.

The glide ratio is a measure of performance. Performance may be improved by increasing lift or decreasing drag; usually both are tried.

To skysurfers, the better angle means being able to fly on gentler slopes and staying up longer. A sailplane may have an L/D of 40:1 but it achieves this figure at 60 mph and it weighs 600 lbs. The skysurfer couldn't lift it or run that fast. The flying speed chart can be used to figure the tradeoffs. Select the speed you wish to fly, pick the best airfoil and find what the aspect ratio must be.

L/D increases 8% for each unit the aspect ratio is increased. If the wing area is increased by 20%, the lift will increase 20% and the minimum landing speed will be reduced by 9%. Speed is the most important element of lift: Double the speed and the lift is increased four times.

Care and a grain of salt should be taken when reviewing manufacturers' claims of performance, especially the glide ratio figures.

STREAMLINING while not so important at low speeds (drag increases at the square of the velocity) must still be considered because the ultra light, ultra slow hang glider needs all the help it can get.

Streamlined tie rods, for example, produce one-sixth the drag of a round one and one-seventh that of stranded cable. A kite will fly at a higher angle with non-fuzzy string than with a greater drag producing fuzzy one.

So wind meeting surfaces should be tear dropped wherever possible. Smoothing and streamlining exterior surfaces will reduce drag and increase the glide ratio.

Gliding parachutes.

LIMP vs RIGID: The limp wing, such as the higher performance gliding parachute type wings, are very light with typical man carrying models weighing 15-20 lbs without the harness but their glide angle is usually 3:1 or less and only stiffening has been able to improve this so far. Foot launching a rigid wing is somewhat easier because it keeps flying and partially supporting the weight of the pilot even when he briefly touches down and again attempts to get airborne. And, of course, limp wings suffer from a lack of pitch control. Limp wings have been successfully foot launched but the hill must be very steep. Some of the earliest activity of this sort took place on the landing portion of the ski jump at Lake Placid, New York. An oversized wing works best as it provides a slow forward speed and a low sink rate; a wing loading of about .65 is good for limp wings.

STRENGTH

Hang gliders designed for high flight should be stressed for at least 3 Gs and all components should be tested prior to installation.

The FAA requires the following stressing: commercial airliners 2.5 Gs, light aircraft 3.17-3.8 Gs, utility aircraft 4.4 Gs and aerobatic aircraft 6 Gs. The increase in strength is required in a banked turn (60 degrees is 2 Gs) and more important to hang gliders, the forces from gust loads. A sharp updraft could fold up the wings. Additionally, hang gliders suffer from abrasion during their repeated landings and ground handling; a safety factor must be built in to accept the wear and tear.

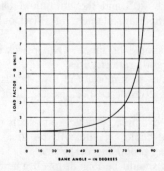

Load factor chart.

The cockpit of the VJ-23 Swingwing is open to the rear.

The padding on the front of this Icarus II may save the face in a rough landing.

THE COCKPIT of the non-Rogallo is normally designed to fit the pilot under the arms and provision is made for a seat or prone harness. 16'' is probably the best support width. The pilot needs as much fore to aft room as possible as self generating dives can result if he cannot move his shoulders rearward. Red line stop places may be indicated by bumps on the parallel bars. The rear should be left open as an escape route in case of emergency. Structure ahead of the pilot will protect him in case of a crash from puncture prone pieces of structure and the terrain.

THE CENTER OF GRAVITY is where the two balance points (fore/aft and side/side) cross. This point must be found to locate the pilot suspension point. The CG may be altered slightly with ballast.

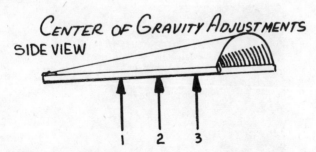

Center of Gravity Adjustments
SIDE VIEW

1   2   3

1, If the pilot is suspended forward of the C.G., the wing will fly fast or dive
2, Where the pilot should be
3, If the pilot is attached behind the C.G., the wing will tend to stall.

If the wing is slightly out of trim, it may not be readily apparent on short flights. However, the constant pressure required will make itself known on long ones. Taras speaks on the Icarus:

"Since hang gliders fly very slowly and weigh much less than the dangling pilot, they respond very quickly if stable.Shifting the pilot weight fore and aft greatly influences the speed and attitude of the craft. This extreme stability means that the glider has to be held in turns and when released quickly resumes straight and level flight. The center of gravity of the craft ALONE should be behind the position where the pilot normally holds the plane; this way he will experience little difficulty keeping the nose up during takeoff and landing because the tail will naturally want to settle to the ground".

TRAPEZE BARS

When Miller and Carmichael were building their ground skimmers, they fitted the craft with parallel bars and it never occurred to them to fly any other way.   Meanwhile, the Australian water ski kitemen, Bennett and Moyes,were towing small kites behind boats and foot launching was far from their minds. Foot launching and the trapeze bar met and both groups benefited.

Bars may be adjusted forward or back by changing the length of the cables.

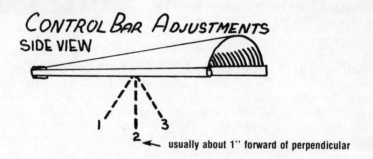

CONTROL BAR ADJUSTMENTS
SIDE VIEW

usually about 1" forward of perpendicular

1, If the bar is too far forward, one cannot reach forward far enough to push out of a dive.
2, This position is correct though the bar should be farther forward for prone flying than for sitting.
3, If the bar is too far back, one cannot pull it back far enough to get the nose down to pick up flying speed.

Russ Velderrain in the first flight of the Rustler. It flew even with the control bar angled too far back.

"The first obstacle to overcome by the practical constructor is that of stability" - Otto Lilienthal.

In high wind conditions, the bar is moved forward a couple of inches to allow the pilot to hold the nose down.

Putting a "belly bulge" in the bar provides the seated pilot with a greater range of control; particularly helpful in high wind stall recovery. Smaller pilots will find that smaller triangle bars are easier to manage in ground handling especially during the learning stages.

Eric Wills poses with the extra wide control bar from Sport Kites.
Mike Riggs shows the cushioned control bar from Seagull Aircraft. It makes launching, carrying and crashing far more comfortable. Material is Armstrong Armaflex refrigerator tubing. Normally only a couple of one foot lengths are used in the shoulder area.

The rounded bar is much nicer looking than the straight triangle and it keeps its fittings out of the dirt but it is not as stable when sitting on the ground and the hinged triangle shaped bar folds flat for transportation.

WHEELS provide several advantages. In landing prone, they contact the ground first causing the nose to pitch up stalling the wing. They are a great help when pulling the craft back to the top of the slope and they save the fingers from "road rash" on landing. Students crash a lot and wheels eliminate the abrupt stop which often encourages him to take up another sport. Poor landings which used to be like hitting a brick wall

"The only disadvantage with the wide triangle is the fact that it's more awkward to handle on the ground. In the air it's superior in every way".-Dave Kilbourne

are now more like being tossed into a snow bank. For training, wheels are an absolute must; for the experienced pilot they are a great aid and a lot of fun. There are several approaches to the finger saving problem; Tom Peghiny simply drills out two inexpensive hockey pucks.

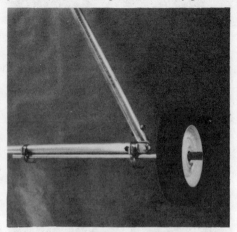

Wheels are easily installed with hose clamps. Sharp edges should be taped.

James Bunn demonstrates his wheels.

Bill Bennett shows his knuckle protectors. Sharp edges should be taped.

PILOT SUSPENSION SYSTEMS consist of seats or harnesses and vary in design according to whether they are being used with trapeze type control bars or parallel bars.

NOTE. YOU SHOULD USE SOME TYPE OF SHOULDER RETAINER ON YOUR SWING SEAT.

Seats and harnesses must be constructed so that the pilot cannot fall inverted; this normally requires shoulder restraints on prone harnesses and back/chest straps on swing seats.

Note: Suspension straps should be routed under the seat in case of seat failure.

One way to fly prone: buckle the swing seat on the front

The swing seat is ordinarily made from a childs' plastic swing and ⅜"polypropylene rope looped under the seat twice and spliced into the upright lengths. A better alternative is Nylon webbing as the Poly rope chafes the arm pits unless heavy clothing is worn. Independent leg straps are preferred over lap belts which sometimes come apart and which must be cinched tighter to stay on making running difficult. However, there must be a release system: lap belt or one above which releases the whole system. A spreader bar above the head allows head movement between the suspension line confluence point. A seat is most comfortable for long flights.

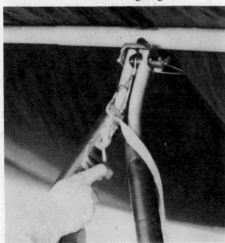

The Sky Sports release system, a 2500 lb. parachute quick ejector snap will not release under load.

This swing seat has independent leg straps.

"There is a lot more physical exertion demanded in the prone harness than with a seat". - Dave Kilbourne

175

The double seat for flying dual used by Bob Wills.

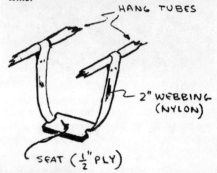

HANG TUBES

2" WEBBING (NYLON)

SEAT ($\frac{1}{2}$" PLY)

Seat for the Icarus II.

Seat for the VJ-23 Swingwing.

Mike Larson flying prone

The Bikini Harness is ideal for students as it allows them to run faster than when strapped to a seat.

For the parallel bar arrangement, one may simply use a disc of plywood on a "Y" suspension system; it will provide support for long flights if not security.

The prone harness allows one to " fly like Superman"; cutting down on wind resistance and lending a feeling of true bird-like flight.

KNEE HANGERS: Manta prone harnesses used by more experienced fliers, has the shoulder-restrainer lines running through (rather than to) the point of suspension (D-ring) and connects them to the knees. This allows the pilot to stand or go prone, and in the prone position supports the legs so that longer flights are both possible and more comfortable. Because of the complexity and need for proper adjustment to the individual flier, knee hangers are not generally recommended for beginners.

BUOYANCY

Some buoyancy may be provided by sealing the tubes in the structure; a great help if one has to ditch. When flying near water, some sort of flotation gear should be used. Floats tied onto the structure often snap off on impact.

TOMORROW

Hang gliders of the future will find their design limited only by imagination. Richard Miller dreams of a "ground bounder", a short spanned model which will permit only brief hopping flights. Wing tip extensions could be added once the basic unit is mastered.

Again, the Rogallo type makes a good glider as it is inexpensive, easy to transport, relatively safe (forgiving) quick to erect and flys well. It could turn better but it is well suited to low, slow flight. Some feel that it isn't stable enough for the beginner.

The biplane is strong, rigid and offers low weight to area but there is a time consuming problem with assembly.

Flying wings are simple, low weight and produce a minimum of drag. They should be swept back and the lateral control problem may be complicated. They can be very sensitive in pitch. A good pilot will fly them all.

INSTRUMENTATION

As hang gliders fly higher and longer, many pilots are looking to instrumentation to prolong their flights. Listening to the sail is not enough and some are mounting air speed indicators, variometers and other equipment designed for more sophisticated craft. Most

"In the future, most will still start with the Rogallo while maybe 10% will pursue the high performance wings" - Carl Boenish

important is an instrument to indicate when lift areas are encountered; the pilot wants to know when he is going up and when he is going down. Thermals are hard to find and stay with and it is important to know not only when one is climbing but at what rate. Most rate of descent indicators are designed for aircraft of larger proportions and are not really suitable for hang gliding. One recent development is an audio variometer designed especially for hang gliding by Frank Colver (3076-P Roanoke Ln, Costa Mesa, CA) which increases its pitch as the glider rises and decreases it as the glider descends. The audio system is less distracting as the pilot needn't turn his head to read a dial.

Colver's Audio Variometer

MODELS

The Rogue, a fine flying scale Rogallo is available in kit form from W.B. Products, 560 So. Helberta Ave., Suite P, Redondo Beach, CA 90277

Chuck Slusarczyk launches GI Joe on a scale model of his Falcon

New designs should always begin with models; let "G.I. Joe" take the bruises and make the design changes on the inexpensive model.

And so we see that no matter how light the new hang glider is made, the heaviest part still remains: the pilot. And this weight dictates within narrow limits the characteristics of the design. To achieve low drag and low sink rate, one must reach for long span

"*The most common problem with hang loose and similar biplanes is stall/turn at low altitude.*" - Doug Fronius

and high aspect ratio but this must be done at the expense of high structural weight and the low speed turning problem. The span must include an aspect ratio sufficient to produce a minimum of induced drag while maintaining a low, workable wing loading. Now, keeping strength and a small safety factor in mind, all elements must be brought into balance. These tradeoffs are the reason why most designs are offered with explanations approaching the apologetic.

TESTING

The recently completed hang glider should be thoroughly tested before being rolled out for its first flight. Before taking to the air, the pilot must be assured that it is properly constructed, has high structural strength, built in stabilities and good control.

As each major assembly is completed, it should be tested for structural rigidity and compatibility with the other components.

Once completely assembled, the new craft should be set on a flat, level surface and visually sighted for proper alignment. Inflate the sail with a breeze and check for symmetry and fullness. Any unbalanced condition will alter the flying characteristics, usually downward. Recheck the glider against the plans.

GLIDE ANGLE may be checked with a glide angle indicator .

The indicator consists of two bearinged discs, one which is plumb and the other which has a wind vane; it reads in degrees.

TUFT TESTING is one method of "seeing" the air as it flows around the glider. To increase performance, either the lift must be increased or the drag decreased and most hang gliders suffer from a great deal of drag which could be easily decreased. Tufting will also help explain the aerodynamic characteristics of the plane. Its simple, effective and the use of the infinite wall wind tunnel is free.

The taped yarn tufts will reveal poor streamlining, wrong wing tip shape, leakage at control surfaces, interference at joint of airframe components, etc. All of these not only add to drag, they affect the performance and the stall characteristics.

Run ordinary knitting yarn around the wing at 8'' intervals and tape every 6'' with a 1'' piece of masking tape. Then cut the yarn just ahead of the tape. This is the fastest way and it assures alignment of the yarns.

Now the flow of air around the glider can be seen. On long, high flights, they may be observed. The otherwise preoccupied pilot will want to view the tufts on low flights but won't have the time. Tests may be conducted on the ground but some terrain interference will occur.

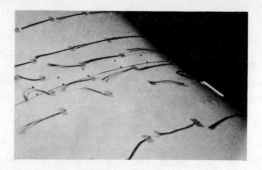

A new craft should be carefully test flown in the beginning. Every glider has its own characteristics and one must determine what they are and then learn to fly it. Low, slow glides with moderate turns should precede the more ambitious leaps.

Taras and his Icarus V.

CHAPTER VIII

HANG GLIDERS AND POWER

Obviously, hang gliders with power are not "gliders" but few deep discussions of hang glider designs conclude without some thought being directed to the subject. Basically, there are two types of power, those produced by man or machine. Man has become airborne under his own power but flight cannot be sustained for long, or at least until now it hasn't been.

MAN POWERED FLIGHT

When the Wright Brothers developed machine powered flight at the turn of the century, man power, like gliding was forgotten. With all of the technological advances of the last half century, man has still been unable to fulfill an age old dream; to fly for extended periods under his own power. But interest has renewed and in 1949 British industrialist Henry Kremer offered a prize which came to be known as the £5000 Kremer Competition (worth nearly $13,000. U.S.).

Originally, the competition was limited to citizens of the British Commonwealth and the requirements were to fly a figure eight course around two pylons spaced a half mile apart while maintaining at least ten feet altitude at the start and finish lines; all this with only muscle power. In March of 1967, the prize was doubled to £10,000 and the gate was thrown open to everyone. A smaller prize with a simplier course was established and reserved for the British. In 1973, the prize was increased to £50,000.

The MPA record so far was set by John Potter in the Jupiter MPA on 29 June 1972 at Benson Airfield, Oxfordshire, England when he flew 1171 yards, 2', 10'' in 1:47. This was one of some 100 flights made over a period of months. The Jupiter has a span of 79' and weighs in at 140 lbs.

There are a number of major technical considerations basic to Man Powered Aircraft design, such as:

Even a champion athlete can only generate .4 to .5 brake horsepower for short periods using leg muscles and then only by going into "oxygen debt". An ordinary individual might generate 70%-80% of this.

Pedaling while seated in a semi-reclined position is reported to be the most efficient means of extracting this leg power.

Since the power available is very low, the craft must fly slowly and must be very efficient aerodynamically.

The craft must be at least 10 feet off the ground at the start and finish and will

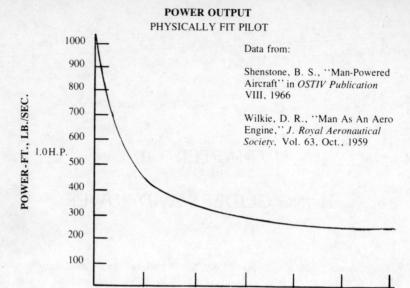

POWER OUTPUT
PHYSICALLY FIT PILOT

Data from:

Shenstone, B. S., "Man-Powered Aircraft" in *OSTIV Publication* VIII, 1966

Wilkie, D. R., "Man As An Aero Engine," *J. Royal Aeronautical Society*, Vol. 63, Oct., 1959

POWER-FT., LB./SEC.

1.0 H.P.

TIME - MINUTES

have to be high on the turns around the pylons or it will drag a wing tip and this dictates large banked turns for nearly the entire flight. Thus the efficiency and handling problem are further complicated.

So there are a number of aerodynamic and structural tradeoffs. A high aspect ratio minimizes induced drag but there is a point at which the weight of the necessary structure sets a limit. A large wing area will reduce wing loading but be too responsive to gusts while a long span will take advantage of ground effect but it increases weight and dictates higher altitudes for turns so that the wing tips won't touch the ground.

One of the greater problems is finding a combination pilot/athlete and it must be realized that one will not be able to generate the same amount of power while concentrating on flying.

Some are attacking the problem by designing ships for two or more people. The problems involved make the whole situation so marginal that it is speculated that while a team may be able to take off and gain enough altitude to cross the starting line at the required ten feet and then descend somewhat to take advantage of ground effect and make the 180 degree turns, they won't have the energy left to climb back to ten feet to cross the finish line.

If the Kremer prize and true man powered flight is ever to be won, a great deal of research will be necessary in the areas of low speed aerodynamics, light weight materials, structures and man as a power plant.

The problems of man powered flight are the same or closely parallel those in hang gliding and much can be learned from past MPA work. One good book in the subject is *Man Powered Flight* by Keith Sherwin ($6.50pp from Soaring Society of America, PO Box 66071p, Los Angeles, CA 90066)

For a good survey of MPAs, see the February 1974 edition of *Popular Science* Magazine. (Try the library).

ROYAL AERONAUTICAL SOCIETY
MAN POWERED FLIGHT
REGULATIONS AND CONDITIONS
for
The £ 50,000 KREMER Competition;
1st March
1967
The Royal Aeronautical Society
4 Hamilton Place London W.1 o1-499 3515

A prize of £ 50,000 is offered by Henry Kremer for a successful controlled flight of a Man Powered Aircraft under conditions laid down by the Man Powered Aircraft Group of the Royal Aeronautical Society. The official observers will be selected from a body approved by the Royal Aeronautical Society and the Royal Aero Club.

The Regulations and Conditions governing the award, which is to be known as the £50,000 Kremer Competition, have now been laid down by the Royal Aeronautical Society and are as follows.

This Competition shall be conducted by the Royal Aero Club of the United Kingdom under the Regulations and Conditions laid down by a Committee called the KREMER COMPETITION COMMITTEE, which shall be composed of members of the Royal Aeronautical Society and of the Royal Aero Club. The Kremer Competition Committee is hereinafter referred to as "The Committee."

NOTE:-In the British Commonwealth the Aircraft will be considered as Gliders and no Permit to Fly or Certificate of Airworthiness will be required and all intending entrants are strongly advised, during trials, to hold adequate insurance cover for all Third Party Risks, and to take every precaution against damages to property, but it is expected that competitors in other countries will observe their own national flying and insurance regulations.

Regulations

1. GENERAL
   The prize will be awarded to the entrant who first fulfills conditions.
2. PRIZE The prize is £50,000 sterling.
3. ELIGIBILITY The competition is international and is open to individuals or teams from any part of the world. Rights of appeal will be governed by the Competition Rules of the Royal Aero Club and the Sporting Code of the Federation Aeronautique Internationale.
4. CONDITIONS OF ENTRY
   4.1 AIRCRAFT
      4.1.1 The machine shall be a heavier-than-air machine.
      4.1.2 The use of lighter-than-air gases shall be prohibited
      4.1.3. The machine shall be powered and controlled by the crew of the machine over the entire flight.
      4.1.4 No devices for storing energy either for take-off or for use in flight shall be permitted.
      4.1.5 No part of the machine shall be jettisoned during any part of the flight including take-off.
   4.2 CREW
      4.2.1 The crew shall be those persons in the machine during take-off and flight, and there shall be no limit set to their number.
      4.2.2 No member of the crew shall be permitted to leave the aircraft at any time during take-off or flight.
      4.2.3 One handler or ground crew shall be permitted to assist in stabilizing the machine at the wing tip during take-off.
   4.3 GROUND CONDITIONS
      4.3.1 All attempts, which shall include the take-off run, shall be made over approximately level ground and on a course to be approved by the Royal Aero Club or

in conjunction with its authorised representatives.

4.3.2 All attempts shall be made in still air, which shall be defined as a wind not exceeding a mean speed of approximately 10 knots, over the period of the flight.

4.4 COURSE

4.4.1 The course shall be a figure of eight, embracing two turning points, which shall be not less than half a mile apart.

4.4.2 The machine shall be flown clear of and outside each turning point.

4.4.3 The starting line, which shall also be the finishing line, shall be between the turning points and shall be approximately at right angles to the line joining the turning pts.

4.4.4 The height, both at the start and the finish, shall be not less than ten feet above the ground; otherwise there shall be no restriction in height.

4.4.5 The machine shall be in continuous flight over the entire course.

4.5 OBSERVATION

Every attempt shall be observed by the Royal Aero Club or by any body or persons authorized by the Royal Club to act as observers.

5. APPLICATION FOR ENTRY

5.1 Entry forms shall be obtained from the Royal Aero Club, Competitions Department, Artillery Mansions, 75 Victoria Street, London, S.W.1.

5.2 The entry fee shall be £ 1 which shall be refunded upon the attempt taking place.

5.3 Each entry form shall contain an application for Official Observation of the competitor's attempt.

5.4 The fee for Official Observations shall be £15 15s. 0d which shall be forwarded with the application.

5.5 The entrant shall undertake to abide by the conditions for Official Observation as set out on the entry form and shall undertake to defray all expenses incurred in connection with the Official Observation of the attempt. In a country not affiliated to the F.A.I. it could be advantageous to fly the course in a neighboring country which is so affiliated.

5.6 Entry forms and application for Official Observation of an attempt must be received by the Royal Aero Club at least thirty days before the proposed date of the attempt. Applications will be considered in order of receipt at the Royal Aero Club, Aviation Centre.

6. GENERAL CONDITIONS

6.1 INSURANCE The entrant must undertake to insure on behalf of himself, his pilot (s), crew, representatives or employees, against third party risks in connection with the attempt to a minimum amount of £ 20,000 within the British Commonwealth and its equivalent in other countries. Evidence that such insurance has been effected must be produced to the Official Observers before the attempt.

6.2 ELIGIBILITY In any question regarding the acceptance of entries, eligibility of entrant, pilot, crew or aircraft under these Regulations, the decision of the Committee shall be final.

6.3 SUPPLEMENTARY REGULATION The Committee reserves the right to add to, amend or omit any of these regulations and to issue supplementary regulations.

6.4 INTERPRETATION OF REGULATIONS The Interpretation of these Regulations or any of the Regulations hereafter issued shall rest entirely with the Committee. The entrant shall be solely responsible to the Official Observers for due observance of these Regulations and shall be the person with whom the Official Observers will deal in respect thereof, or any other question arising out of this Competition.

6.5 REVISION OF REGULATIONS These Regulations shall remain in force until 31st December 1973. After this time, the Royal Aeronautical Society reserves the right to review and amend these Regulations if the prize has not been won.

* By "height" is meant ground clearance, everywhere in these rules.

The above regulations in facsimile of the original (3 pages of 8½ by 11 inches) are available from the Society in London.

ORNITHOPTERS

Ornithopters are any type of flying machine, man or machine powered, modeled after the flapping action of bird wings. Icarus and Daedalus became part of the ornithopter when they mythically attached feathers to their arms with wax.

Degen's Orthogonal Flier.

In 1809 Degen built the first recorded ornithopter consisting of 16 sq. feet of taffeta bands which produced a valvular action similar to that of the feathers in a bird's wing and while he rose some 54 feet by flapping violently, most accounts report that the majority of the weight was supported by a balloon or to a counterweighted rope over a pulley.

Trouve's Flapping Flier.

Trouve's Flapping Flier had wings connected by a flattened tube which would straighten out when subjected to internal pressure which was supplied by successive explosions from cartridges in a revolver barrel.

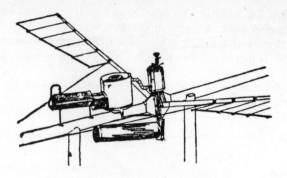

Laurence Hargrave of Sydney, Australia, inventor of the box kite, built some 18 machines between 1883 and 1893 with several different means of propulsion. His most successful were steam powered and one flew for 343 feet in 1891.

The Hargrave's machine used the flapping motion only for propulsion, however, the machine flew because of plane surfaces to the rear. So the flapping was really a propeller and the new machine lies on the border between ornithopters and airplanes.

The major difficulty is that man is quite heavy. Large birds flap their wings rarely except for takeoff; they rely on winds to soar. As scale is increased, there is a problem with the effect of inertia; the larger the ornithopter becomes, the more power that is required to make it flap.

MACHINE POWERED HANG GLIDERS

From the simple hang glider, a powered minimum airplane with folding wings is an intriguing and logical step.

Barry Palmer began building and flying Rogallo type hang gliders in California in 1961. In 1969, he added a chain saw motor then two chain saw motors and later a skimobile engine with 15 hp. All had empty weights of about 150 lbs. and the last one, at least, flew quite well.

Ryan built a "Flex-Wing" and a "Fleep", flying flat bed trucks, for the U. S. Army.

One of the most intriguing possibilities is a Rogallo wing automobile which could fold its wings into the trunk after landing.

It has been speculated that a 1.5 hp. motor might sustain some of the most efficient hang gliders but only if upcurrents of air were also used, more power would be required for level flight in calm conditions. Less efficient Rogallos require much more.'

Bill Bennett with a 12.5 hp back pack engine used as a glide extender for a Rogallo type glider.

There are a few very interesting small jet engines on the market, write: EMG Engineering Co., 18518P South Broadway, Gardena, CA 90248. and Thermo-Jet, P.O. Box 1528P, Kerrville, TX 78028.

EMG has engines with 10, 18 and 40 lbs of thrust and tests have been made with some of them mounted on a Rogallo glider. With the 40 lb. model, 10 minutes of flight consumes about 8 gallons of fuel. Weight of the engine is just 10 lbs.

Motorgliding is a monthly publication devoted to self-launching sailplanes ($6. yr.) From Soaring Society of America, Box 66071P, Los Angeles, CA 90066.

Winners of the First Alpine World Hang Gliding Championships in Kossen, Austria. 1st Dave Cronk (USA), 2nd Werner Tscherne (Switzerland), and 3rd Roy Haggard (USA).

Dave Cronk in his Cumulus.

APPENDIX

AC NO: 60-10

DATE: 5/16/74

ADVISORY CIRCULAR

DEPARTMENT OF TRANSPORTATION
FEDERAL AVIATION ADMINISTRATION
SUBJECT:
RECOMMENDED SAFETY PARAMETERS FOR OPERATION OF HANG GLIDERS

1. **PURPOSE.** Since the sport of "hang gliding" or "sky sailing" has become popular, numerous questions have arisen as to the FAA position on the regulation and operation of these vehicles. The purpose of this Advisory Circular is to suggest safety parameters for the operation of "hang gliders" and to present the current FAA intent with respect to the regulation and operation of those vehicles.

2. **DEFINITION.** For purposes of this Advisory Circular, "hang glider" means an unpowered, single place vehicle whose launch and landing capability depends entirely on the legs of the occupant and whose ability to remain in flight is generated by natural air currents only.

3. **BACKGROUND.** There has been a recent revival of popular interest in the almost forgotten art of powerless flight. This is now being accomplished by very light vehicles that are self-launched and unpowered. The sport is referred to as "hang gliding" or "sky sailing." New materials, modern construction techniques, improved knowledge of stability and control requirements, and imaginative configurations have all been applied. Coupled with low cost and an aviation adventure that has attracted both young and old, this increasingly popular sport is expected to grow dramatically in the near future. The revival of early Lilienthal days is being conducted primarily in open unpopulated areas where favorable wind conditions exist and terrain features provide an acceptable glide ratio clearance. The glide ratio of most of these vehicles is 4 to 1 or less. In a few instances, a higher glide ratio has been obtained through a hard wing construction; however, they still retain the feature of being self-launched and landed. Several corporations have been formed to manufacture these craft, along with a manufacturer's association that intends to provide minimum materials criteria to ensure safe construction. Numerous clubs have been formed, and many more may be formed in the future, which will provide safety guidance through both operational control and educational media.

4. **REGULATORY INFORMATION.** The FAA is interested in this activity, but at this time does not have sufficient data and information with respect to "hang glider" design and operational capabilities to make any determination as to the need for new specific action. It is the FAA's intent to observe the growth and safety status of this activity as it progresses and to continually assess the need for FAA involvement. The following, however, are certain regulatory areas of which "hang glider" operators should take cognizance:

a. <u>Federal Aviation Regulations, Part 101.</u> Part 101 specifies rules applicable to kite operations. Those rules are applicable to any vehicle intended to be flown at the end of a rope, having as its only means of support the force of the wind moving past its surfaces, and that is not capable of sustained flight when released from its tether. No person should operate a "hang glider" at the end of a surface towline without first becoming fully familiar with Part 101.

b. <u>Federal Aviation Regulations, Sections 91.17 and 91.18.</u> Section 91.17 provides rules applicable to the towing by an aircraft of gliders as that term is defined in FAR Part 1. Section 91.18(a) provides, in part, that no pilot of a civil aircraft may tow anything with that aircraft (other than under §91.17) except in accordance with the terms of a certificate of waiver issued by the Administrator.

5. <u>SAFETY SUGGESTIONS.</u> The following guidelines are suggested for the use of all participants in "hang gliding," manufacturers of "hang gliders" and operating clubs:

a. Suggestions relating to operation of the vehicle:

   (1) Limit altitude to 500 feet above the general terrain. It must be remembered, however, that there are certain aircraft operations conducted below 500 feet above the terrain and "hang glider" operators should be alert to this.

   (2) Do not fly them within controlled airspace, specifically a control zone, airport traffic area, or within five miles of the boundary of an uncontrolled airport unless authorized by airport authorities.

   (3) Do not fly them within any prohibited or restricted area without prior permission from the controlling or using agency, as appropriate.

   (4) Do not fly them within 100 feet horizontally of, or at any altitude over, buildings, populated places, or assemblages of persons.

   (5) Remain clear of clouds.

   (6) Questions regarding operations in conflict with the above recommended safety parameters should be discussed with the nearest FAA district office.

b. Suggestions to manufacturers and clubs:

   (1) Develop criteria for materials and construction techniques. (It is recommended that aircraft quality hardware and materials be utilized in construction as appropriate.)

   (2) Ensure that adequate quality control procedures are utilized during manufacture of the vehicle.

   (3) Pay particular attention to ensure that a good training program is established. (The United States Hang Glider Association can be helpful in this area.) Students should be taught early to recognize their individual limitations as well as the limitations of the "hang glider."

   (4) Provide adequate instructions in "do-it-yourself" kits so that proper hardware is utilized and good construction

190

techniques are employed.

    (5) Coordinate with local municipalities and property owners for recognized flying sites.

    (6) Establish strong safety programs and distribute safety related materials to clubs, associations, and operators of "hang gliders."

    (7) Develop close coordination with the Federal Aviation Administration.

    (8) Operators of "hang gliders" should be encouraged to wear protective clothing, including a helmet.

6. **CONCLUSION**. The Federal Aviation Administration is willing to devote time and effort, within reason, to assist manufacturers and clubs during this developmental period. District Offices are encouraged to work with manufacturers and clubs so that the sport is conducted in a safe manner. Safety related materials developed by clubs and manufacturers' associations will be disseminated to all Regions as it is developed. Appropriate material coming to the attention of field offices should be forwarded to Headquarters as well as related safety information developed by local FAA personnel. The "hang glider" community should, on the other hand, make a vigorous effort to develop safety criteria and instructions usable in the manufacture and operation of "hang gliders."

7. **DISTRIBUTION**. This Advisory Circular should be given the widest distribution possible by district offices to ensure that all persons interested in this activity are aware of the information contained in this document.

JAMES F. RUDOLPH
Director, Flight Standards Service

(Membership usually includes a magazine)

U.S. Hang Gliding Association
P.O. Box 66306-P
Los Angeles, CA 90066

Self Soar Assn.
P.O. Box 1860-P
Santa Monica, CA 90406

Hang Glider Manufacturers Assn.
137-P Oregon St.
El Segundo, CA 90245

Professional Pilots Assn.
775-P Merry Ln.
Boulder, CO 80302

Windward Gliding Club
901 B/P Plum St.
Ft. Devens, MA 01433

New England Hang Gliding Assn.
P.O. Box 356-P
Stoughton, MA 02072

Connecticut Hang Gliding Assn.
145-P Day Street
Newington, Conn. 06111

New Jersey Water Ski Kite Assn.
40-P Center St.
Springfield, N.J. 07081

Homdel Hang Gliding Club
Room 1C-433-P Bell Labs
Homdel, NJ 07733

Clarkson College Hang Glider Club
Star Route (P)
Potsdam, NY 13676

Pittsburgh Hang Gliding Assn.
RD 1, Box 67-A/P
Trafford, PA 15085

Eastern Penna H. G. Assn.
620-P Walnut St.
Reading, PA 19601

Glide on Assn.
323-P Bradley Ave.
Rockville, MD 20851

Capitol Hang Glider Assn.
7358-P Shenandoah Ave.
Annandale, VA 22003

The H. G. Club of Virginia
1618-P Jefferson Pk #2A
Charlottesville, VA 22903

Tidewater Hang Glider Club
5624-P Hampshire Ln. #102
Virginia Beach, VA 23462

N.C. Hang Glider Society
104-P Wright St.
Lewisville, NC 27023

Atlanta Ultralight Assn.
190-P Shiloh Rd.
Kenesaw, GA 30144

Ascension Island Hang Glider Assn.
NASA/SDTN STM Ascension Island
P.O. Box A-P
Patrick AFB, Fla. 32975

Ohio Hang Glider Assn.
26875-P Bagley Rd.
Olmstead Falls, Ohio 44138

Cincinnati H. G. Assn.
P.O. Box 26012-P
Cincinnati, OH 45226

Michigan Skysurfers
1361-P Oregon
Pontiac, Mich. 48054

Michigan U.F.O. Hang Glider Club
1554-P Park Lane
Livonia, MI 48154

Betsie Bay Bluff Buzzards
P.O. Box 1593-P
Frankfort, MI 49635

Wisc. Ultralite Pilots Soc.
S45 W22360-P Quinn Rd.
Waukesha, WI 53186

Madison Sky Sailors
2861-P Guilford Rd. #5
Madison, Wisc. 53713

Miss. Valley A.S. Assn.
676-P Summit Ave. #12
St. Paul, MN 55102

Normandale H. G. Club
9700-P France Ave. So.
Bloomington, MN 55431

Inland Empire Aeronauts
P.O. Box 2009-P
Missoula Mt. 59801

Midwest Hang Glider Assn.
11959-P Glenvalley Dr.
Maryland Heights, MO 63043

North Texas Hang Glider Soc.
1716-P Jasmine Ln.
Plano, TX 75014

Hill Country Glider Club
Rt. #1, Box 326-P
Wimberly, TX 78676

Mountain Home Glider Riders
Box 3414-P
Mt. Home AFB, ID 83648

Utah Ultralight Gliders Assn.
143-P East 500 North
Kaysville, Utah 84037

Ultralight Flyers Organization
P.O. Box 81665-P
San Diego, CA 92138

Orange County Sky Sailing Club
916-P Delaware
Huntington Beach, CA 92648

Escape Country Sky Surfing Club
c/p Escape Country, RT#P
Trabuco Canyon, CA 92678

Kydid Flyer Club
323-P Euclid #140
Santa Ana, CA 92703

Channel Island H.G. Assn.
1806 J/P Cliff Drive
Santa Barbara, CA 93109

San Joaquin Valley H.G. Club
1505-P East Magill
Fresno, CA 93710

California Condors
P.O. Box 5474-P
Carmel, CA 93921

The Fellow Feathers
2123-P Junipero Serra Blvd.
Daly City, CA 94015

Wings of Rogallo
1137-P Jamestown Dr.
Sunnyvale, CA 94087

Sierra H. G. Assn.
Box 443-P
Sutter Creek, CA 95685

Pacific Tradewind Sky-Sailors
3142-P Hinano St.
Honolulu, Hawaii 96815

Oregon Hang Glider Assn.
P.O. Box 3815-P
Portland, Ore. 97208

Pacific Northwest Hang Glider Assn.
417-P Harvard Ave. #4
Seattle, WN 98102

Eastern Washington Hang Gliders Assn.
1425-P Marshall
Richland, WN 99352

━━ ━━ ━━ ━━ ━━ ━━ ━━

AUSTRALIA
T.A.S.S.A.
42-P Lansdowne Parade
Oatley N.S.W. 2223

AUSTRIA
International Hang Gliding Secretariat
WOC-P
A-6345 Kossen

CANADA
Westcoast Skysurfers Hang Gliding Club
4660-P W. Tenth Ave. #1205
Vancouver, B.C. V6R 2J6

Terrace Hang Glider Assn.
4616-P Grieg Ave.
Terrace, BC

Alberta Hang Glider Assn.
131-P 10th Ave. S.E.
Calgary, Alberta

Southern Ontario Hang Glider Association
12-P Foundry St.
L9H 5G1
Dundas, Ontario

SW Ont. Air Riders
33-P Plymouth Ave.
London, Ont. N6H 3T2

ENGLAND
National Hang Gliding Assn.
9 the Drive #P
West Wickham, Kent BR4 OEF

Sussex Para Kite Club
20-P Surrenden
Brighton 6, Sussex
BNI 6PP

British Kite Soaring Assn.
c/o Dick Bickel
8A-P Richman Close
Woodley, Berkshire

British Hang Gliding Assn.
Monksilver #P
Taunton, Somerset

FRANCE
Federation Francaise de Vol Libre
29-P Rue de Severs
75006 Paris

NEW ZEALAND
New Zealang Hang Gliding Assn.
62-P Nile Rd.
Westlake, Auckland 10,

BOOKS

Write for latest price and delivery information

Hang Flight
by Adleson & Williams
Eco-Nautics
P.O. Box 1154-P
Redlands, CA 92373

Delta
by Jean-Bernard Desfayes
Haessner Publishing, Inc.
P.O. Drawer B/P
Newfoundland, NJ 07435

Guide to Rogallo Flight-Basic
by Skinner and Finley
Flight Realities
1945-P Adams Ave.
San Diego, CA 92116

KITING, the basic handbook of tow launched
hang gliding
by Dan Poynter P.O. Box 4232-P
Santa Barbara, CA 93103

FLY, the complete book of Sky Sailing
by Rich Carrier
McGraw-Hill Book Company
New York City

Skysurfing, A Guide to Hang Gliding
by Eddie Paul
Crown Publishers
419-P Park Avenue South
New York City, NY 10016

Rapture of the Heights
by Lorraine M. Doyle
Lion Press
P.O. Box 836-P
National City, CA 92050

MAGAZINES

Write for sample copy and latest rates

Up Draft Magazine
35-P Mill Drive
St. Albert Alberta
T8N 1J5 Canada

Hang Glider Magazine
3333-P Pacific Ave.
San Pedro, CA 90731

Wings Unlimited
P.O. Box 5421-P
Topeka, KS 66605

MANUFACTURERS AND DEALERS
FOR MORE INFORMATION WRITE TO THE FIRMS NEAREST YOU.

Help them to expedite your inquiry for the latest flying and equipment information by sending a stamped, self addressed envelope.

Sky-High Glider Co.
P.O. Box 311-P
Turners Falls, MA 01376

Walt Niemi
25-P Willow St.
Fitchburg, MA 01420

Worcester County Aircraft
270-P Boylston Street
Shrewsbury, MA 01545

Man Flight Systems, Inc.
P.O. Box 872-P
Worcester, MA 01613

Get High East
84-P Boxborough Road
Stow, MA 01775

Abate Aircraft
P.O. Box 1-P
Lawrence, MA 01842

U.F.M., Inc.
Main Ave. #P
South Hampton, NH 01913

Sky Sports, Inc. (Mass.)
Pine and High Streets
Whitman, Mass. 02382

Wings and Things
338-P Granite St.
Manchester, NH 03102

Terry Sweeney
RFD #2 Box P
Concord, NH 03301

Sky People, Inc.
P.O. Box 898-P
North Conway, NH 03860

Sky Truckin', Inc.
P.O. Box 234-P
Biddeford, ME 04005

194

Portland Bicycle Exchange
396-P Fore St.
Portland, ME 04111

Gliders of Mt. Abram
Mt. Abram Ski Slopes (P)
Lockemills, ME 04255

Jim Thomann Sky Sports
RD #4, Spauldings E. Shore (P)
Malletts Bay
Winooski, VT 05404

Sky Sports, Inc. (Conn)
Ellington Airport
Bldg. #P
Ellington, Conn. 06029

Zephyr Aircraft Corp.
25-P Mill St.
Glastonbury, Conn. 06033

Gene Hilborn
122-P Strathmore Gardens
Matawan, NJ 07747.

Bennett Delta Wings East
Box 36-P
Berkeley Heights, NJ 07922

Appalachian High
38-P Sussex Ave.
Morristown, NJ 07960

Go Fly a Kite Store, Inc.
1613-P Second Avenue
New York, NY 10028

Bob & Jill Inc.
55-P Lyncroft Road
New Rochelle, NY 10804

New York Hang Gliders Inc.
144-45-P 35 Ave.
Flushing, NY 11354

Wings for Man
P.O. Box 249-P
East Islip, NY 11730

Dixson Hang Glider Supplies & School
5-P Arden Lane
Farmingville, NY 11738

Long Island Kite Distributors
5-P Bethpage Road
Hicksville, NY 11801

Cole Hill Recreational Inc.
Box 193-P
Berne, NY 12023

The Hang Gliding Store
Box 57-P Ridge Road
Marlboro, NY 12542

Chandelle Birch Hill Inc.
P.O. Box 283-P
Patterson, NY 12563

McCarron Aeronautical Corp.
17-P Vichy Drive
Saratoga Springs, NY 12866

David Deming
Hoag Lane #P
Fayetteville, NY 13066

David Inglehart
160-P Ten Eyck St.
Watertown, NY 13601

Delta Wing Kites & Gliders NE
RD #1, #, Upper East Street
Oneonta, NY 13820

Mark Flight Ltd.
104-P Gettysburg
Kenmore, NY 14223

Sutton Brothers
222-P Verbeke St.
Marysville, PA 17053

Icarus, Inc.
P.O. Box 51-P
Broomall, PA 19008

Jim Hutchings
7526-P Rogers Ave.
Upper Darby, PA 19080

Phila. Hang Glider Sales
Box 466-P
Conshohocken, PA 19428

J. R. McTammany, M.D.
620-P Walnut St.
Reading, PA 19601

Chandelle Maryland
5603-P McKinley
Bethesda, MD 20034

East Coast Hang Gliders Ltd.
P.O. Box 961-P
Washington, DC 20044

Sport Flight
3305-P Ferndale St.
Kensington, MD 20795

Econ-O-Flight Systems
10711-P Liberty Road
Randallstown, MD 21133

John Luck
4610-P Killam Ave.
Norfolk, VA 23508

J.J. Sky Surfing, Inc.
P.O. Box 1181-P
Martinsburg, WV 25401

Free-Flight of Greensboro
2300-P Phoenix Drive
Greensboro, NC 27406

Emory Gliders
409-P S. Dawson St.
Raleigh, NC 27601

Kitty Hawk Kites
P.O. Box 386-P
Nags Head, NC 27959

Land, Sea and Air Ventures
P.O. Box 275-P
Wrightsville Beach, NC 28480

Appalachian Mountaineering
5725-P Binford Highway
Atlanta, GA 30340

Jimmy Spears
128-P Reynolds St.
Augusta, GA 30901

Hollymatic Corp.
2001-P NW 51st St.
Boca Raton, Fla. 33432

Don R. Hill
P.O. Box 2868-P
Sarasota, Fla. 33578

Cloudmen Glidercraft Co.
905-P Church St.
Nashville, TN 37203

Butterfly Industries
1191-P West Cumberland Ave.
Knoxville, TN 37916

Ron Oakley
8400-P Blue Lick Rd.
Louisville, KY 40219

Chuck's Glider Supplies
860-P Jefferson Ave.
Cleveland, OH 44113

Troyer Kite Supply
4299-P Kent Road
Stow, OH 44224

Flight-Tri State Hang Gliders
5725-P Dragon Way, #400
Cincinnati, OH 45227

Dyna-Soar
P.O. Box 236-P
Carmel, IN 46032

Hoosier Hang Gliders
707-P Highwood
Greencastle, Inc. 46135

Eco-Flight Systems
2275-P South State
Ann Arbor, MI 48104

Free Flight of Ann Arbor
304-P South Thayer St.
Ann Arbor, MI 48104

Foot Launched Fliers
11411-P Hyne
Brighton, Mich. 48116

Ski & Sail
7949-P West Grand River
Brighton, MI 48116

Free Flight of Detroit
19366-P Kelly Rd.
Harper Woods, MI 48225

Great Lakes Sky Sails
5125-P North River Road
Freeland, MI 48623

Aero Float Flights
82-P Fremont
Battle Creek, MI 49017

Delta Kites of Indian Lake
7844-P Shaver Road
Portage, MI 49081

Easy Traveling Crop.
12173-P East D Ave.
Richland, MI 49083

A A Flight Systems
10-P North Barton
New Buffalo, MI 49117

Skyscape Sports
25-P West Ninth
Holland, MI 49423

D & D Skysailing Shops
1853-P Ruddiman
No. Muskegon, MI 49445

Delta Wing of Michigan
1434-P Lake Drive S.E.
Grand Rapids, MI 49506

Gar's Sport Center
2531-P South Division Avenue
Grand Rapids, Mich. 49507

Sail Boat Center
22-P 44th St. S.E.
Grand Rapids, MI 49508

Michigan Manta
327-P Main Street
Frankfort, MI 49635

Big Powderhorn Mt. H.G. School
P.O. Box 136-P
Bessemer, MI 49911

Sea & Ski
4248-P North 76th
Milwaukee, Wisc. 53222

Delta Wing Kites
8620-P West Auer
Milwaukee, Wisc. 53222

H.H. Petrie Sporting Goods
P.O. Box 5427-P
Madison, Wisc. 53705

Fish Creek's Cycles
Rt. #P
Exploration Outfitter
Fish Creek, Wisc. 54212

Hawk of Lacrosse
P.O Box 378-P
Lacrosse, WI 54601

Aspen Enterprises
Box 423-P
Neenah, Wisc. 54956

Aircraft Unlimited
P.O. Box 1616-P
Mpls. St. P. Intl. Airport
Minneapolis, Minn. 55111

L & R Sales Corp.
2548-P Nicollet South
Mpls, MN 55404

Midwest Hang Gliders Spec.
2002 Garfield South #24-P
Mpls, MN 55405

Northwestern Hang Glider Inc.
1215-P Washington Ave. So.
Minneapolis, MN 55415

Blackhills Sailbird
1510-P Tenth Street
Belle Fouche, SD 57717

Upward Bound
Box 2009-P
Missoula, Mont. 59801

Chandelle Chicago
109-P West Prospect
Mt. Prospect, ILL. 60056

Sailbird of Illinois
305-P South Wright
Naperville, Ill. 60540

Phantom Sport Gliders
5405-P Hollis Ave.
Loves Park, Ill. 61111

Al Signorino
11959-P Glenvalley Dr.
Maryland Heights, MO 63043

United Skysports
3314-P Dix Ave.
St. Louis, MO 63114

Joe Goodrich
101-P Dunbar St.
Excelsior Springs, MO 64024

Voyageur Enterprises
5935-P Merriam Drive
Merriam, KS 66203

Harold Steves, Jr.
P.O. Box 5421-P
Topeka, KS 66605

Sailbird of Kansas
1306-P North B Street
Wellington, KS 67152

Pliable Moose Delta Wing
243-P Matthewson
Wichita, KS 67214

Outdoor Actions
422 B/P East 9th St.
Hays, KS 67601

J & J Hang Glider Supplies
P.O. Box 6064-P
Lincoln, NEB 68506

Kondor Kite Co.
P.O. Box 603-P
Lewisville, TX 75067

South Central Kite & Glider Enterprises
6205 Shady Brook #153-P
Dallas, TX 75206

Sky Sails Inc.
3432-P Dalworth
Arlington, TX 76011

High Trails
7051-P Tamarack Rd.
Ft. Worth, TX 76116

Flight Systems
8718-P Dale Valley
San Antonio, TX 78227

Delta Kites
6123-P Grand Point
San Antonio, TX 78239

High Plains Hang Gliders
300-A/P West Sixth
Amarillo, TX 79101

Sport Haus
2309-P Broadway
Lubbock, TX 79401

Life Cycle
1224-P 15th St.
Larimer Square
Denver, Colorado 80202

Sun Sail Corporation
Airport Business Center
6753 E. 47th Ave. Dr. Suite D/P
Denver, Colo. 80216

Rocky Mountain Marine
5411-P Leetsdale Drive
Denver, Colo. 80222

D & D Enterprises, Inc.
572-P Orchard St.
Golden, CO 80401

Leaf, Inc.
1508-P Newcastle
Colorado Springs, CO 80907

Sailbird Flying Machines
Box 9990-P
Colorado Springs, CO 80932

Jeff Campbell
Box 103-P
Telluride, Colo. 81435

Get High, Inc.
Box 4551-P
Aspen, Colo. 81611

Gorsuch Ltd.
P.O. Box 1508-P
Vail, Colo. 81657

Chandelle Idaho
P.O. Box 1221-P
Sun Valley, Idaho 83353

Glide Path Soaring School
322-P "H" Street
Idaho Falls, Idaho 83401

Sailbird of Utah
847-P North 750 East
Layton, Utah 84041

The Lift House
3698-P East 7000 South
Salt Lake City, Utah 84121

Fox Distributing, Inc.
3147-P 31st Ave.
Phoenix, Ariz. 85017

U.S. Hang Gliders, Inc.
11024 N. 22nd Ave., Unit 5-P
Phoenix, Ariz. 85029

Rainco
P.O. Box 20944-P
Phoenix, Arizona 85036

Hang Gliders Inc.
1300-P East Valencia
Tucson, Arizona 85706

Ski Haus Action Sports
2823-P East Speedway
Tucson, AZ 85716

New Mexico Sky School
4007-P Central, NE
Albuquerque, NM 87108

Sky Sailors
7208-P Arroyo del Oso N.
Albuquerque, NM 87109

S.W. Hang Gliding Center
3119-P San Mateo N.E.
Albuquerque, NM 87110

Base Camp
121-P West San Francisco St.
Santa Fe, NM 87501

Wings
906-P South Fourth St.
Las Vegas, Nev. 89101

Ultralite Products
137-P Oregon St.
El Segundo, CA 90245

Sail Wing Sales & Service Center
1116-P 8th St.
Manhattan Beach, CA 90266

Hang Glider Shoppe & School
P.O. Box 1671-P
Santa Monica, CA 90401

Seagull Aircraft
3021-P Airport Ave.
Santa Monica, CA 90405

Soaring Emporium
20123-P Hawthorne Blvd.
Torrance, CA 90503

Eipper-Formance
P.O. Box 246-47
Lomita, CA 90717

Velderrain Kite Co.
P.O. Box 314-P
Lomita, CA 90717

Volmer Aircraft
Box 5222-P
Glendale, CA 91201

Sunbird Ultralight Gliders
21420 Chase St. Bldg. #7-P
Canoga Park, CA 91304

Free Flight Systems
12424-P Gladstone Ave.
Sylmar, CA 91342

Delta Wing Kites
P.O. Box 483-P
Van Nuys, CA 91408

Windways Flying Machines
1368-P Max
Chula Vista, CA 92011

Taras Kiceniuk, Jr.
Palomar Observatory
Box P
Palomar Mountain, CA 92060

Britt Reynolds
3046-P Whittier St.
San Diego, CA 92106

Free-Flight of Orange County
P.O. Box 485-P
Costa Mesa, CA 92627

Jack G. Hall
12561-P Pearce St.
Garden Grove, CA 92643

Solo Flight
1141-P Citrus
Orange, CA 92667

Pacific Gull
1321 Calle Valle
(Unite F/P)
San Clemente, CA 92672

Escape Country Hang Gliding School
Robinson Ranch, Rt #P
Trabuco Canyon, CA 92678

Sport Kites, Inc.
1208 H/P E. Walnut
Santa Ana, CA 92701

Windsong Division
Tapioka Enterprises
27-P North Garden St.
Ventura, CA 93001

Free-Flight of Ventura
P.O. Box 2094-P
Ventura, CA 93001

Free Flight of Santa Barbara
1806 Cliff Drive, Suite J/P
Santa Barbara, CA 93109

The Bike & Sport Shoppe
P.O. Box 404-P
Bishop, CA 93514

Monarch Skysails
136-P East Olive
Fresno, CA 93728

Chandelle San Francisco
2123-P Junipero Serra Blvd.
Daly City, CA 94015

Manta Products
1647-P E. 14th St.
Oakland, CA 94606

Eagle Wings, Inc.
2627-P Hillegass
Berkeley, CA 94704

Northern California Sun
P.O. Box 1624-P
Sausalito, CA 94965

Angel Wing Kite Sales
236-P Santa Cruz Ave.
Aptos, CA 95003

Ultralight Flying Machines
Box 59-P
Cupertino, CA 95014

Aeolus Hang Gliders
631-P Redwood Rd.
Felton, CA 95018

True Flight
1719-P Hillsdale Avenue
San Jose, CA 95124

Sacramento Valley Hang Gliders
3210-P Balmoral
Sacramento, CA 95821

Cecil Hall
848-P West Ninth St.
Chico, CA 95926

Air Performance Hawaii
217-P Prospect
Honolulu, Hawaii 96813

Aeron Ltd., Inc.
9985-P S.E. Eastmont Dr.
Gresham, OR 97030

Hang Gliders of America
829-P N.E. Imperial
Portland, OR 97232

Pacific Hang Gliders of Eugene
1265-P Brickley Road
Eugene, OR 97401

Pacific Hang Gliders
1729-P Labona Dr.
Eugene, OR 97401

Soaring Unlimited
4023-P Donald St. #C
Eugene, OR 97405

Hang Ups Inc.
30003-P 112th SE
Auburn, Wash. 98002

Chandelle Northwest
77-P Madison St.
Seattle, Wash. 98104

Recreational Equipment Inc.
P.O. Box 22088-P
Seattle, Wash. 98122

The Flying Burrito Bros.
17036-P 44th NE
Seattle, WA 98155

Kleen Fun Kites
P.O. Box 4-2990-P
Anchorage, Alaska 99509

Sailbird of Alaska
1738-P Hilton
Faribanks, Alaska 99701

ARGENTINA
Apolo Especialidades
Psje. El Hornero 190-P
Cap. Federal (suc 8)

AUSTRALIA
Southern Cross
Box 21-P
Doveton, Victoria

Bill Moyes
173-P Bronte Road
Waverly, Sydney 2024

McDonald Hovering Craft
22-P Crown Street
Belmont 2280

Lite Feet Publishing
Box 307-P
Parramatta, NSW 2150

AUSTRIA
Sepp Himberger
Delta School (P)
A-6345 Kossen

CANADA
Werner Kausche Co.
215-P 11th Ave. S.W.
Calgary, Alta T2R OC2

Mini Sport
12-P Foundry Street
Dundas, Ontario L9H 5G1

Peter's Cross Country Skiing
1610-P Tenth Avenue
Regina, Sask. S4P OE6

Müller Kites Ltd.
Box 4062 Postal Station C/P
Calbary, Alberta
T2T 5M9

Birdman Enterprises
8011-P Argyll Road
Edmonton, Alberta
T6C 4A9

Tod Mountain Flying School
749-P Victoria
Kamloops, B.C.

Pat Bates
352-P Oughtred St.
Kimberley, BC

B.C. School of Sp. Para.
1359-P Kingway
Vancouver 10, BC

Kits Marine
1502-P West 2nd Ave.
Vancouver, B.C.

High Perspective
RR #2-P Claremont
Ontario LOH 1E0

Skysurfing Unlimited
621-P Redwood Ave.
Ottawa, Ont. K2A 3E8

DENMARK
Para-Fun International, Ltd.
Jaegersborggade 25-P
2200 Copenhagen

ENGLAND
Hawksworth Skysport Center
18-P Coombe Terrace
Brighton, Sussex

McBroom Sailwings, Ltd.
12-P Manor Court Dr.
Horfield Common, Bristol
BS7 OXF

L. Gabriels
4-P Thornlea Ave.
Hollinwood, Oldham,
Lancs. OL8 3PX

Alec M. Hunt
130 Houslow Rd. #P
Whitton, Twickenham,
Middlesex

GERMANY
Mike Harker
Postfach 123-P
81 Garmisch

Delta Glider
7021-P Stetten Filder
Bernhauser Str 31

IRELAND
Tony Morelli
12-P Capel Street
Dublin 1,

ITALY
Aquilone Delta
39033 Corvara Badia

JAPAN
Japan Hang Gliders, Inc.
5-12-18 Yagumo Meguro-ku
Tokyo 152-P

NETHERLANDS
A. Celeen
Pieter Stockmanslaan 53-P
Eindhoven 4508

NEW ZEALAND
Pacific Kites Ltd.
P.O. Box 45-087-P
Te Atatu
Auckland 8

SOUTH AFRICA
South African Aviation Centre
P.O. Box 33191-P
Jeppestown, Transvaal

SWITZERLAND
Para Centro Locarno
Aeroporto Cantonale
6596-P Gordola, Locarno

Swiss Delta FFA
7550-P Schuls

Felix Zbinden
Dort 19-P
1711 Plasselb

Now that you have read *HANG GLIDING,*

pick up a copy of *KITING* and learn

even more about these aviation sports.

KITING is devoted to tow launching

and covers flying, materials, design

and construction of towed hang gliders

in great detail. Over 100 pages and

150 illustrations.

See your nearest dealer, or send $3.95 to:

MANNED KiTiNG

THE BASIC HANDBOOK OF TOW LAUNCHED HANG GLIDING

By
Dan Poynter